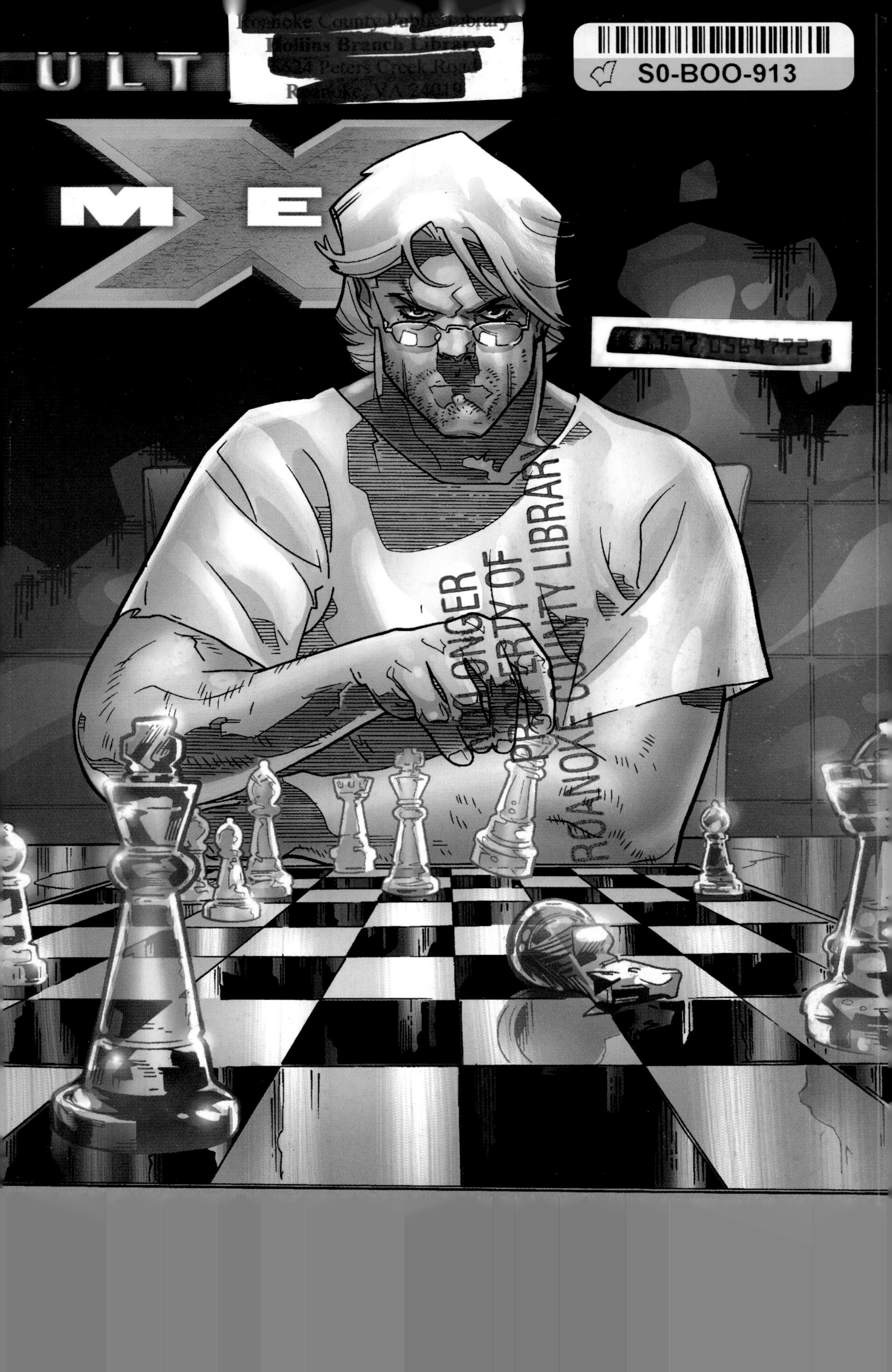

ULT
X
ME

ULTIMATE X-MEN

MAGNETIC NORTH

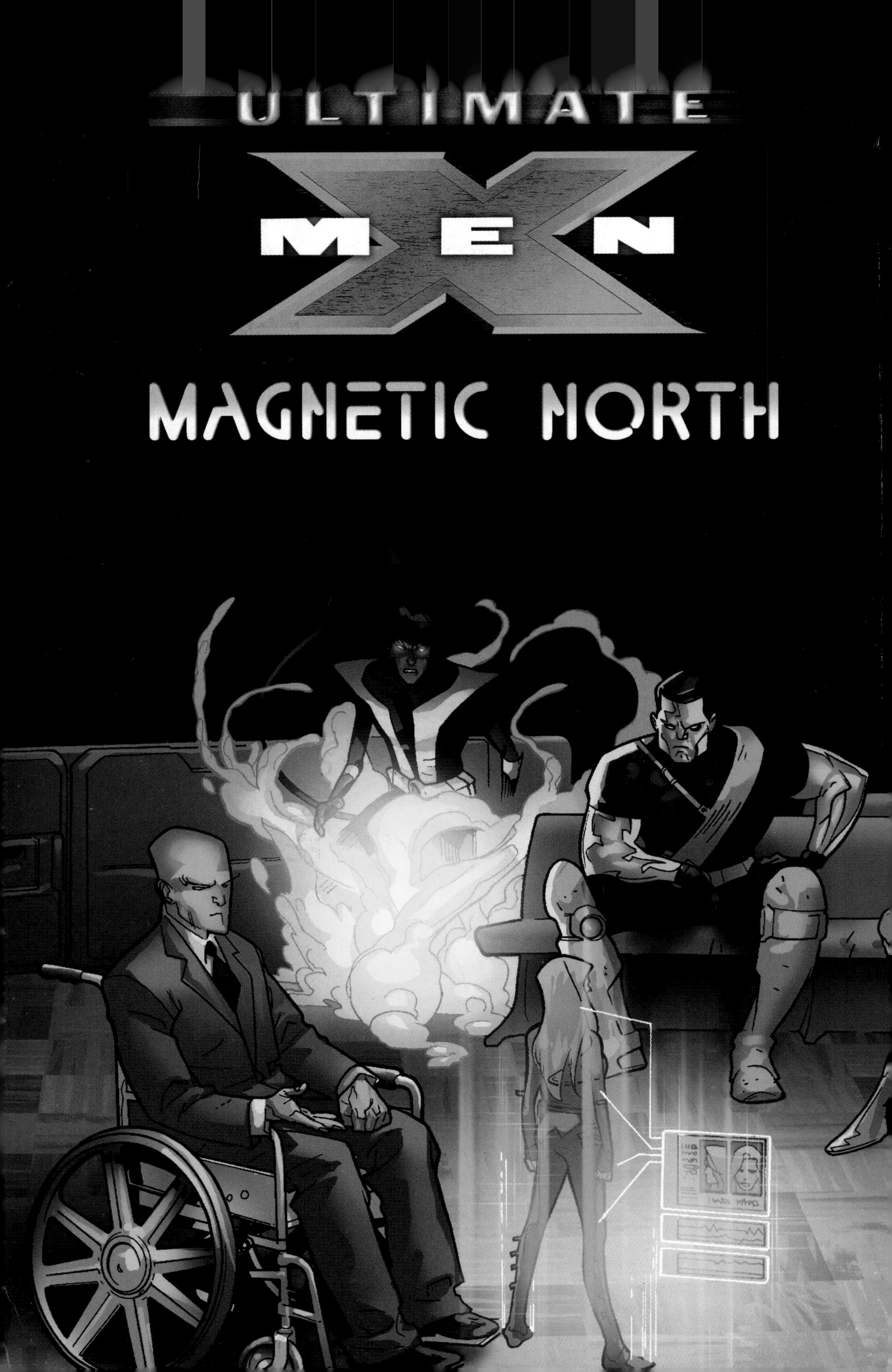

Writer
Brian K. Vaughan
Pencils
Stuart Immonen
Inks
Wade vonGrawbadger
Colors
Justin Ponsor
with Paul Mounts
Letters
Chris Eliopoulos
Assistant Editors
John Barber & Nicole Wiley
Editor
Ralph Macchio

Collection Editor
Jennifer Grünwald
Assistant Editor
Michael Short
Senior Editor,
Special Projects:
Jeff Youngquist
Vice President of Sales
David Gabriel

Production
Jerron Quality Color
Creative Director
Tom Marvelli

Editor in Chief
Joe Quesada
Publisher
Dan Buckley

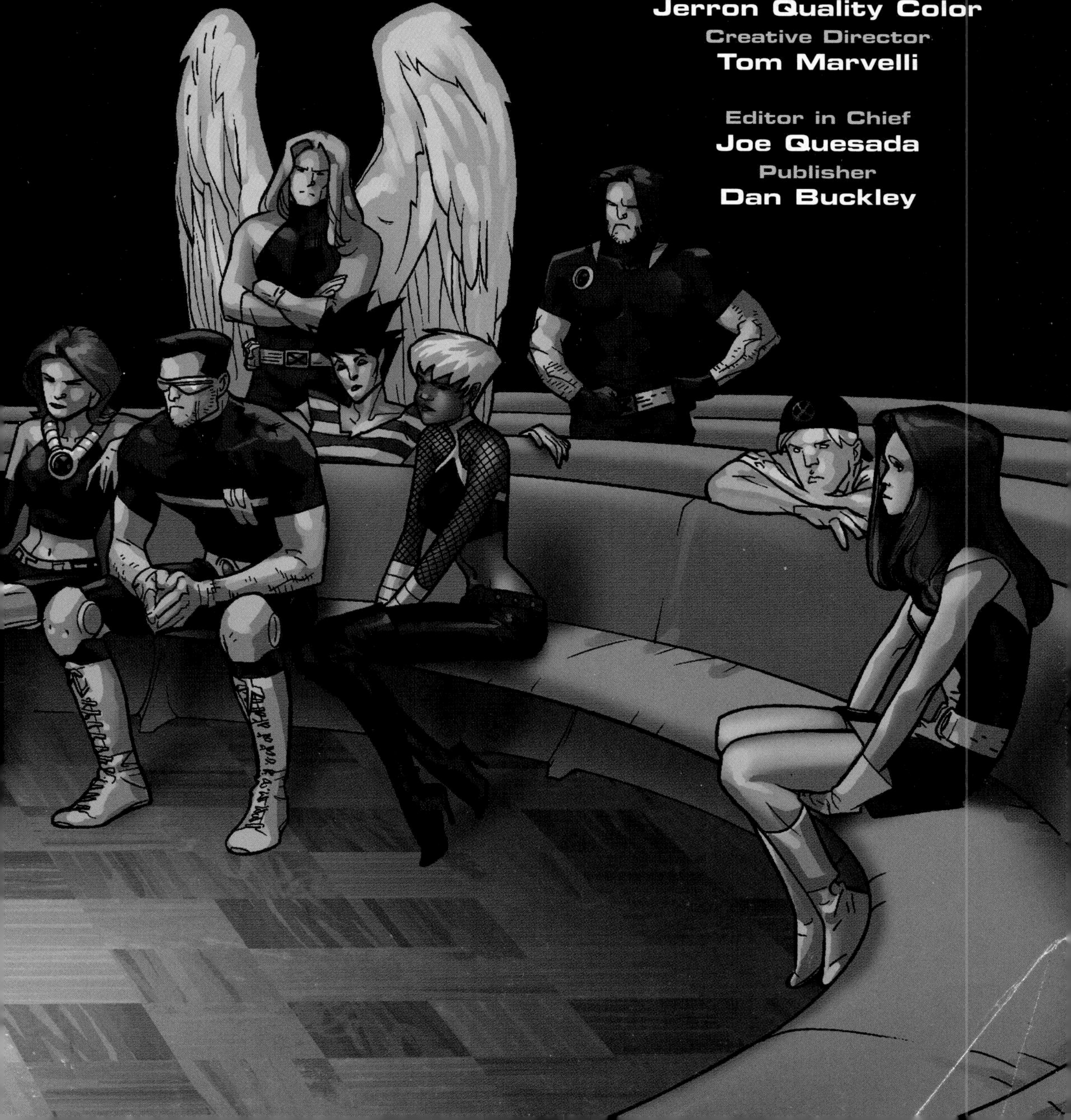

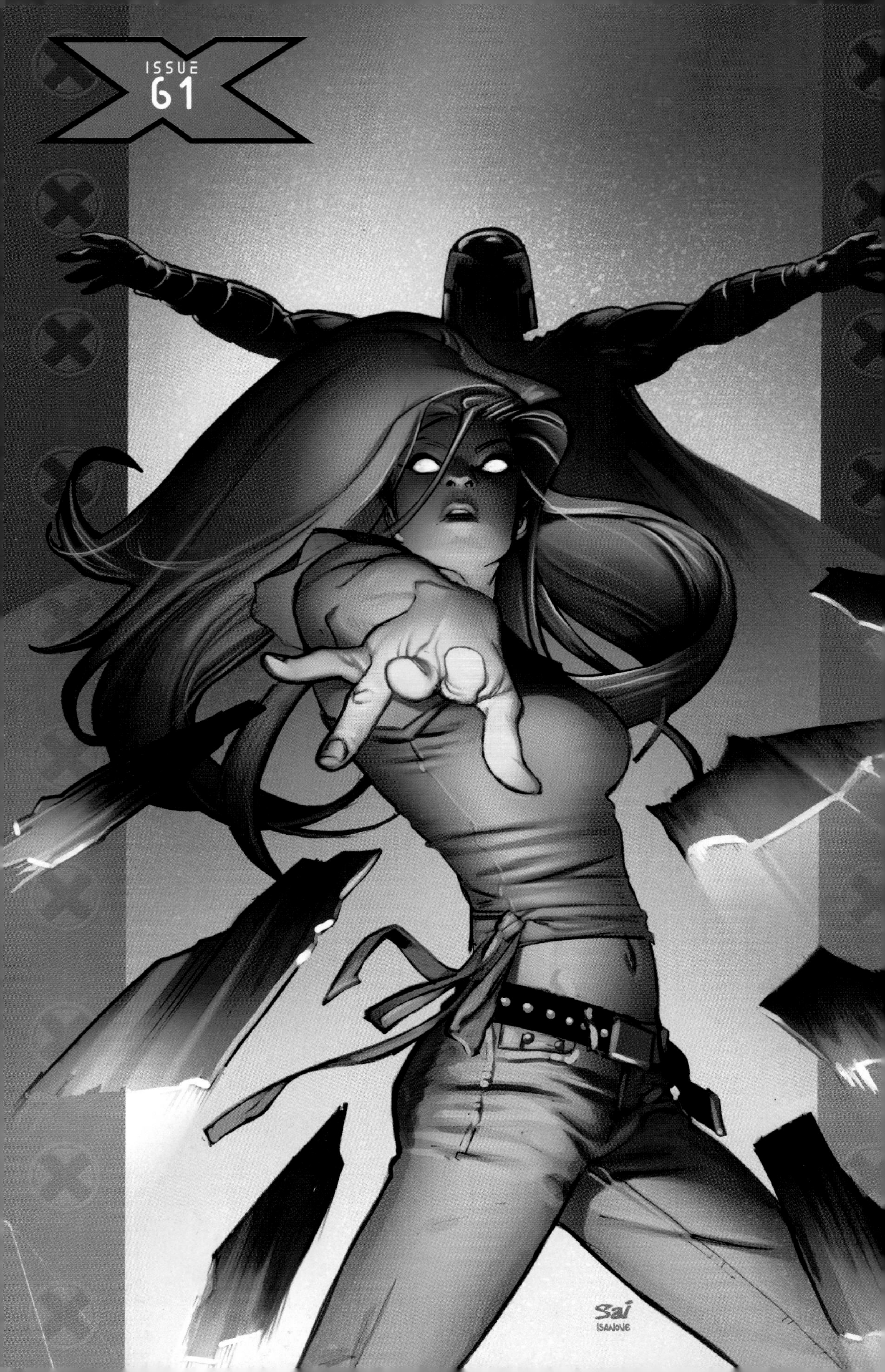
ISSUE
61
SAI
ISANOVE

PREVIOUSLY IN ULTIMATE X-MEN:

Born with strange and amazing abilities, the X-Men are young mutant heroes, sworn to protect a world that fears and hates them.

Their moral compass is a man named Professor Charles Xavier, an avowed pacifist, and the most powerful telepath on the planet.

Their friends are few. Their enemies are not.

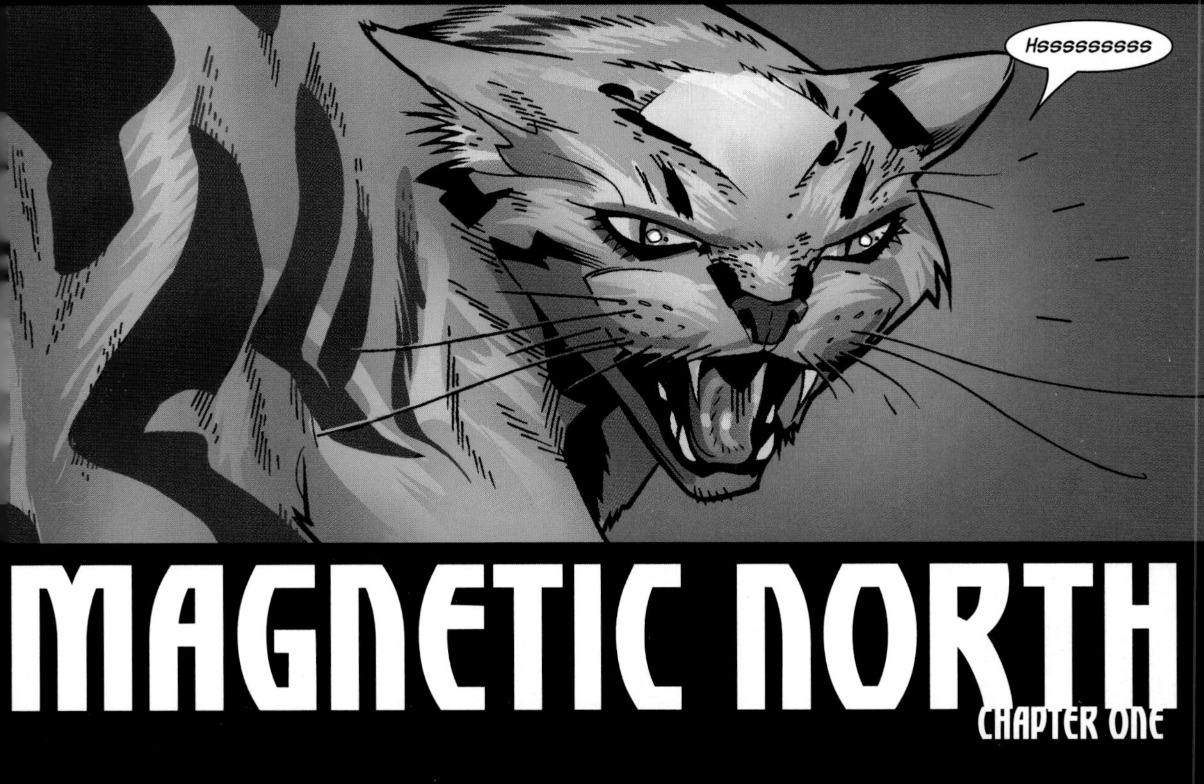
Hssssssssss

MAGNETIC NORTH

CHAPTER ONE

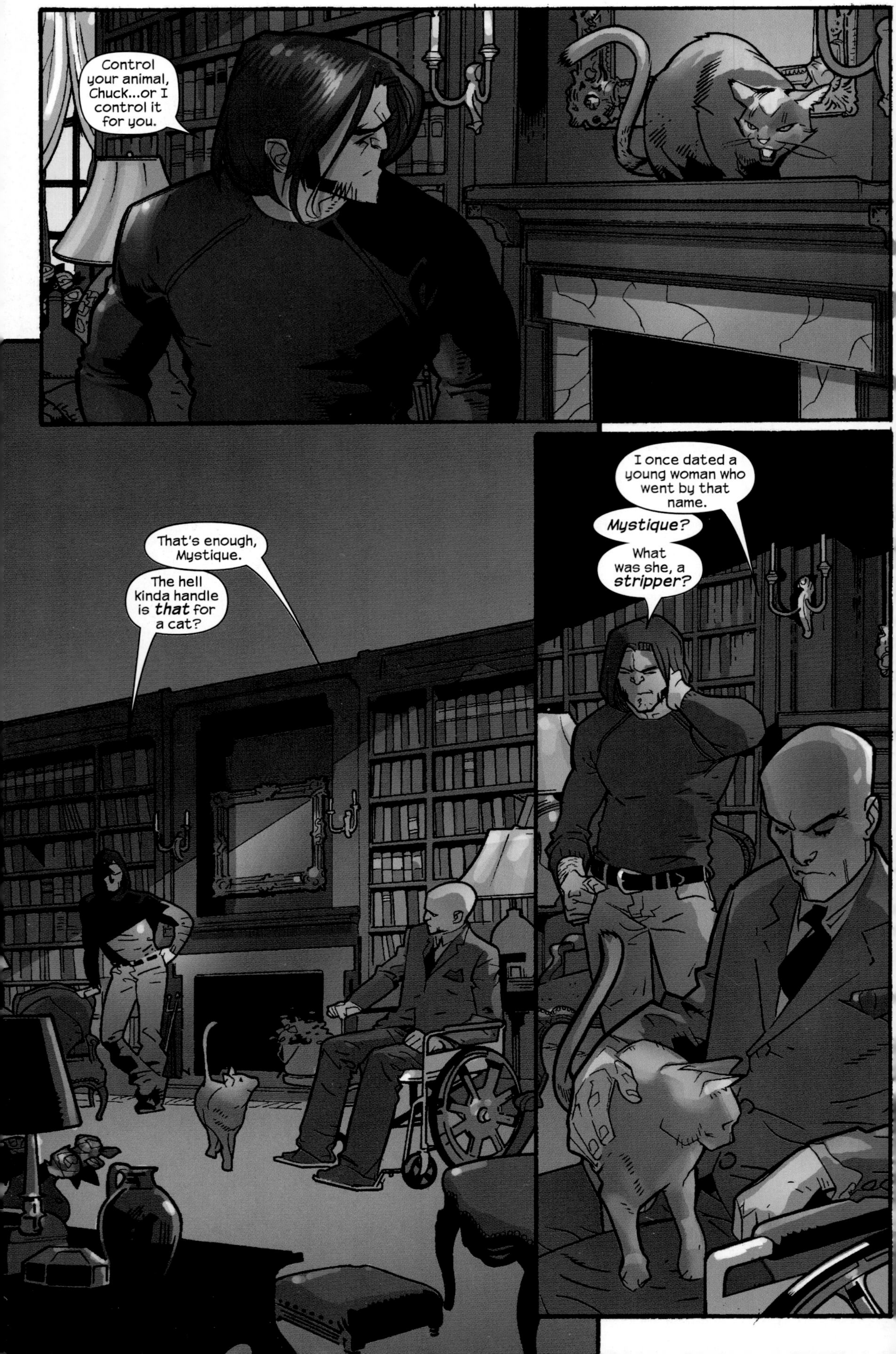
Control your animal, Chuck...or I control it for you.
That's enough, Mystique.
The hell kinda handle is *that* for a cat?
I once dated a young woman who went by that name.
Mystique?
What was she, a *stripper?*

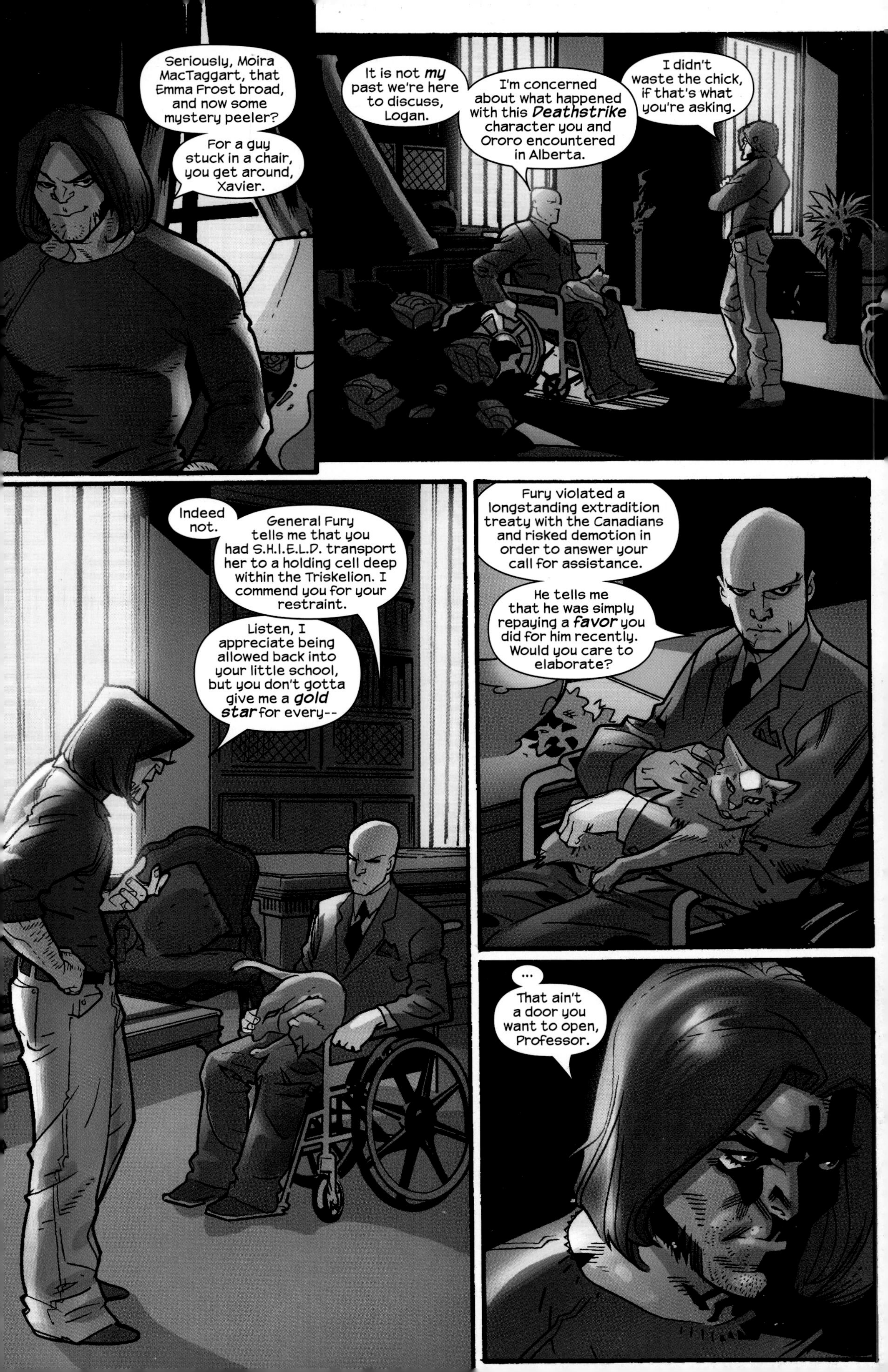
Seriously, Moira MacTaggart, that Emma Frost broad, and now some mystery peeler?
For a guy stuck in a chair, you get around, Xavier.
It is not *my* past we're here to discuss, Logan.
I'm concerned about what happened with this *Deathstrike* character you and Ororo encountered in Alberta.
I didn't waste the chick, if that's what you're asking.
Indeed not.
General Fury tells me that you had S.H.I.E.L.D. transport her to a holding cell deep within the Triskelion. I commend you for your restraint.
Listen, I appreciate being allowed back into your little school, but you don't gotta give me a *gold star* for every--
Fury violated a longstanding extradition treaty with the Canadians and risked demotion in order to answer your call for assistance.
He tells me that he was simply repaying a *favor* you did for him recently. Would you care to elaborate?
...
That ain't a door you want to open, Professor.

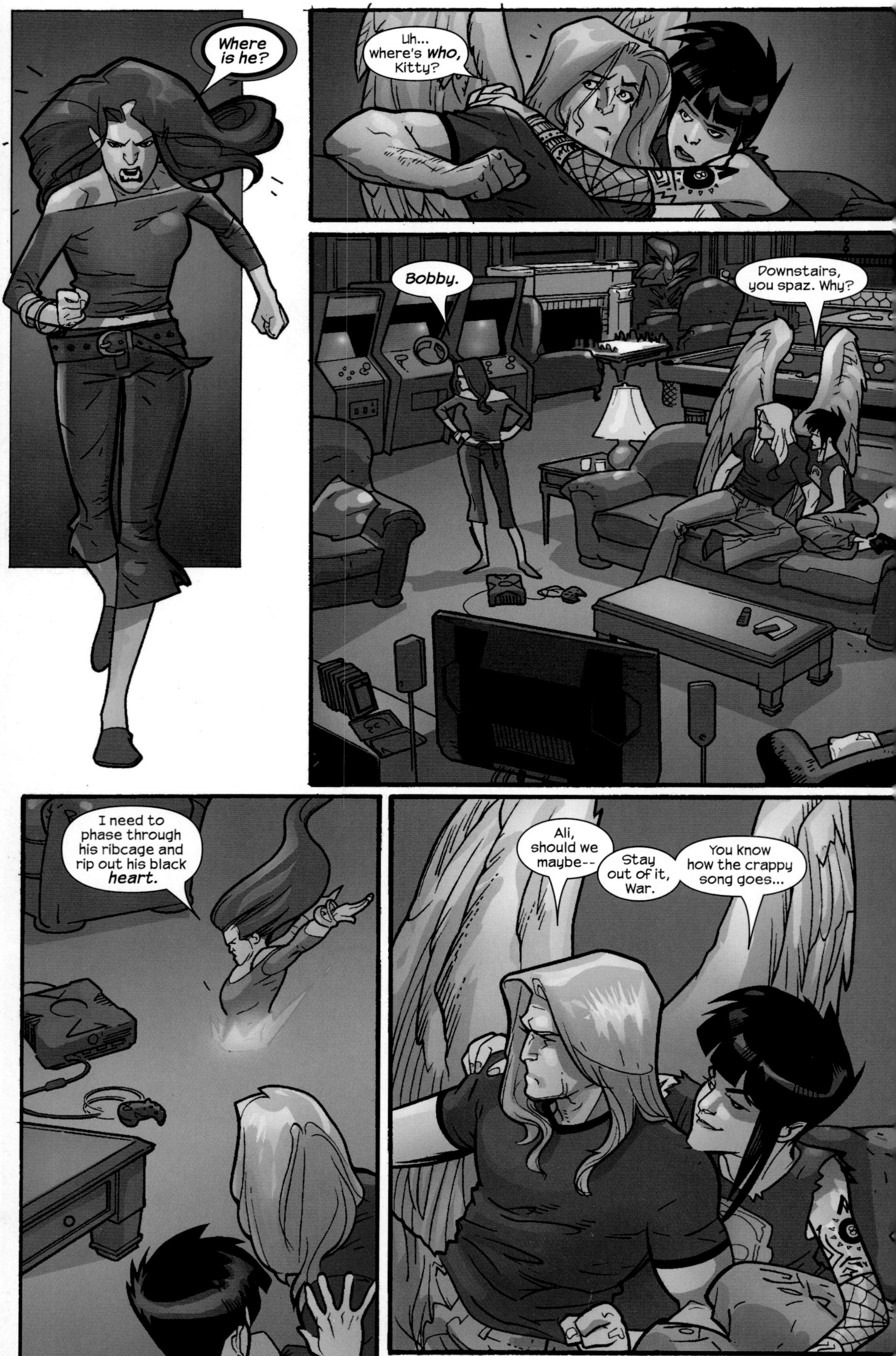

Where is he?
Uh... where's who, Kitty?
Bobby.
Downstairs, you spaz. Why?
I need to phase through his ribcage and rip out his black heart.
Ali, should we maybe--
Stay out of it, War.
You know how the crappy song goes...

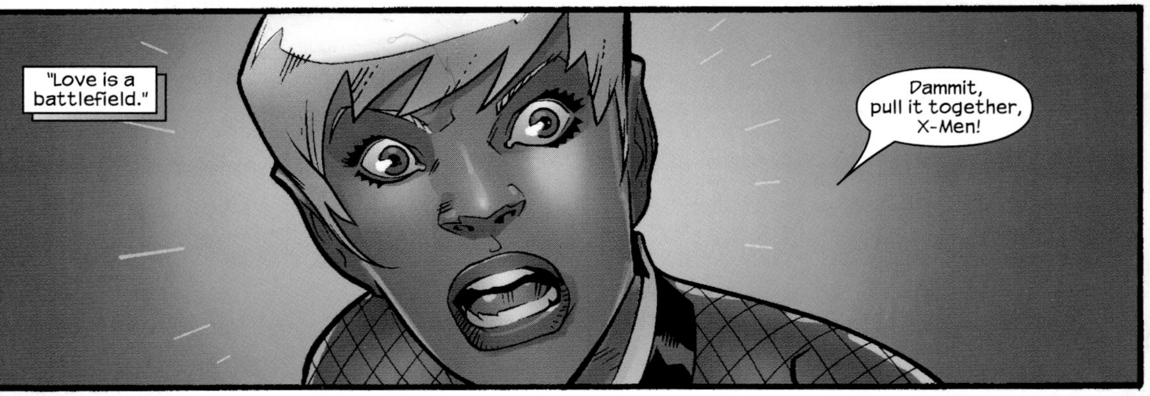
"Love is a battlefield."
Dammit, pull it together, X-Men!

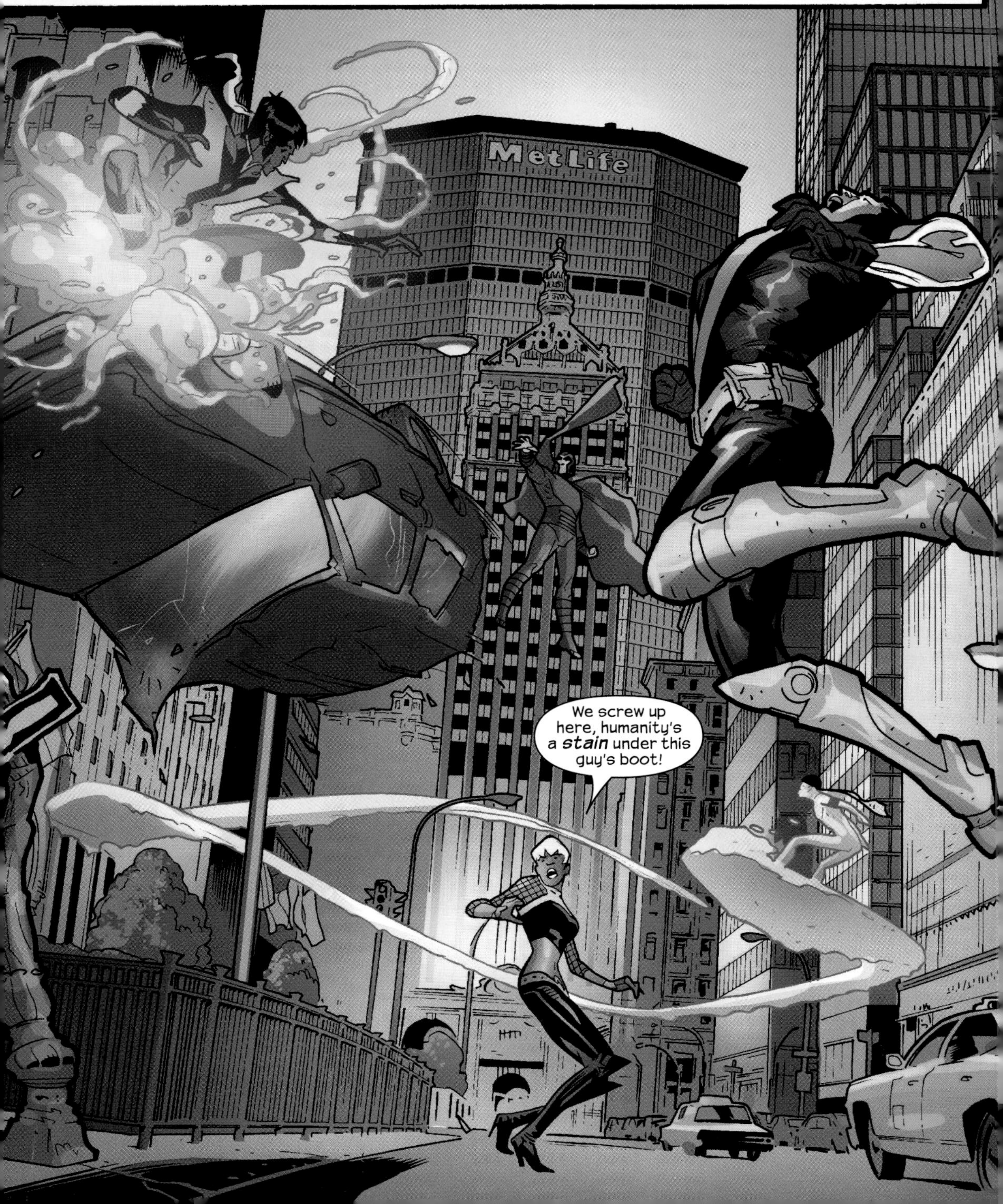
MetLife
We screw up here, humanity's a *stain* under this guy's boot!

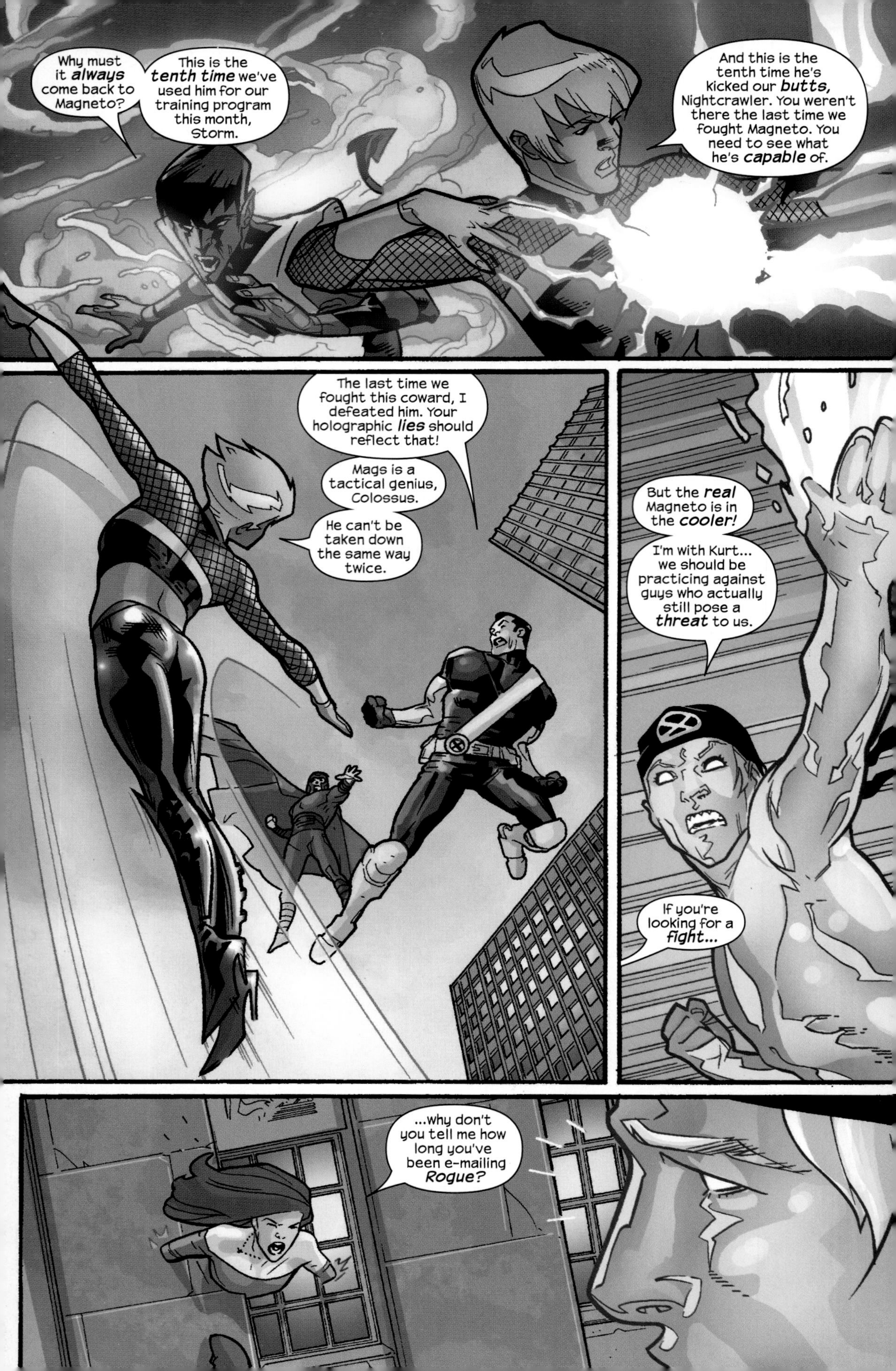
Why must it always come back to Magneto?
This is the tenth time we've used him for our training program this month, Storm.
And this is the tenth time he's kicked our butts, Nightcrawler. You weren't there the last time we fought Magneto. You need to see what he's capable of.
The last time we fought this coward, I defeated him. Your holographic lies should reflect that!
Mags is a tactical genius, Colossus.
He can't be taken down the same way twice.
But the real Magneto is in the cooler!
I'm with Kurt... we should be practicing against guys who actually still pose a threat to us.
If you're looking for a fight...
...why don't you tell me how long you've been e-mailing Rogue?

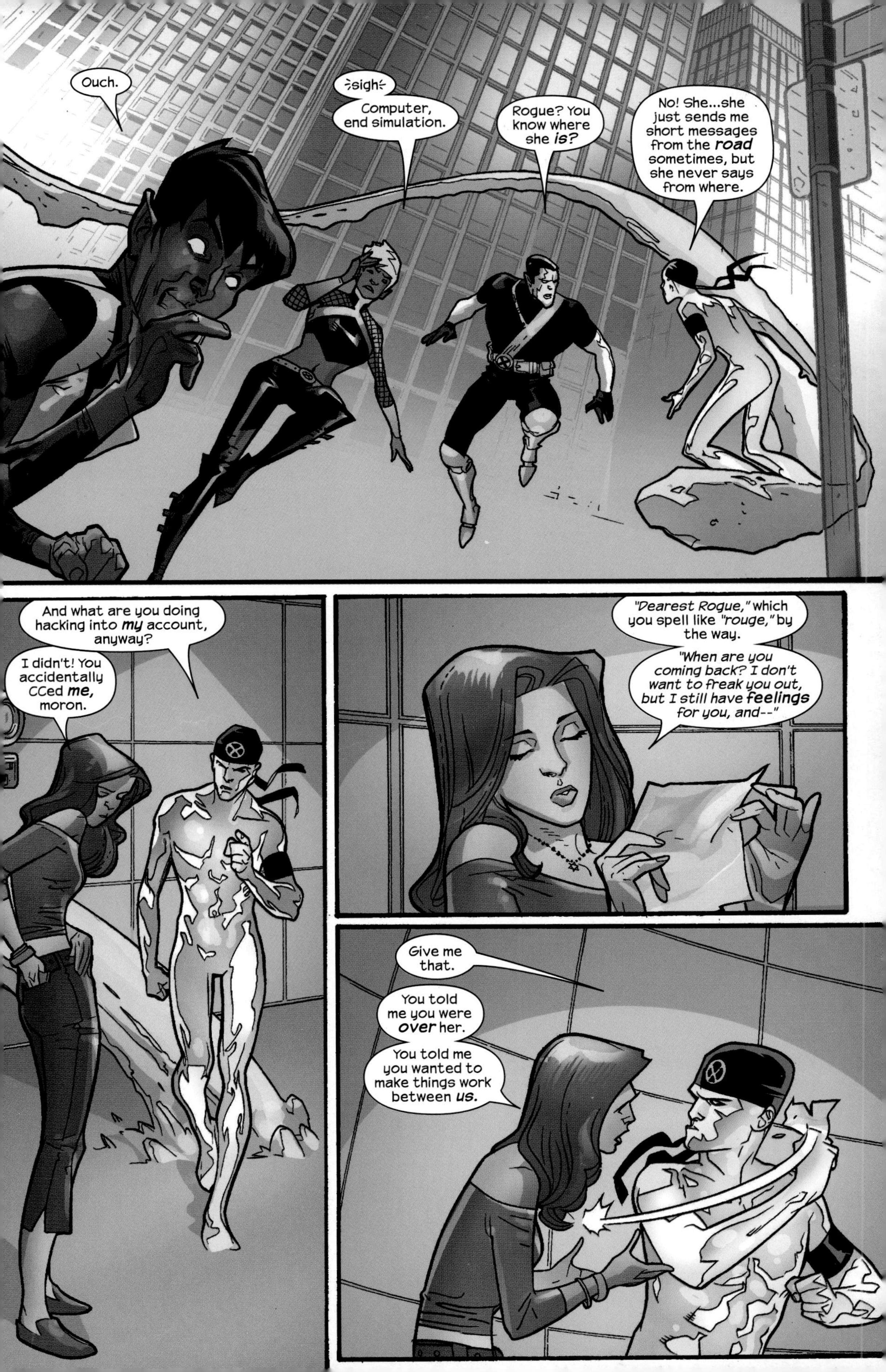
Ouch.
-sigh-
Computer, end simulation.
Rogue? You know where she *is?*
No! She...she just sends me short messages from the *road* sometimes, but she never says from where.
And what are you doing hacking into *my* account, anyway?
I didn't! You accidentally CCed *me,* moron.
"Dearest Rogue," which you spell like "rouge," by the way.
"When are you coming back? I don't want to freak you out, but I still have *feelings* for you, and--"
Give me that.
You told me you were *over* her.
You told me you wanted to make things work between *us.*

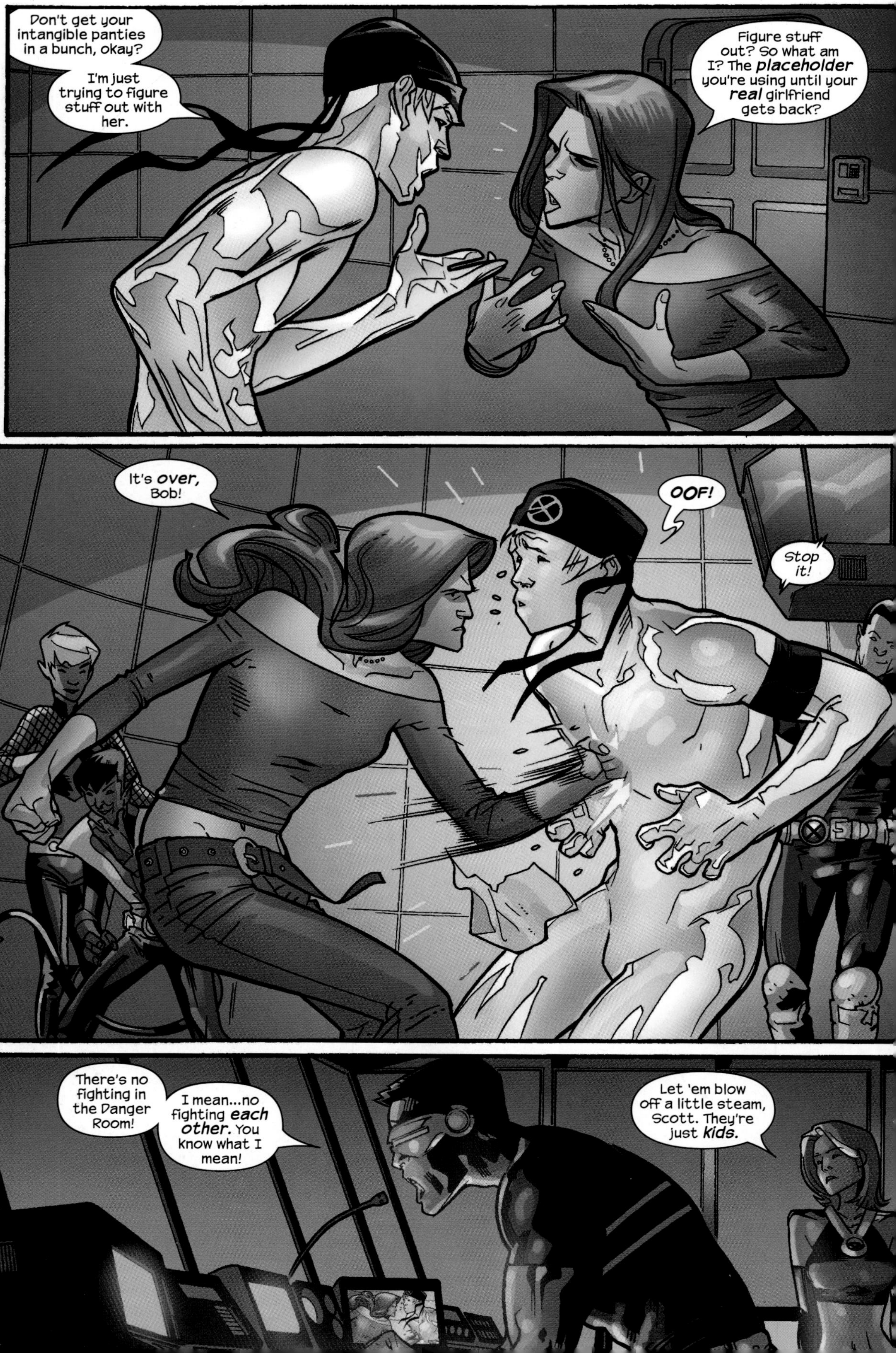
Don't get your intangible panties in a bunch, okay?
I'm just trying to figure stuff out with her.
Figure stuff out? So what am I? The *placeholder* you're using until your *real* girlfriend gets back?
It's *over,* Bob!
OOF!
Stop it!
There's no fighting in the Danger Room!
I mean...no fighting *each other.* You know what I mean!
Let 'em blow off a little steam, Scott. They're just *kids.*

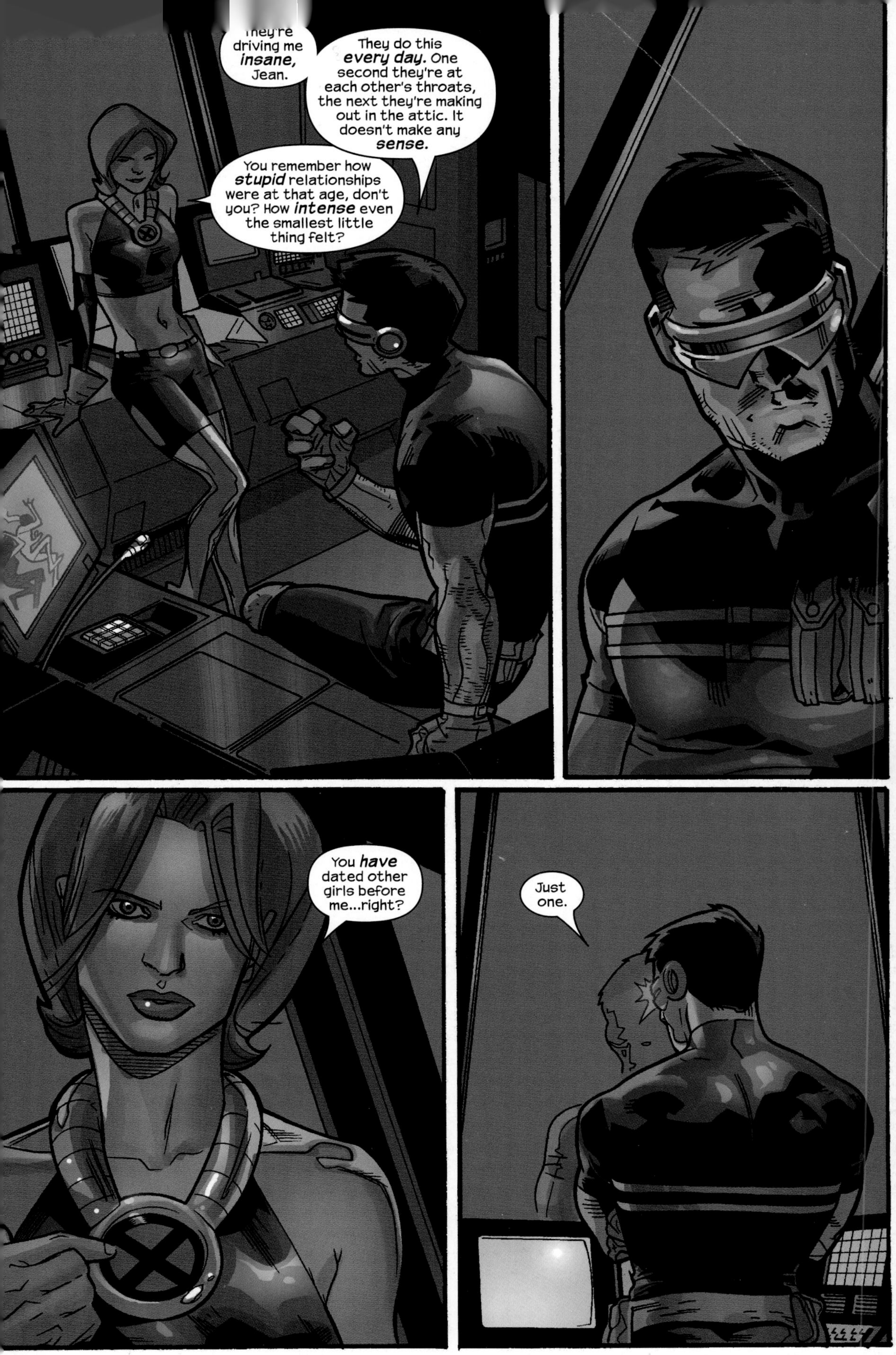
They're driving me *insane,* Jean.
They do this ***every day.*** One second they're at each other's throats, the next they're making out in the attic. It doesn't make any ***sense.***
You remember how ***stupid*** relationships were at that age, don't you? How ***intense*** even the smallest little thing felt?
You ***have*** dated other girls before me...right?
Just one.

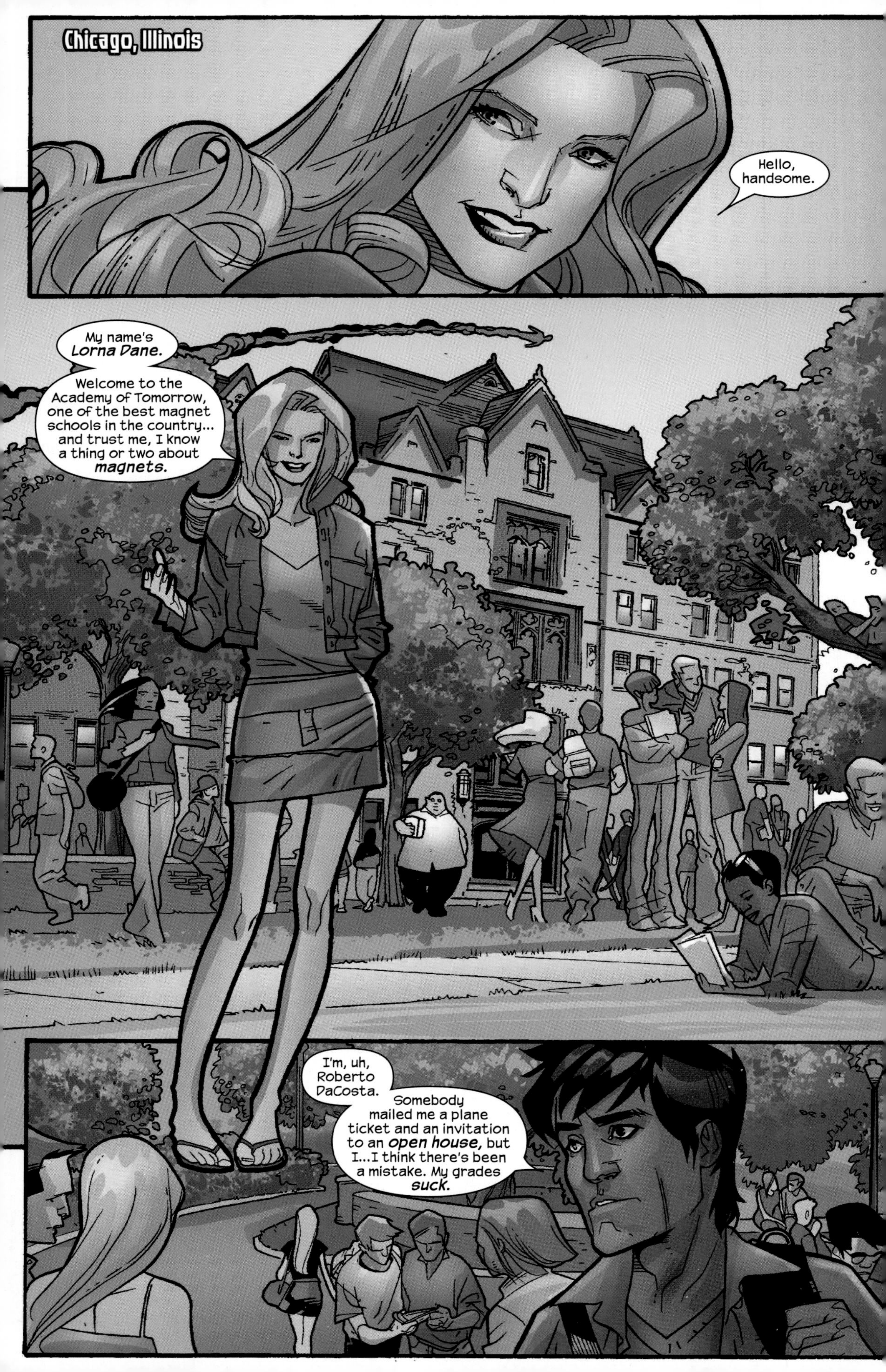
Chicago, Illinois
Hello, handsome.
My name's *Lorna Dane.*
Welcome to the Academy of Tomorrow, one of the best magnet schools in the country... and trust me, I know a thing or two about ***magnets.***
I'm, uh, Roberto DaCosta.
Somebody mailed me a plane ticket and an invitation to an ***open house,*** but I...I think there's been a mistake. My grades ***suck.***

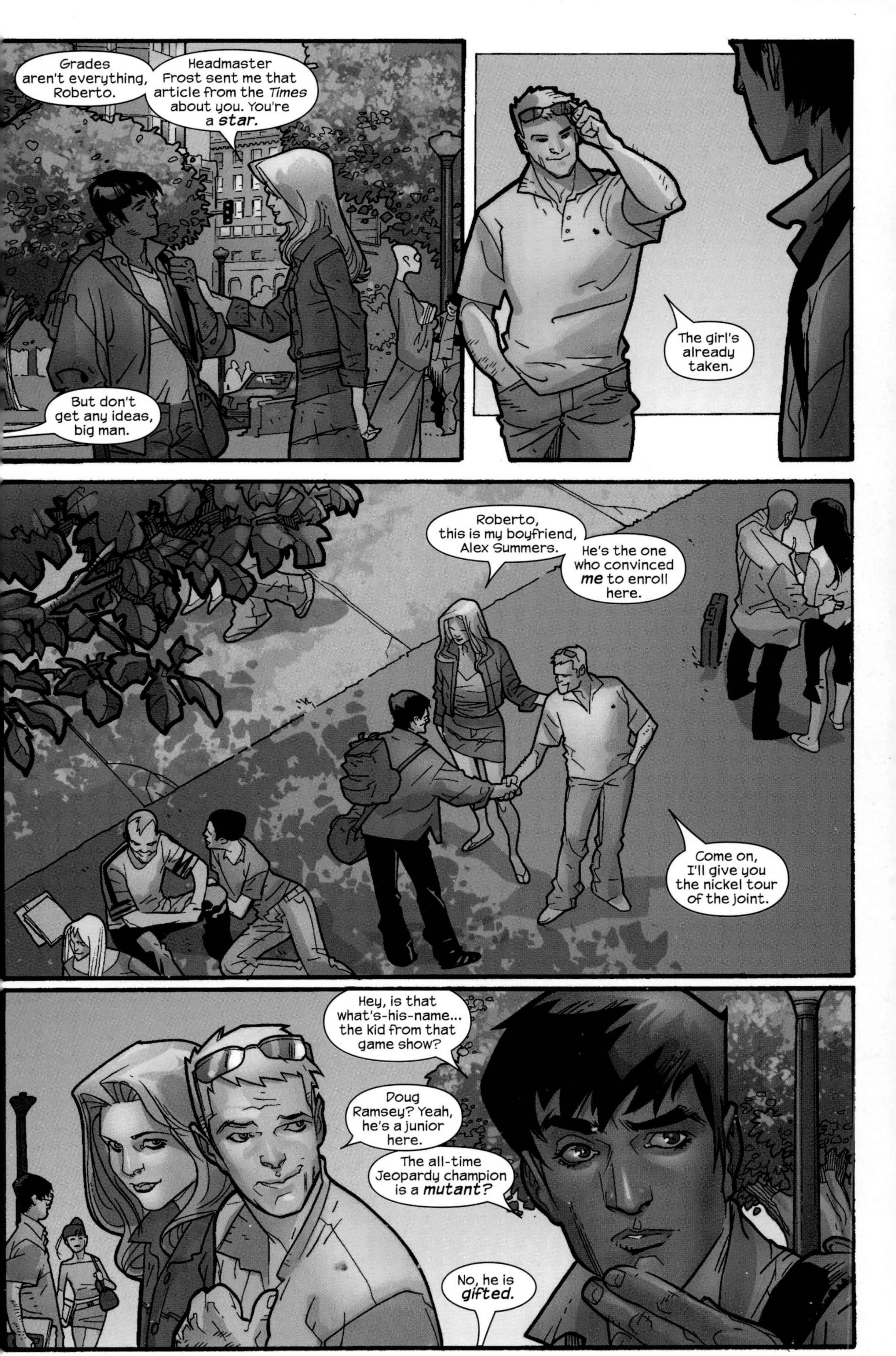
Grades aren't everything, Roberto.
Headmaster Frost sent me that article from the *Times* about you. You're a ***star.***
But don't get any ideas, big man.
The girl's already taken.
Roberto, this is my boyfriend, Alex Summers.
He's the one who convinced ***me*** to enroll here.
Come on, I'll give you the nickel tour of the joint.
Hey, is that what's-his-name... the kid from that game show?
Doug Ramsey? Yeah, he's a junior here.
The all-time Jeopardy champion is a ***mutant?***
No, he is ***gifted.***

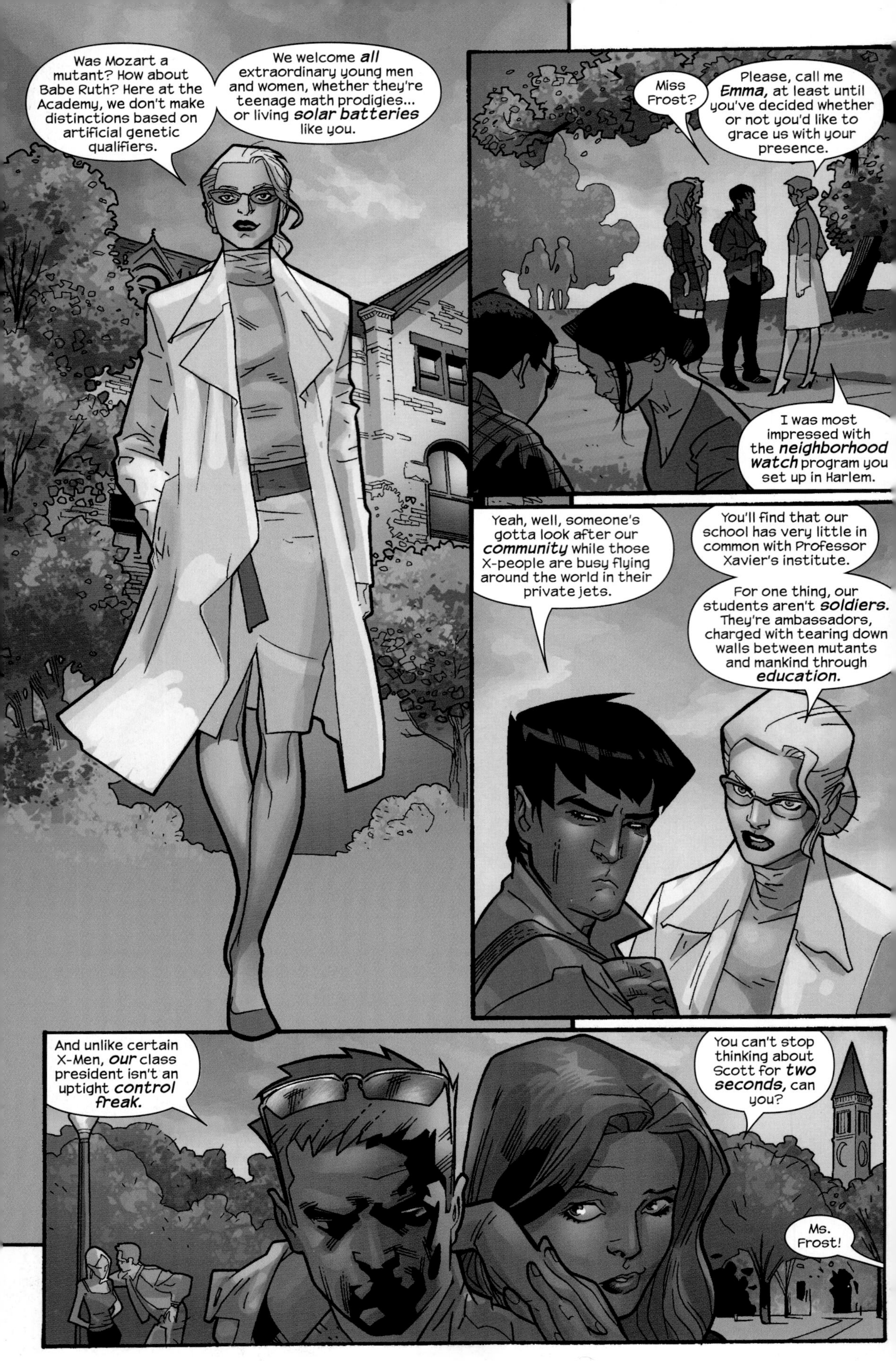

Was Mozart a mutant? How about Babe Ruth? Here at the Academy, we don't make distinctions based on artificial genetic qualifiers.
We welcome all extraordinary young men and women, whether they're teenage math prodigies... or living solar batteries like you.
Miss Frost?
Please, call me Emma, at least until you've decided whether or not you'd like to grace us with your presence.
I was most impressed with the neighborhood watch program you set up in Harlem.
Yeah, well, someone's gotta look after our community while those X-people are busy flying around the world in their private jets.
You'll find that our school has very little in common with Professor Xavier's institute.
For one thing, our students aren't soldiers. They're ambassadors, charged with tearing down walls between mutants and mankind through education.
And unlike certain X-Men, our class president isn't an uptight control freak.
You can't stop thinking about Scott for two seconds, can you?
Ms. Frost!

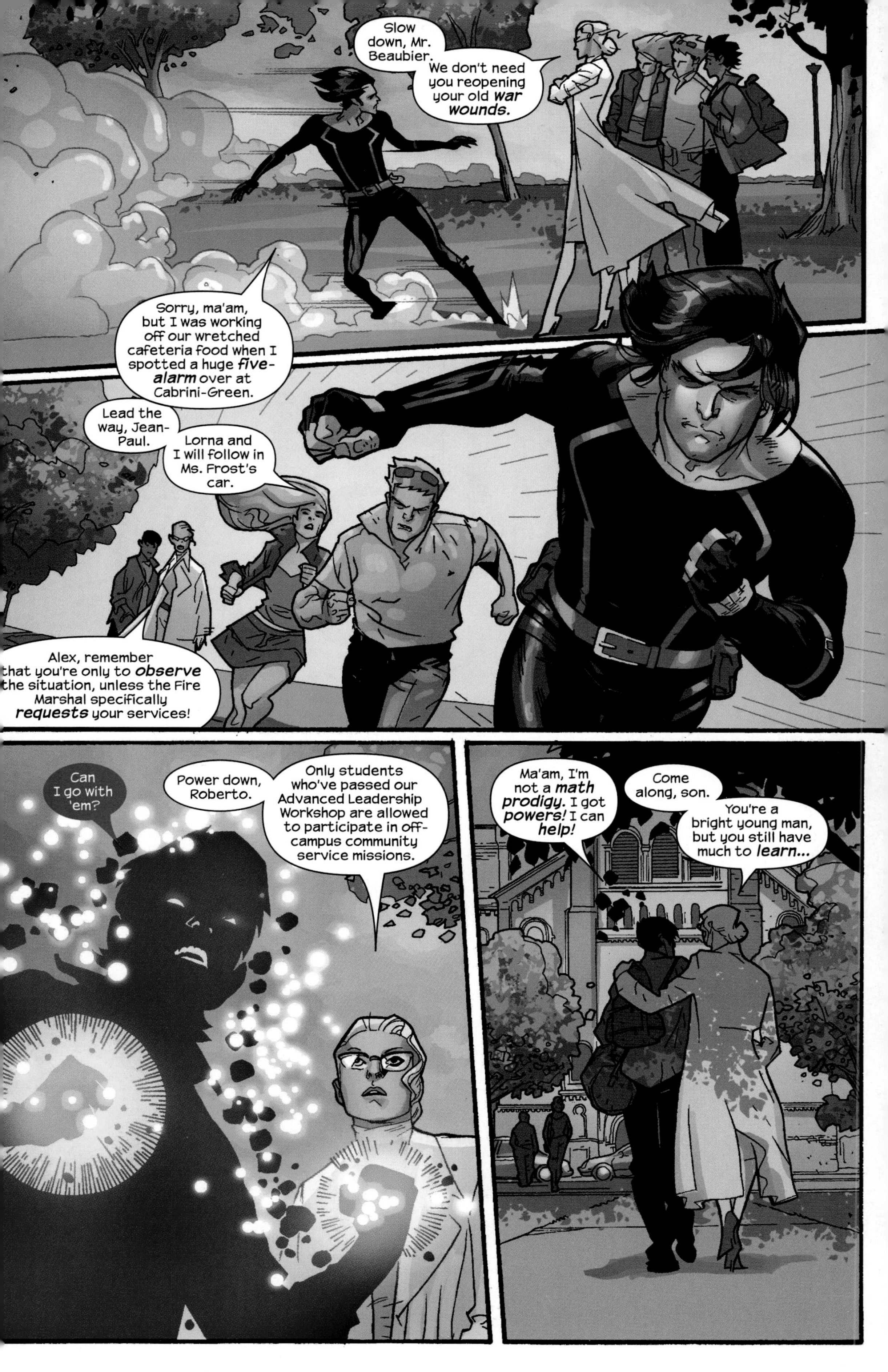
Slow down, Mr. Beaubier.
We don't need you reopening your old *war wounds.*
Sorry, ma'am, but I was working off our wretched cafeteria food when I spotted a huge *five-alarm* over at Cabrini-Green.
Lead the way, Jean-Paul.
Lorna and I will follow in Ms. Frost's car.
Alex, remember that you're only to *observe* the situation, unless the Fire Marshal specifically *requests* your services!
Can I go with 'em?
Power down, Roberto.
Only students who've passed our Advanced Leadership Workshop are allowed to participate in off-campus community service missions.
Ma'am, I'm not a *math prodigy.* I got *powers!* I can *help!*
Come along, son.
You're a bright young man, but you still have much to *learn...*

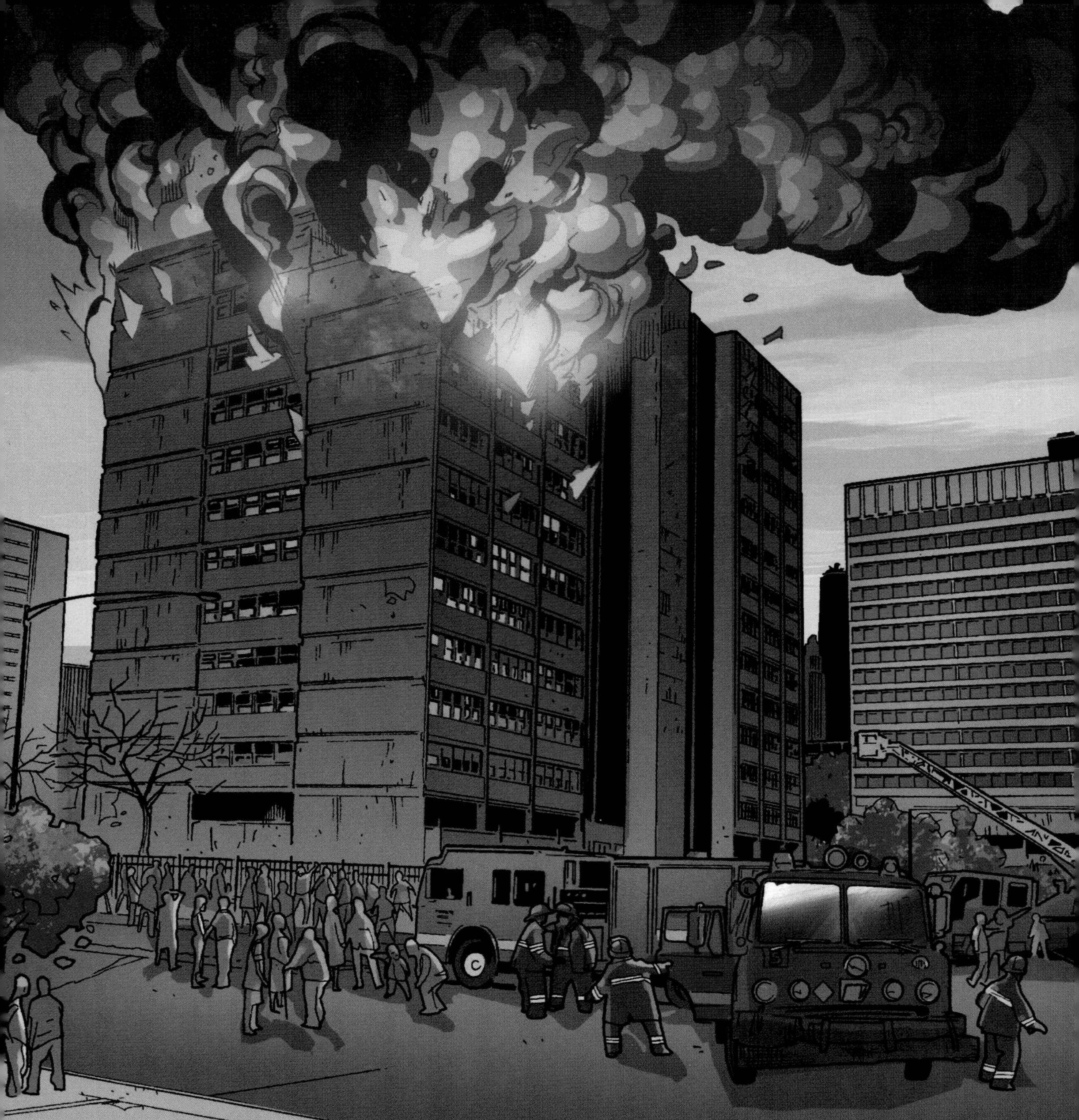

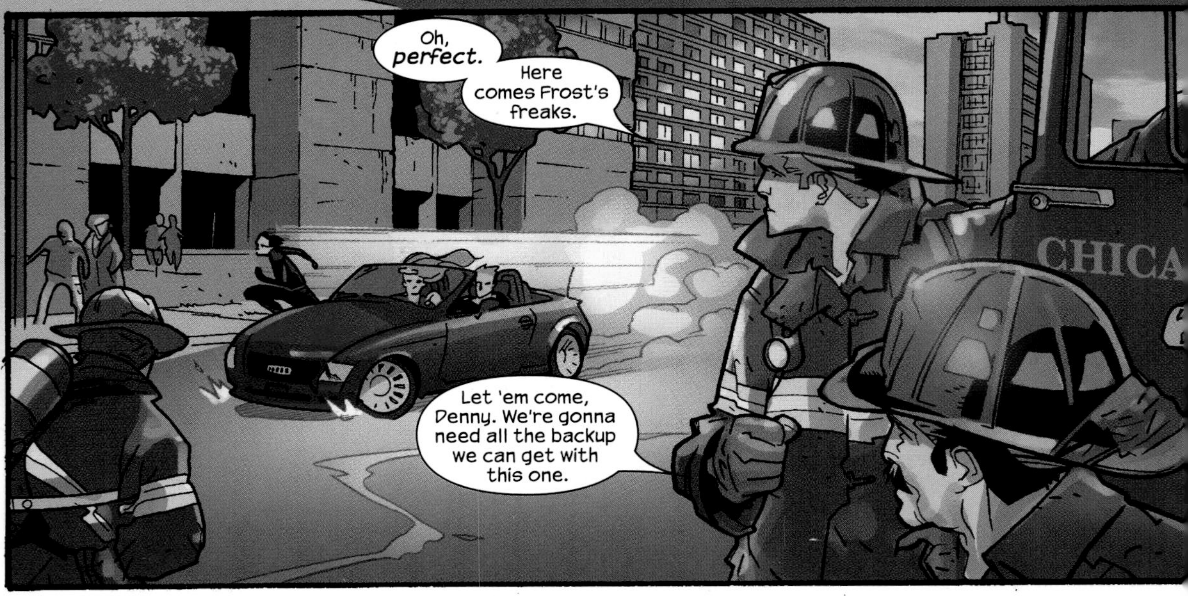
Oh, *perfect.*
Here comes Frost's freaks.
CHICA
Let 'em come, Denny. We're gonna need all the backup we can get with this one.

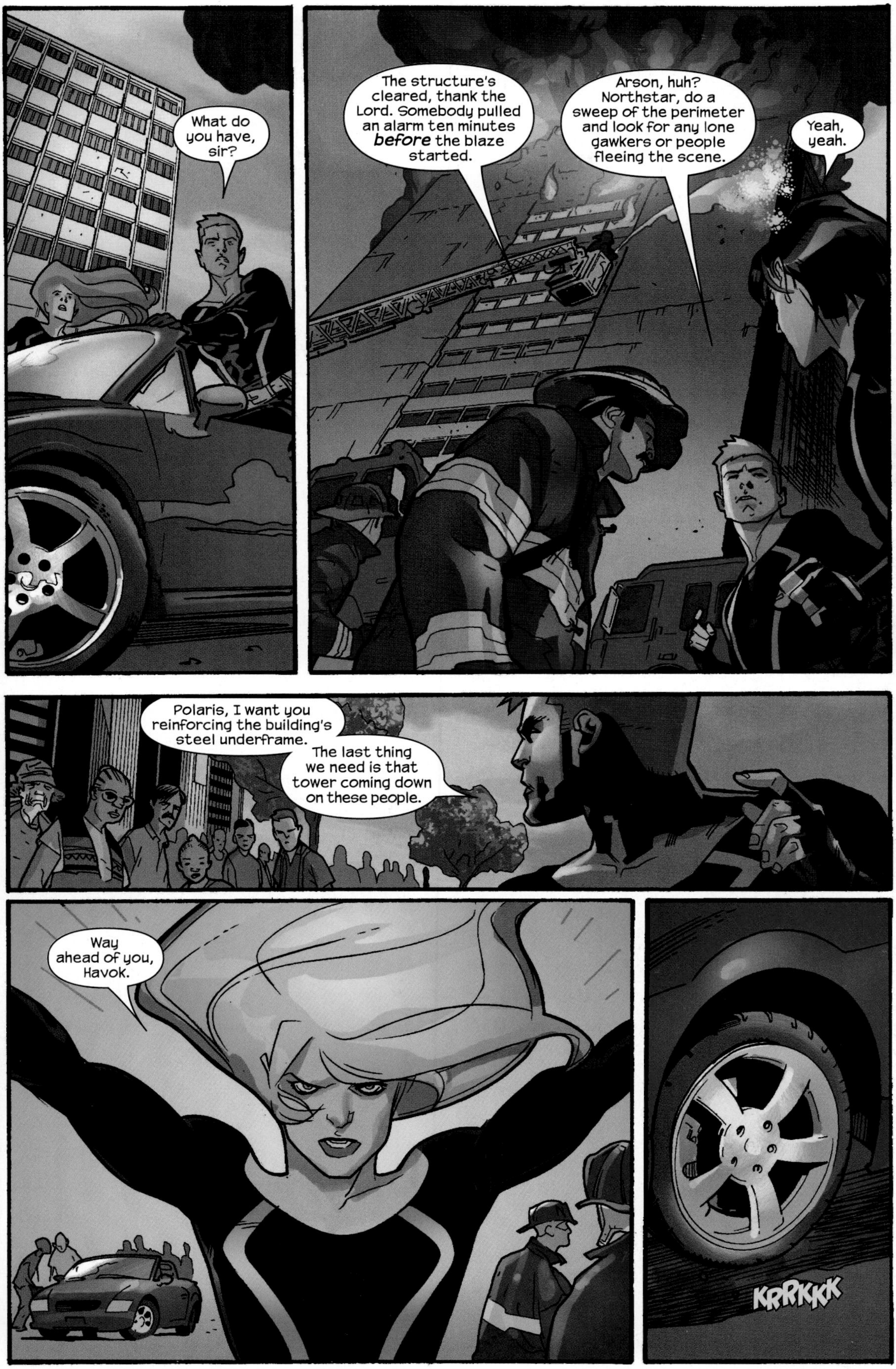
What do you have, sir?
The structure's cleared, thank the Lord. Somebody pulled an alarm ten minutes *before* the blaze started.
Arson, huh? Northstar, do a sweep of the perimeter and look for any lone gawkers or people fleeing the scene.
Yeah, yeah.
Polaris, I want you reinforcing the building's steel underframe.
The last thing we need is that tower coming down on these people.
Way ahead of you, Havok.
KRRKKK

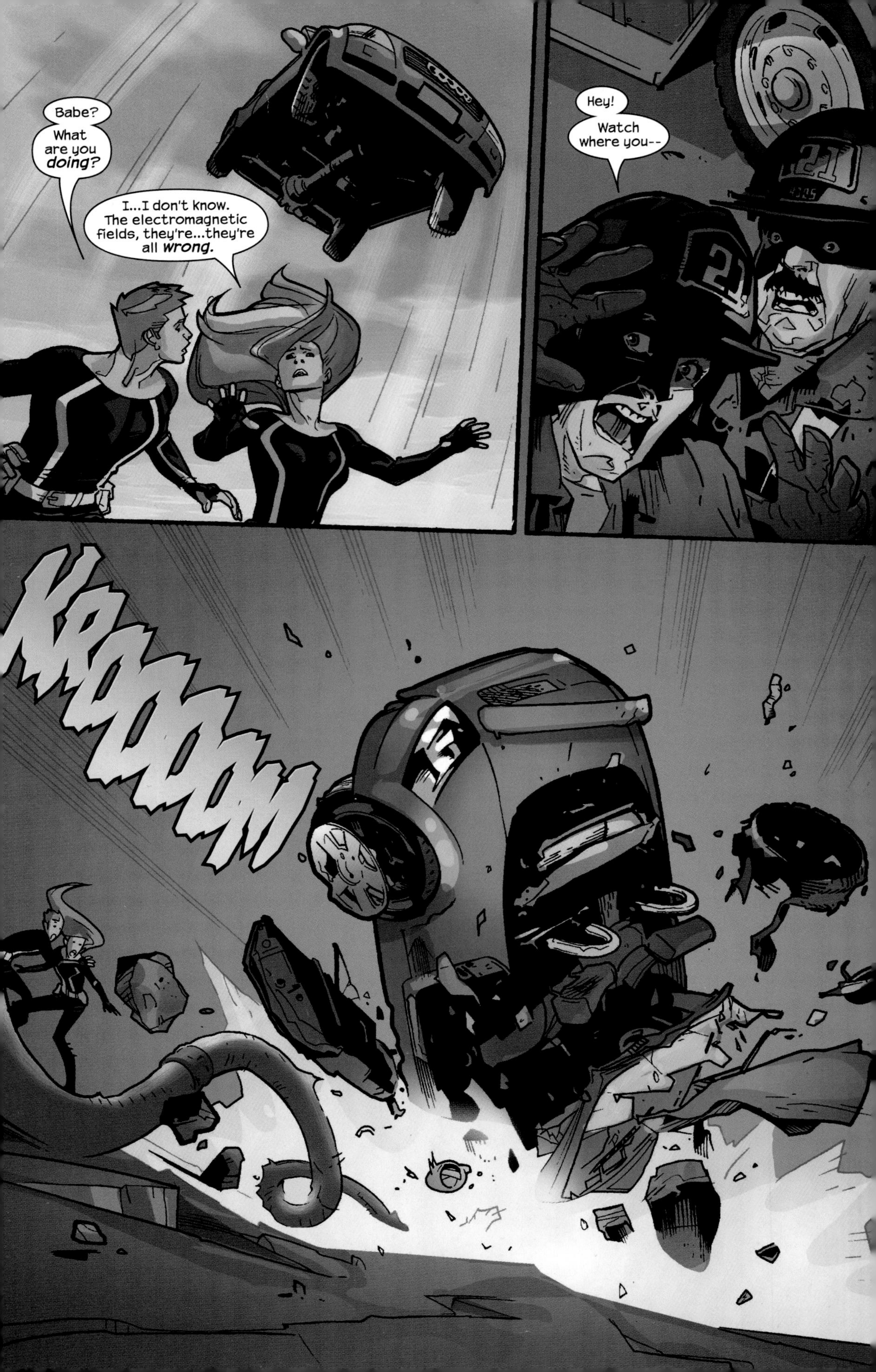
Babe?
What are you *doing?*
I...I don't know. The electromagnetic fields, they're...they're all *wrong.*
Hey!
Watch where you--
KRAOOOM

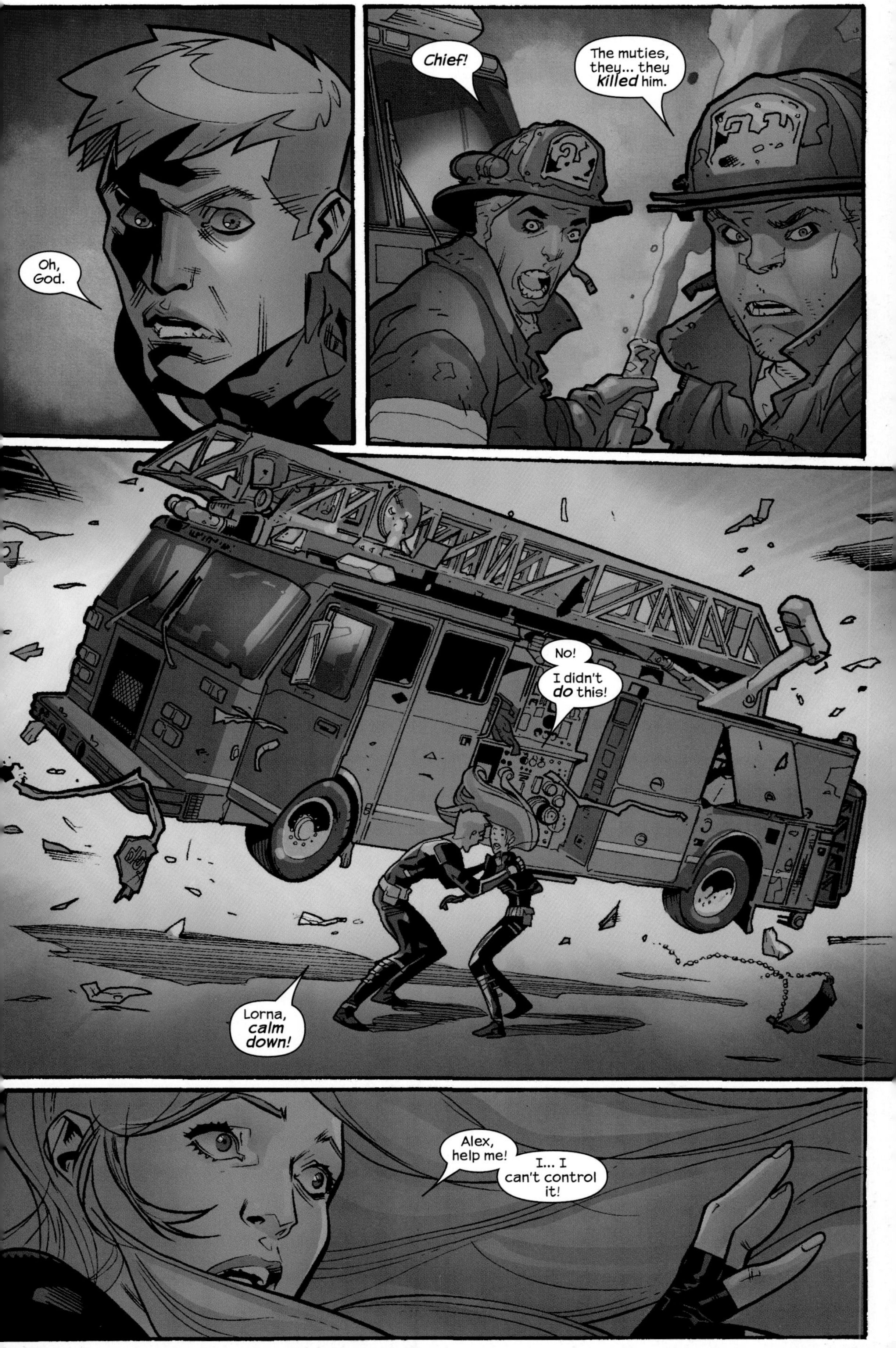
Oh, God.
Chief!
The muties, they... they *killed* him.
No!
I didn't *do* this!
Lorna, *calm down*!
Alex, help me!
I... I can't control it!

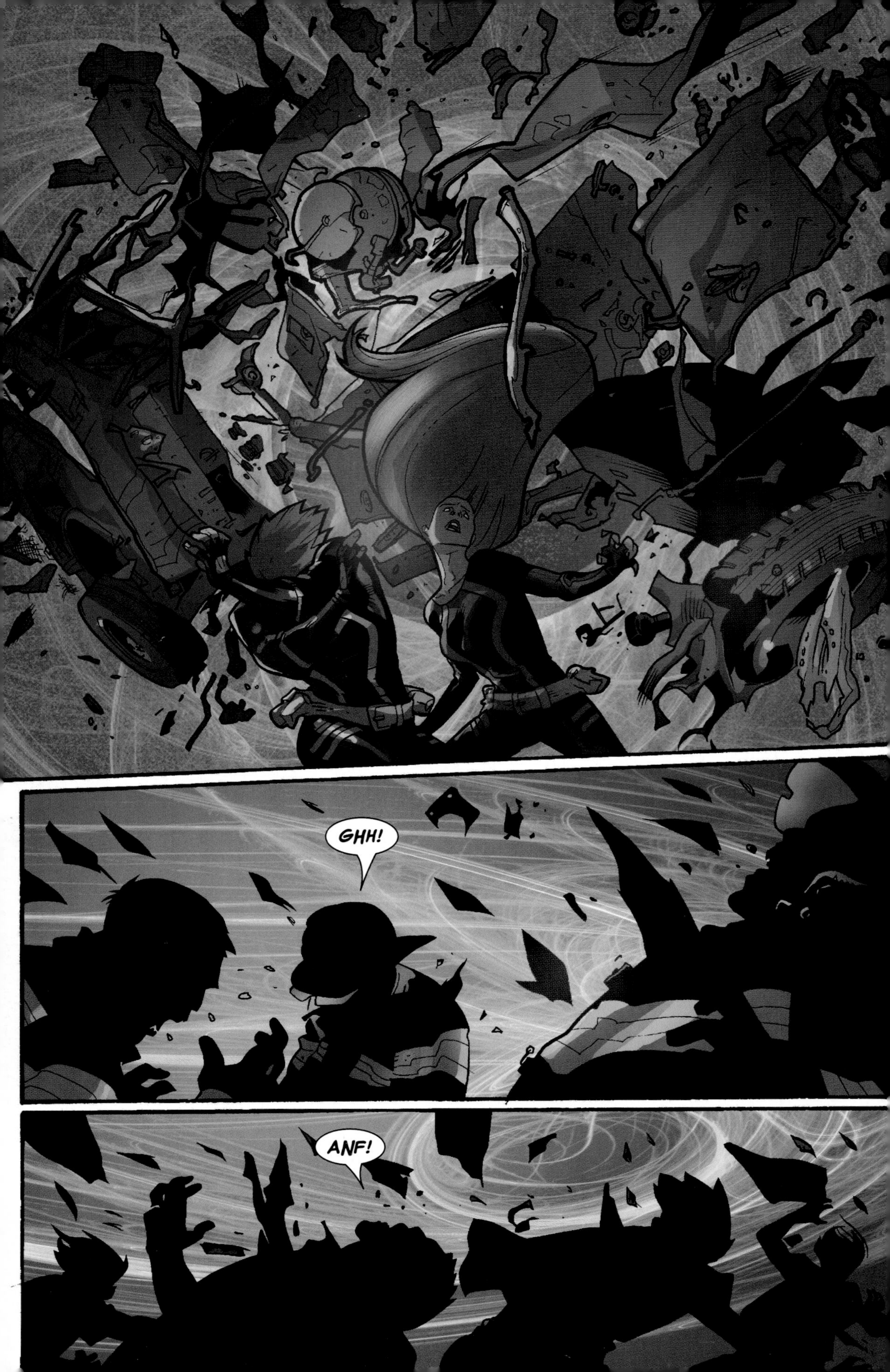
GHH!
ANF!

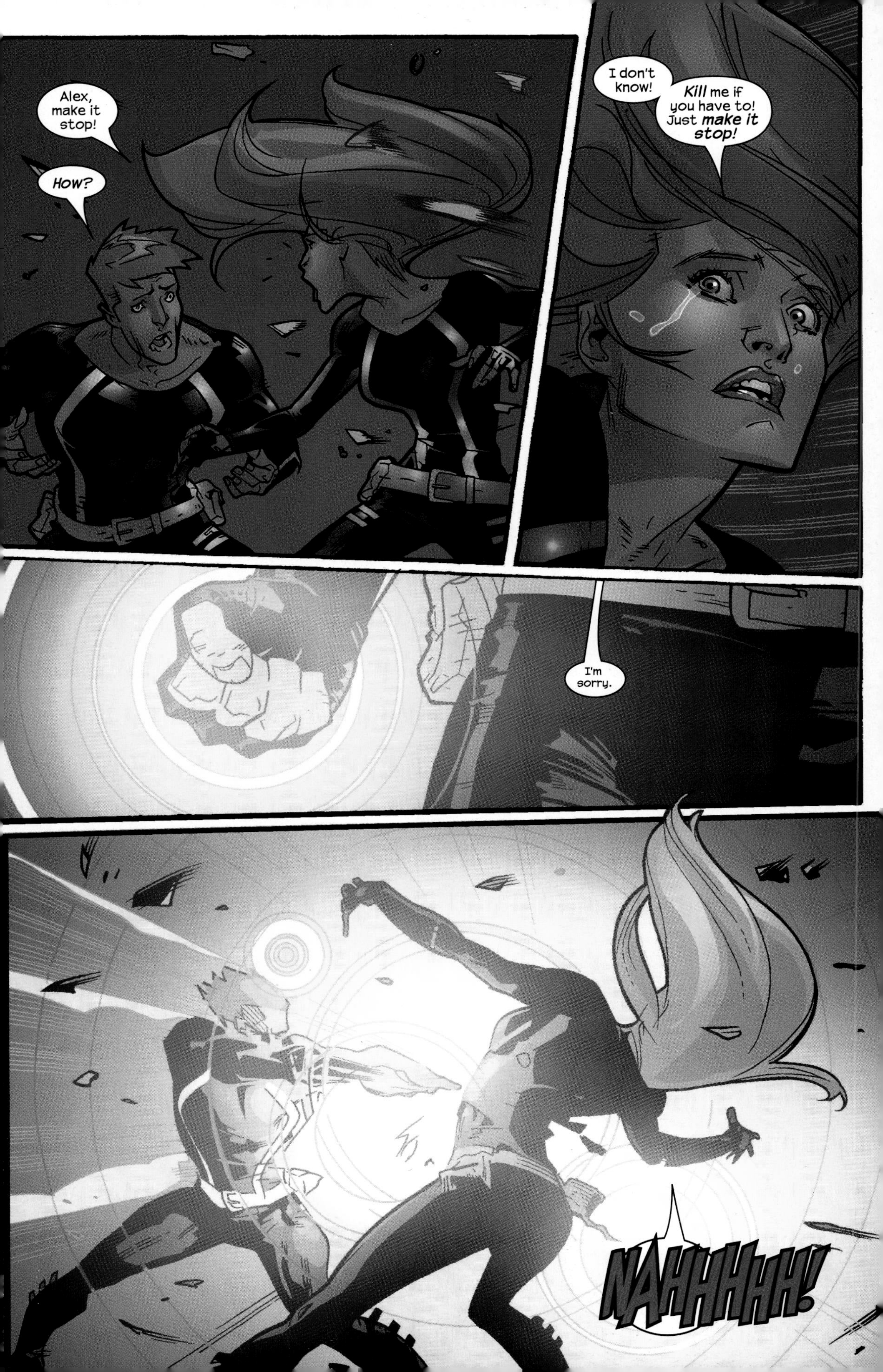
Alex, make it stop!
How?
I don't know!
Kill me if you have to! Just make it stop!
I'm sorry.
NAHHHHH!

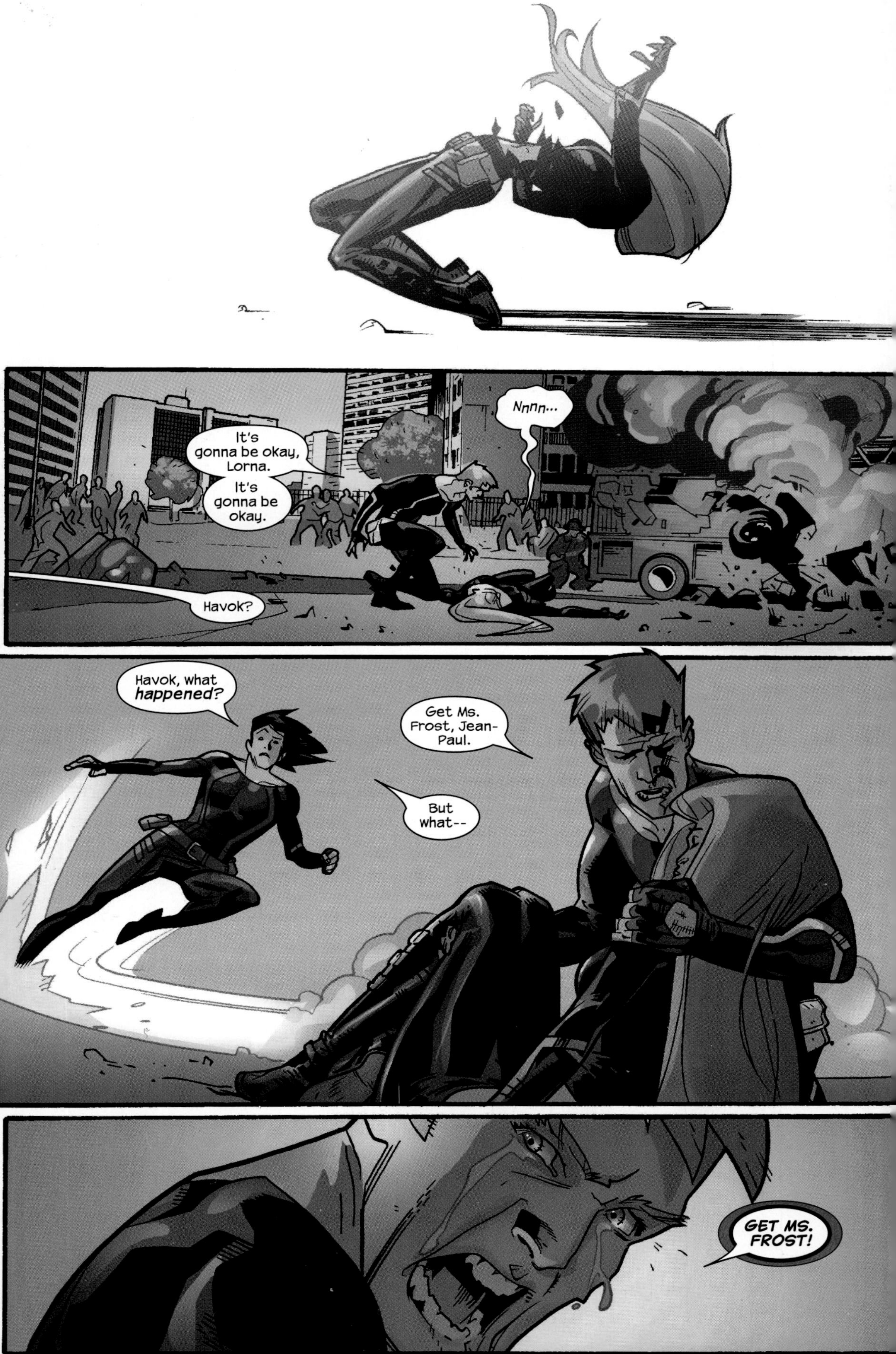
Nnnn...
It's gonna be okay, Lorna.
It's gonna be okay.
Havok?
Havok, what *happened*?
Get Ms. Frost, Jean-Paul.
But what--
GET MS. FROST!

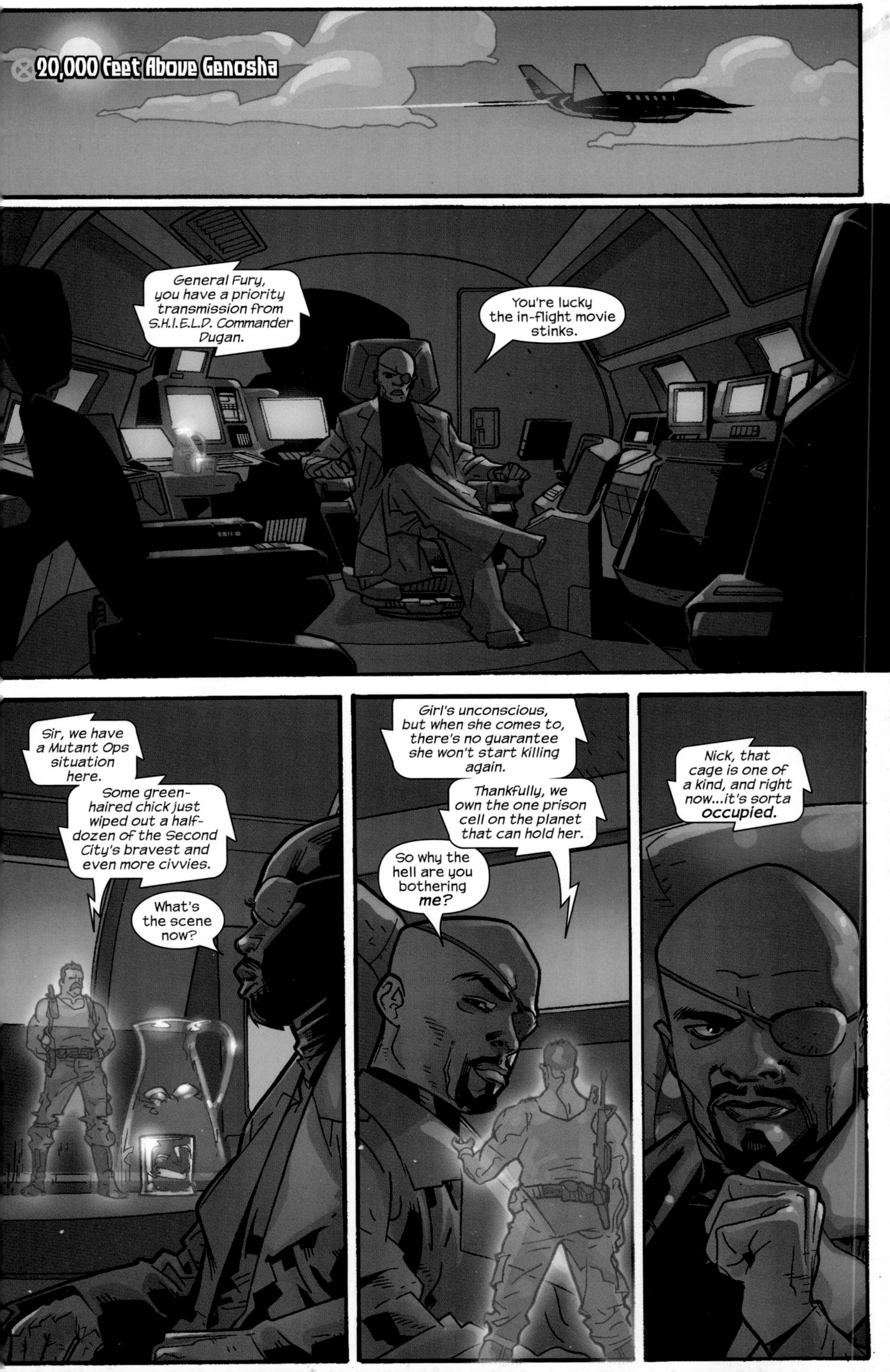
20,000 Feet Above Genosha
General Fury, you have a priority transmission from S.H.I.E.L.D. Commander Dugan.
You're lucky the in-flight movie stinks.
Sir, we have a Mutant Ops situation here.
Some green-haired chick just wiped out a half-dozen of the Second City's bravest and even more civvies.
What's the scene now?
Girl's unconscious, but when she comes to, there's no guarantee she won't start killing again.
Thankfully, we own the one prison cell on the planet that can hold her.
So why the hell are you bothering me?
Nick, that cage is one of a kind, and right now...it's sorta occupied.

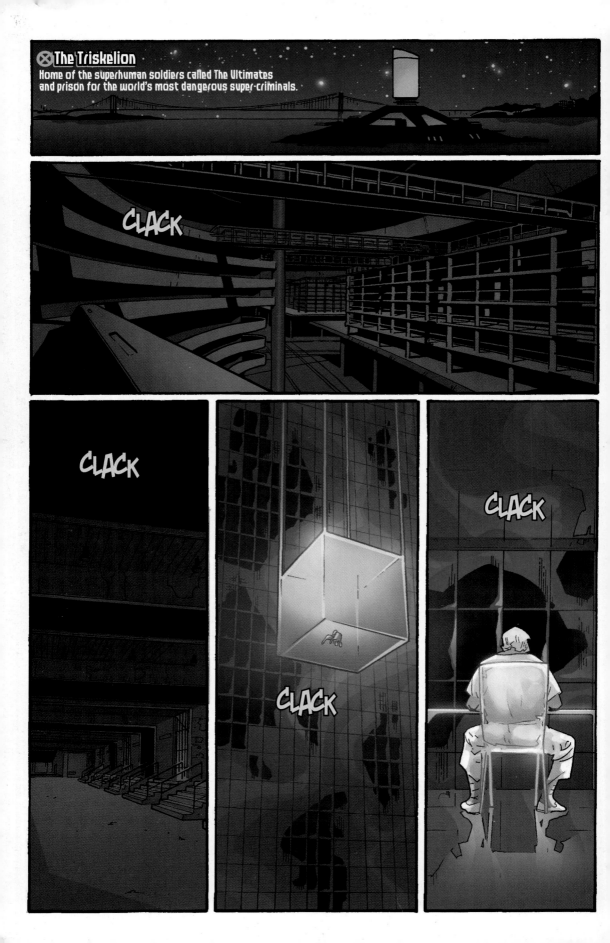

The Triskelion
Home of the superhuman soldiers called The Ultimates
and prison for the world's most dangerous super-criminals.

CLACK

CLACK

CLACK

CLACK

CLACK

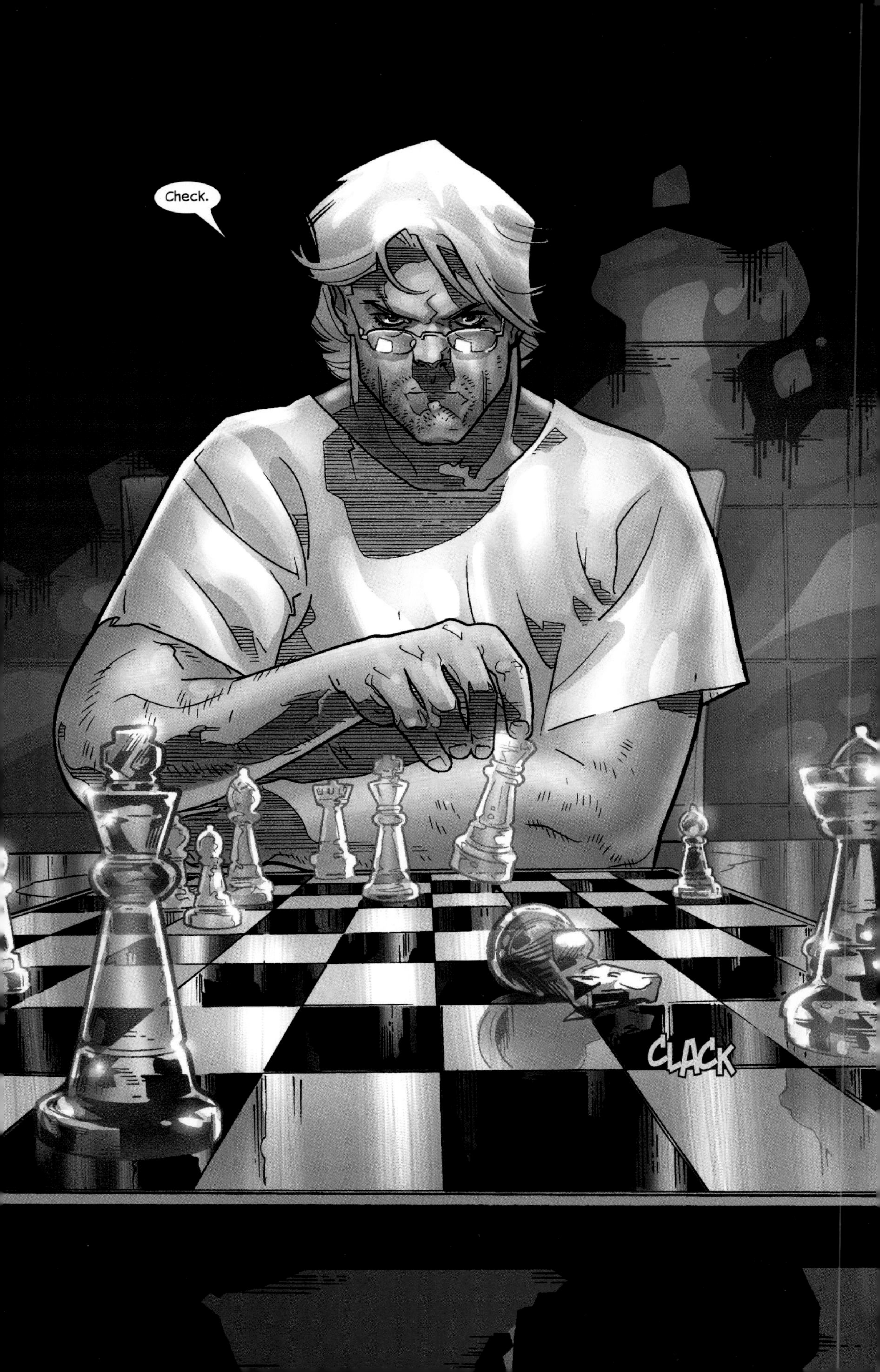
Check.
CLACK

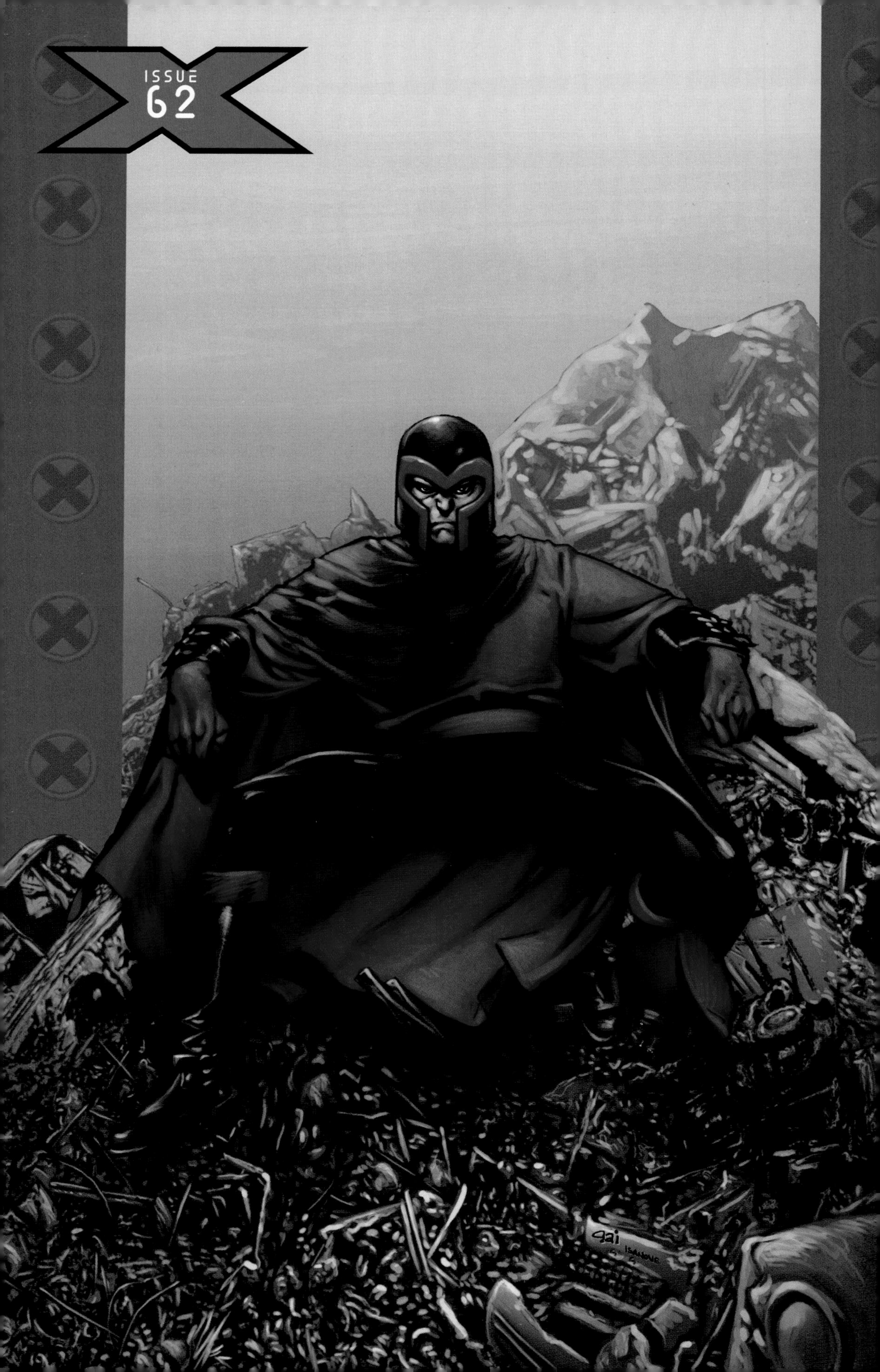
ISSUE
62

"The Savage Land" Somewhere in the South Pacific

KRAAAAAAA

MAGNETIC NORTH

CHAPTER TWO

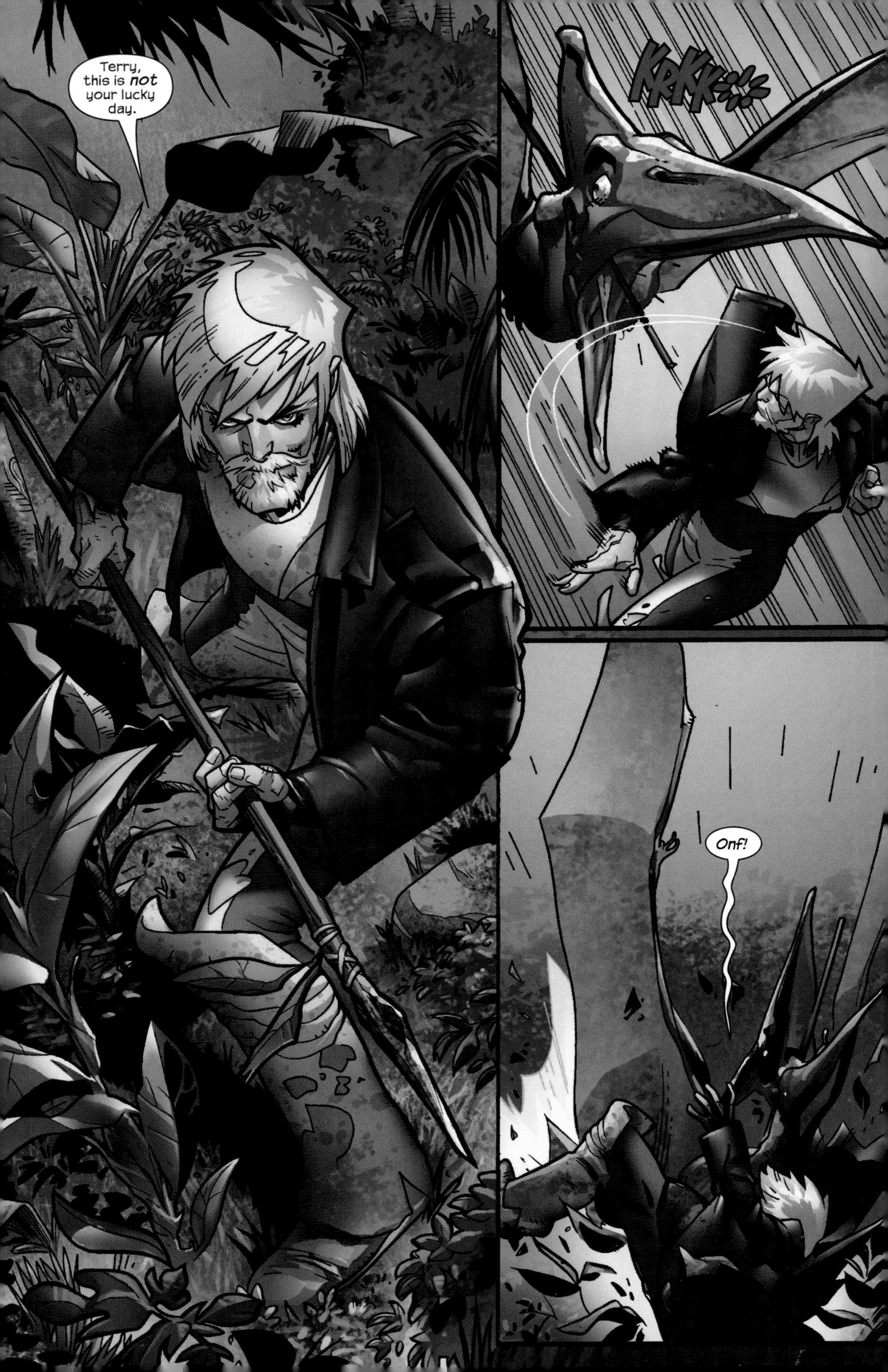
Terry, this is *not* your lucky day.
KRKKK
Onf!

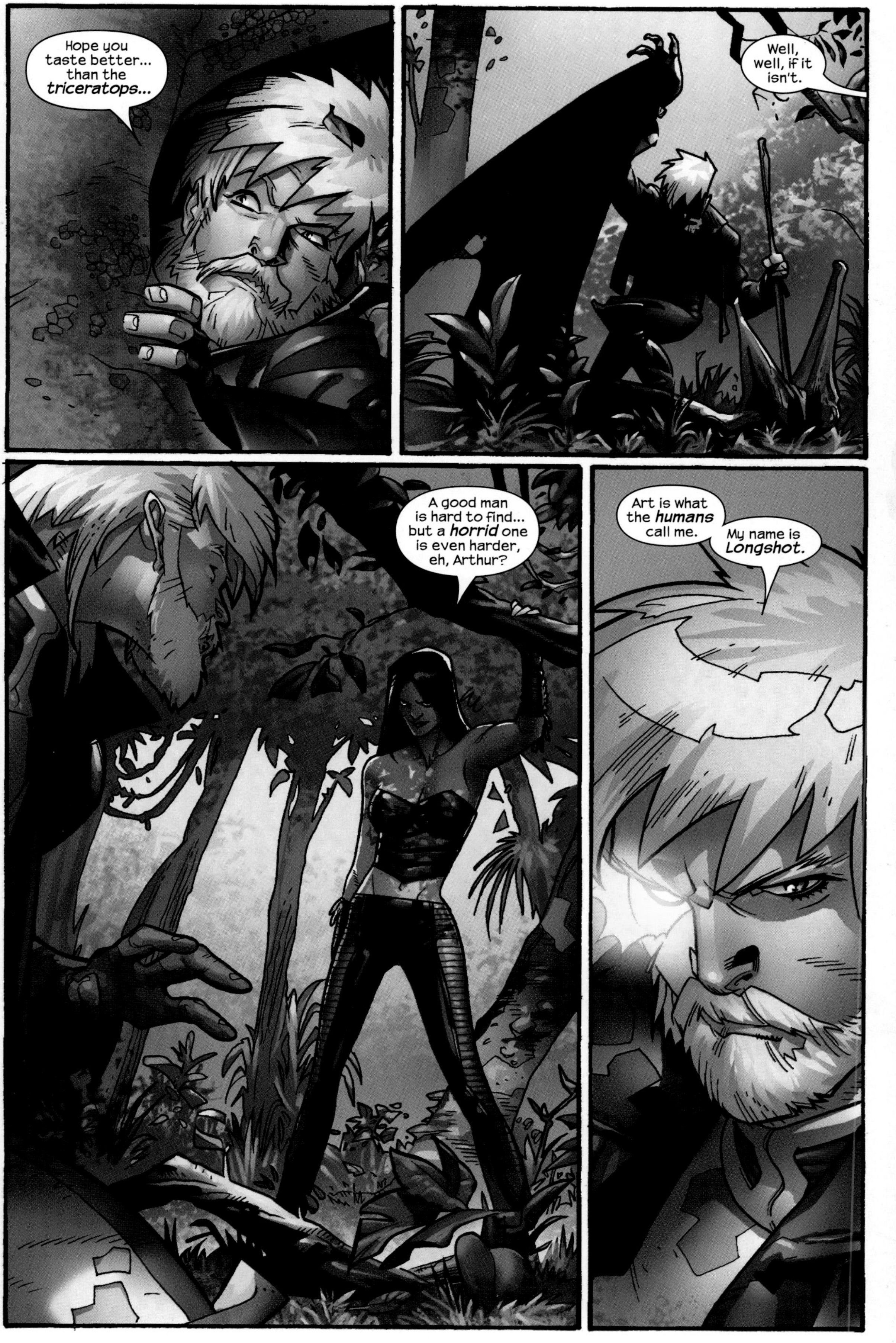
Hope you taste better... than the *triceratops...*
Well, well, if it isn't.
A good man is hard to find... but a *horrid* one is even harder, eh, Arthur?
Art is what the *humans* call me.
My name is *Longshot.*

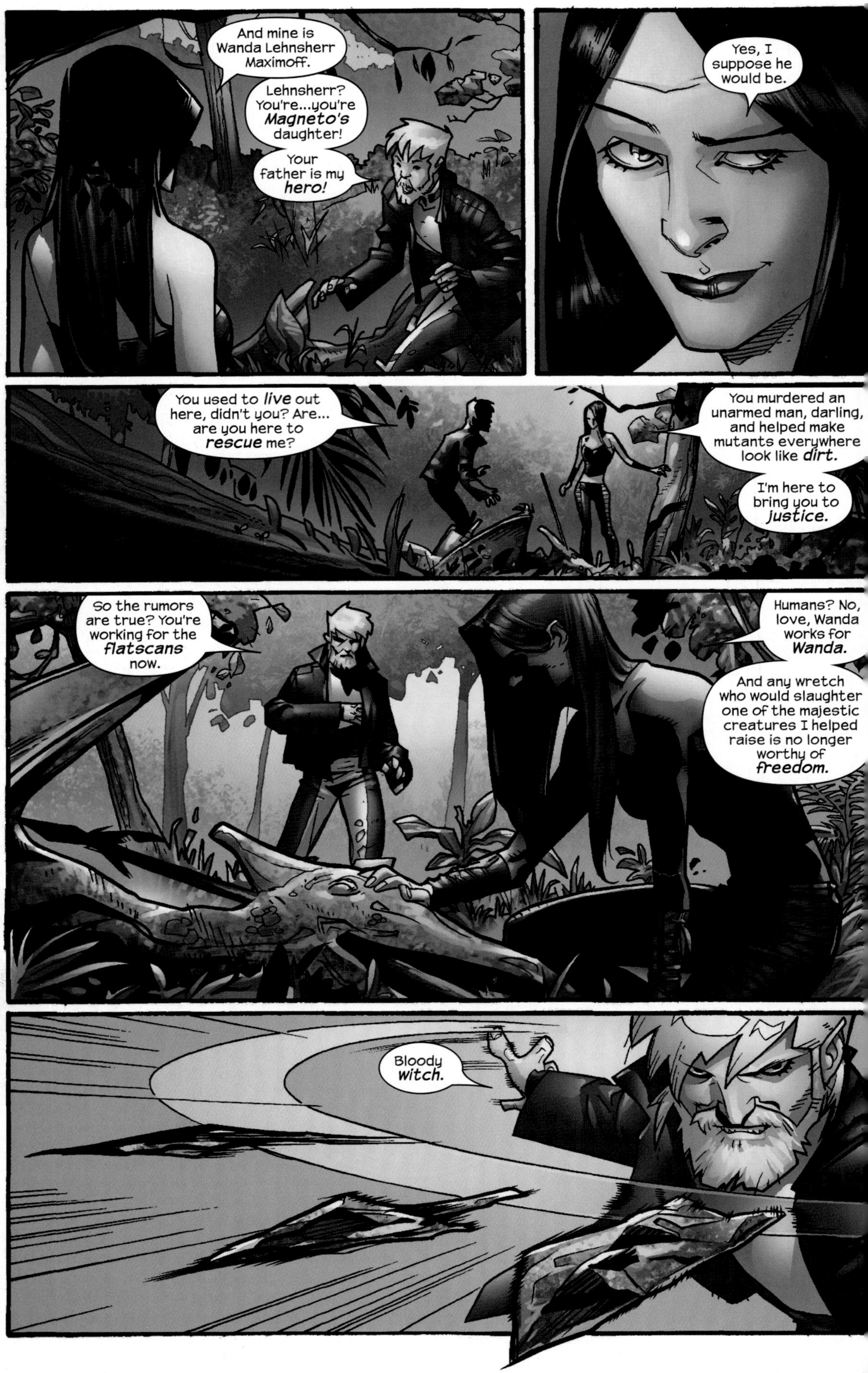
And mine is Wanda Lehnsherr Maximoff.
Lehnsherr? You're...you're *Magneto's* daughter!
Your father is my *hero!*
Yes, I suppose he would be.
You used to *live* out here, didn't you? Are... are you here to *rescue* me?
You murdered an unarmed man, darling, and helped make mutants everywhere look like *dirt.*
I'm here to bring you to *justice.*
So the rumors are true? You're working for the *flatscans* now.
Humans? No, love, Wanda works for *Wanda.*
And any wretch who would slaughter one of the majestic creatures I helped raise is no longer worthy of *freedom.*
Bloody *witch.*

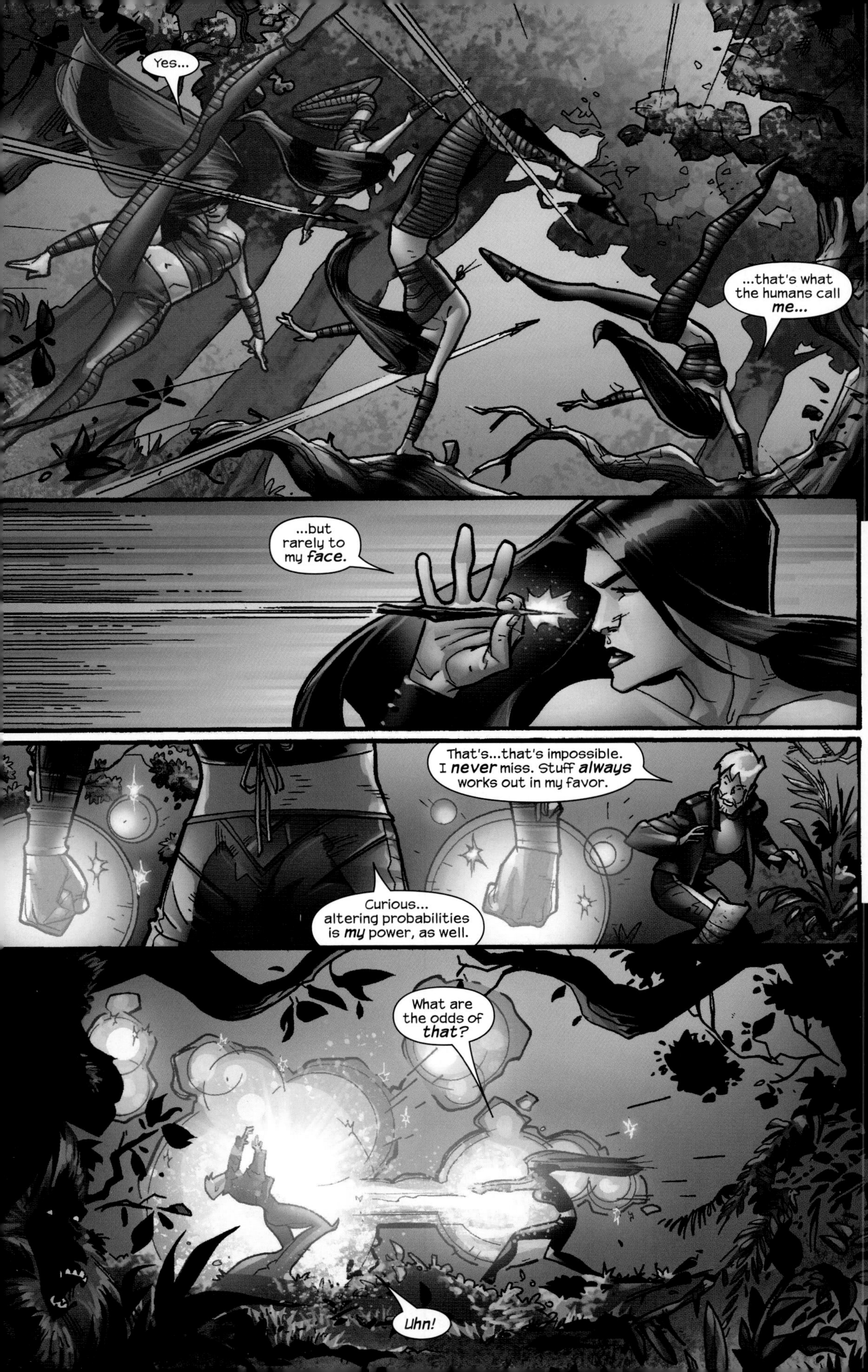
Yes...
...that's what the humans call *me*...
...but rarely to my *face*.
That's...that's impossible. I *never* miss. Stuff *always* works out in my favor.
Curious... altering probabilities is *my* power, as well.
What are the odds of *that*?
Uhn!

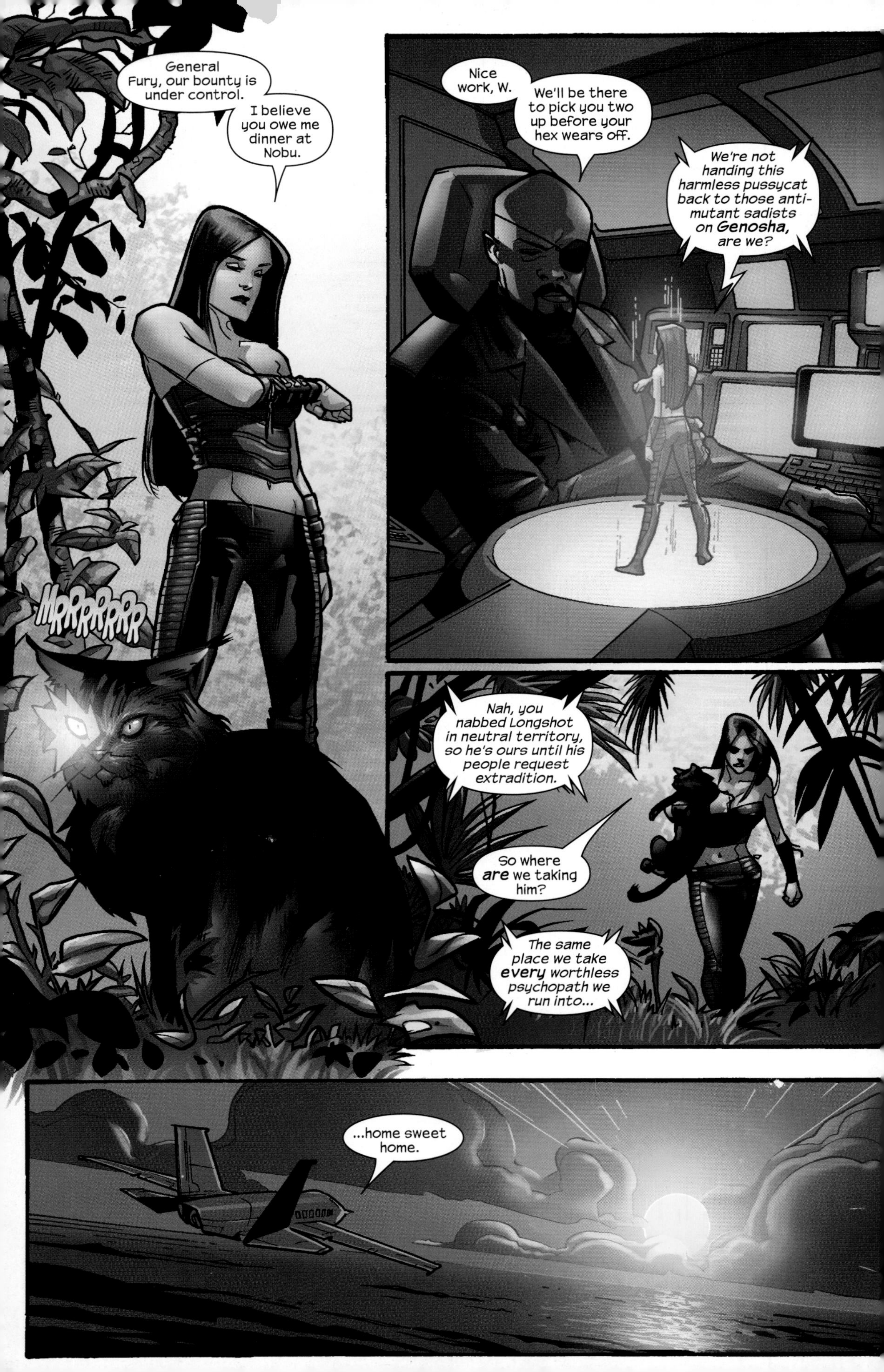
General Fury, our bounty is under control.
I believe you owe me dinner at Nobu.
MRRRRRRR
Nice work, W.
We'll be there to pick you two up before your hex wears off.
We're not handing this harmless pussycat back to those anti-mutant sadists on Genosha, are we?
Nah, you nabbed Longshot in neutral territory, so he's ours until his people request extradition.
So where are we taking him?
The same place we take every worthless psychopath we run into...
...home sweet home.

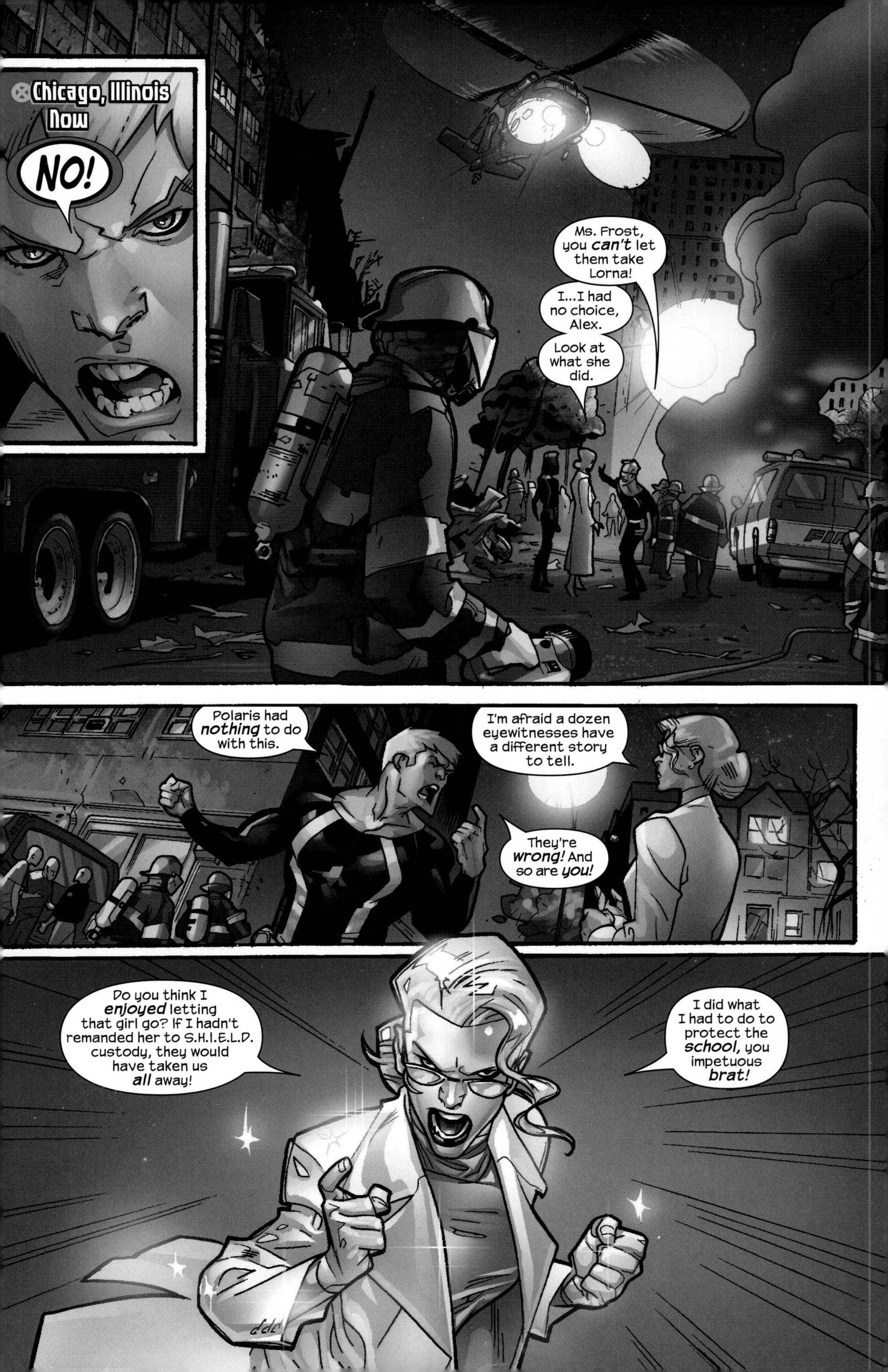
Chicago, Illinois
Now
NO!
Ms. Frost, you can't let them take Lorna!
I...I had no choice, Alex.
Look at what she did.
Polaris had nothing to do with this.
I'm afraid a dozen eyewitnesses have a different story to tell.
They're wrong! And so are you!
Do you think I enjoyed letting that girl go? If I hadn't remanded her to S.H.I.E.L.D. custody, they would have taken us all away!
I did what I had to do to protect the school, you impetuous brat!

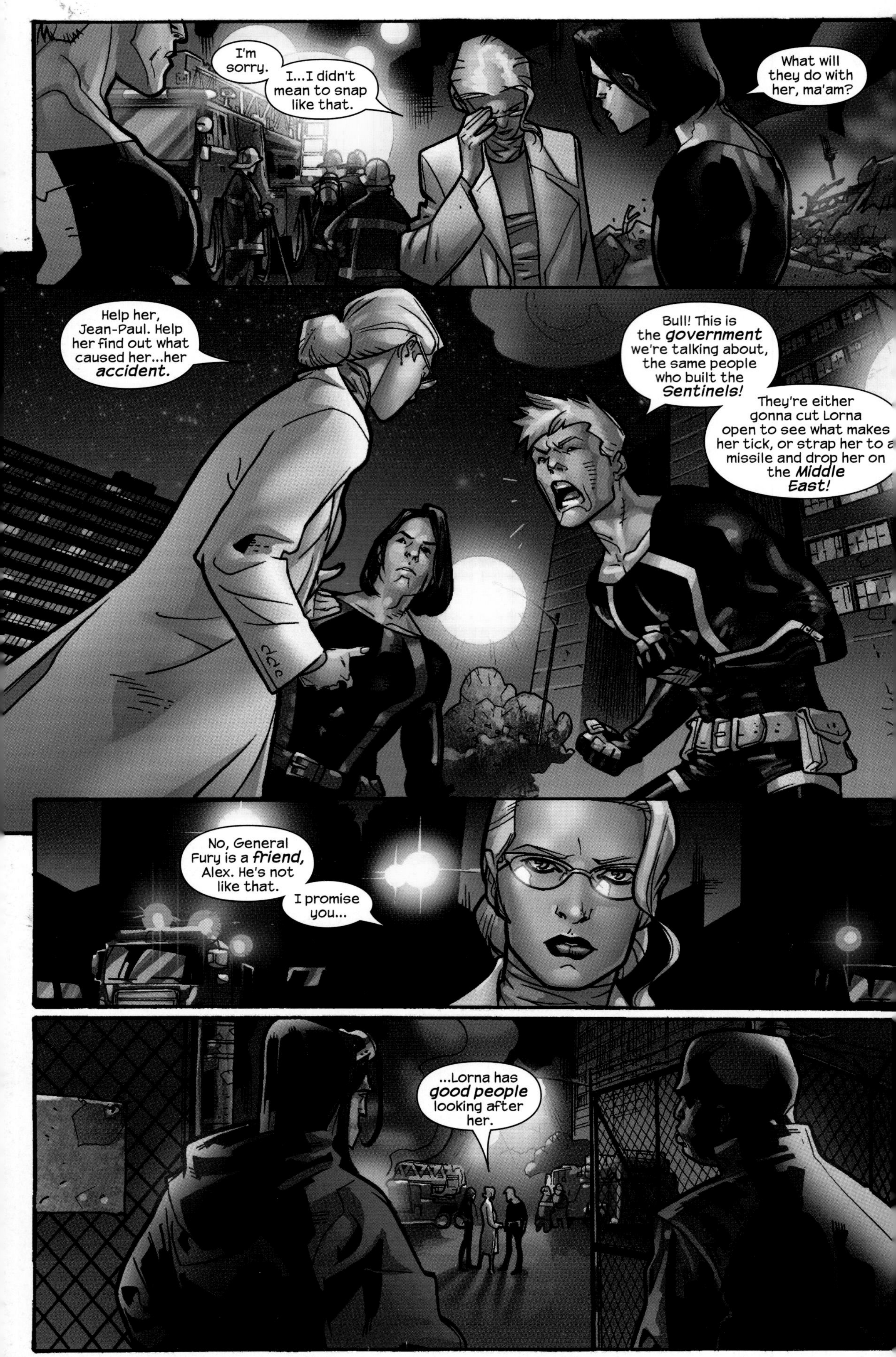
I'm sorry.
I...I didn't mean to snap like that.
What will they do with her, ma'am?
Help her, Jean-Paul. Help her find out what caused her...her *accident.*
Bull! This is the *government* we're talking about, the same people who built the *Sentinels!*
They're either gonna cut Lorna open to see what makes her tick, or strap her to a missile and drop her on the *Middle East!*
No, General Fury is a *friend,* Alex. He's not like that.
I promise you...
...Lorna has *good people* looking after her.

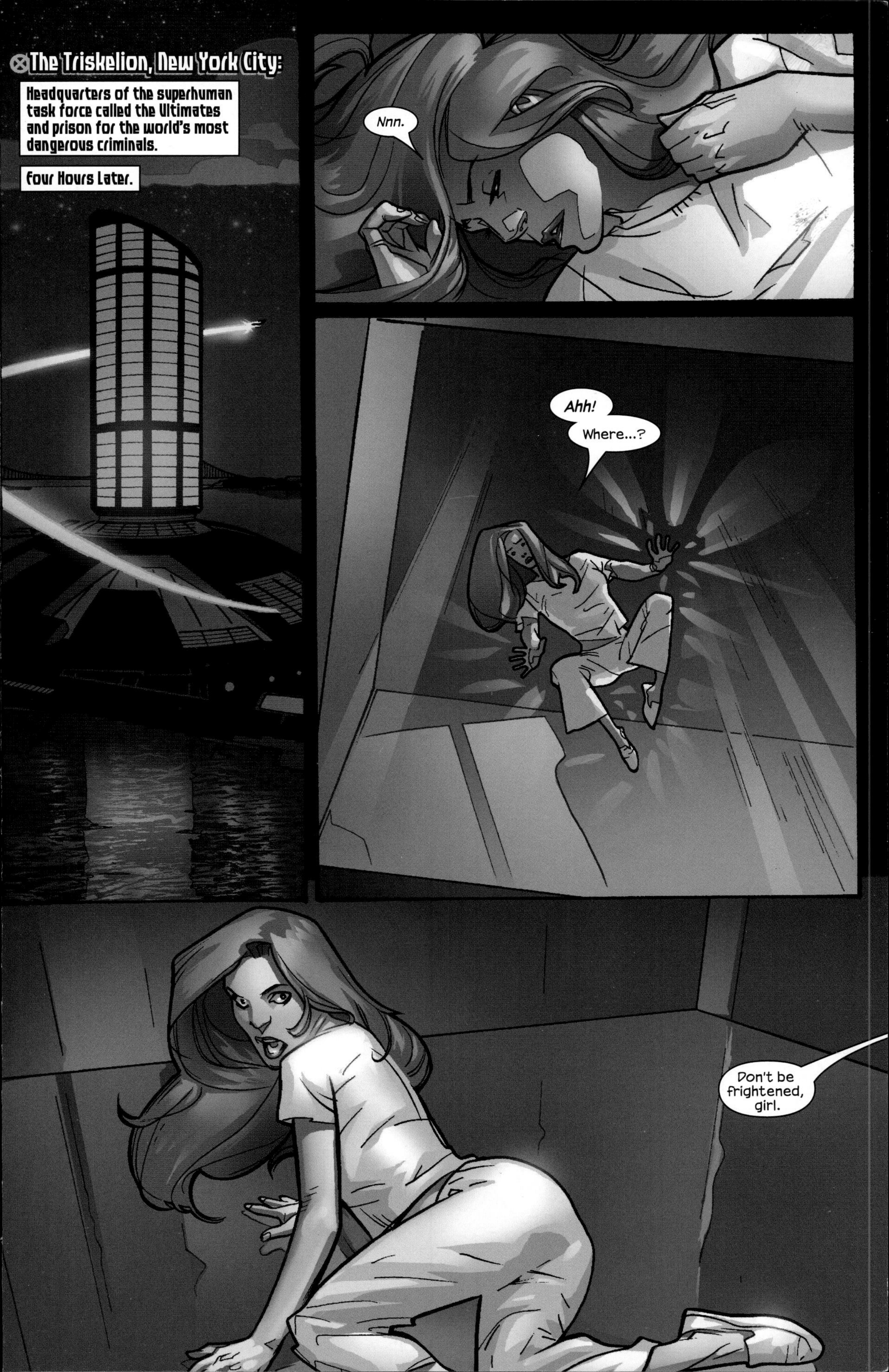
The Triskelion, New York City:
Headquarters of the superhuman task force called the Ultimates and prison for the world's most dangerous criminals.
Four Hours Later.
Nnn.
Ahh!
Where...?
Don't be frightened, girl.

You're among friends.

No.

You're... you're...

Indeed. Congratulations, your magnetic abilities must be *formidable* if they put you in here.

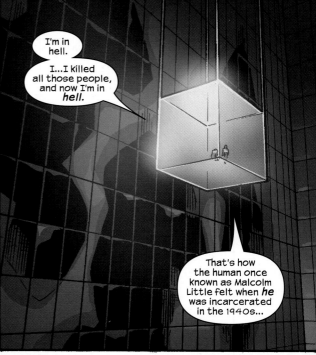

I'm in hell.

I...I killed all those people, and now I'm in *hell*.

That's how the human once known as Malcolm Little felt when *he* was incarcerated in the 1940s...

...but over the years, prison proved to be Malcolm X's *salvation*. He--

Get away from her, old man.

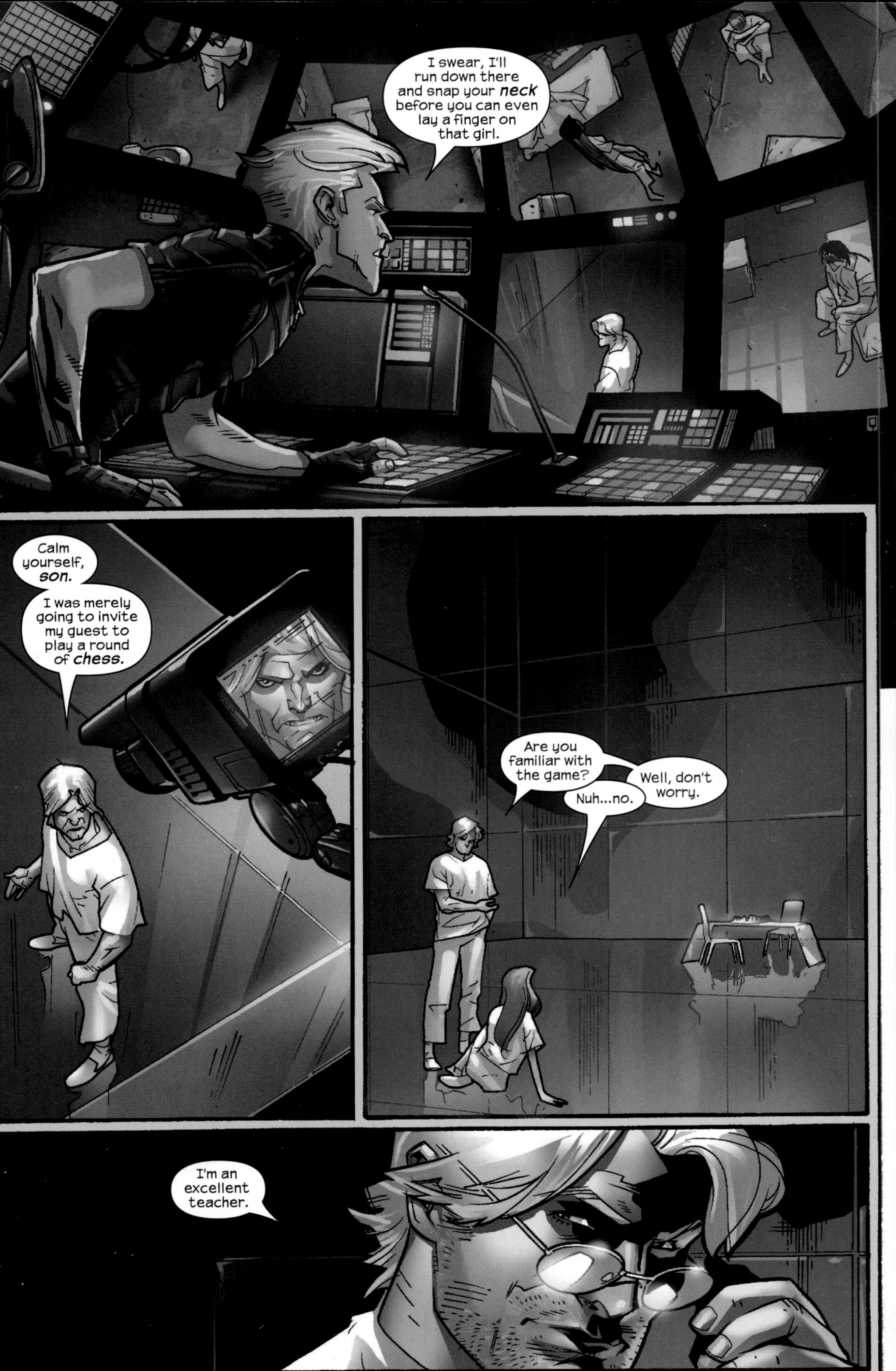
I swear, I'll run down there and snap your **neck** before you can even lay a finger on that girl.
Calm yourself, **son.**
I was merely going to invite my guest to play a round of **chess.**
Are you familiar with the game?
Nuh...no.
Well, don't worry.
I'm an excellent teacher.

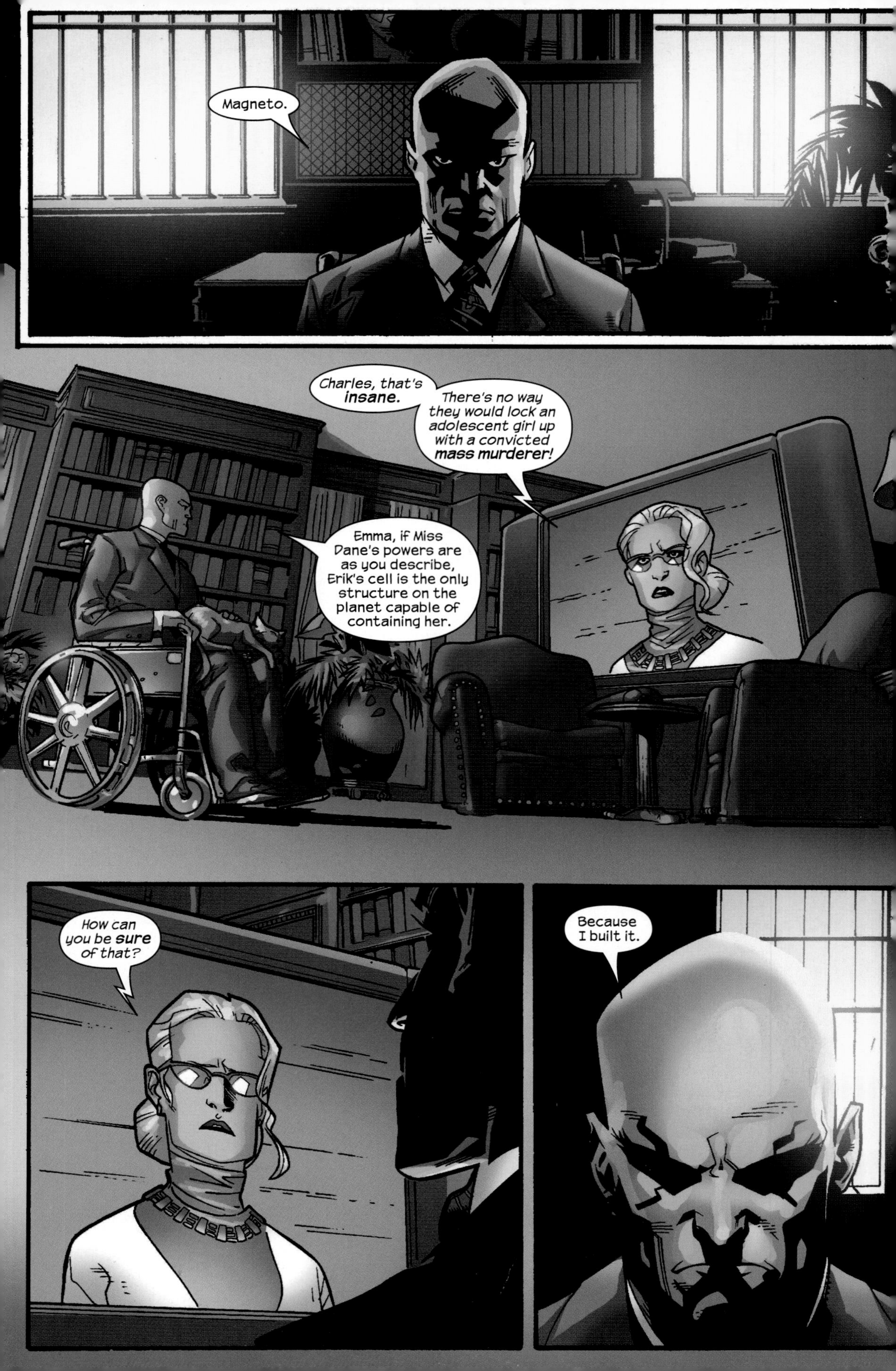
Magneto.
Charles, that's **insane.**
There's no way they would lock an adolescent girl up with a convicted **mass murderer!**
Emma, if Miss Dane's powers are as you describe, Erik's cell is the only structure on the planet capable of containing her.
How can you be **sure** of that?
Because I built it.

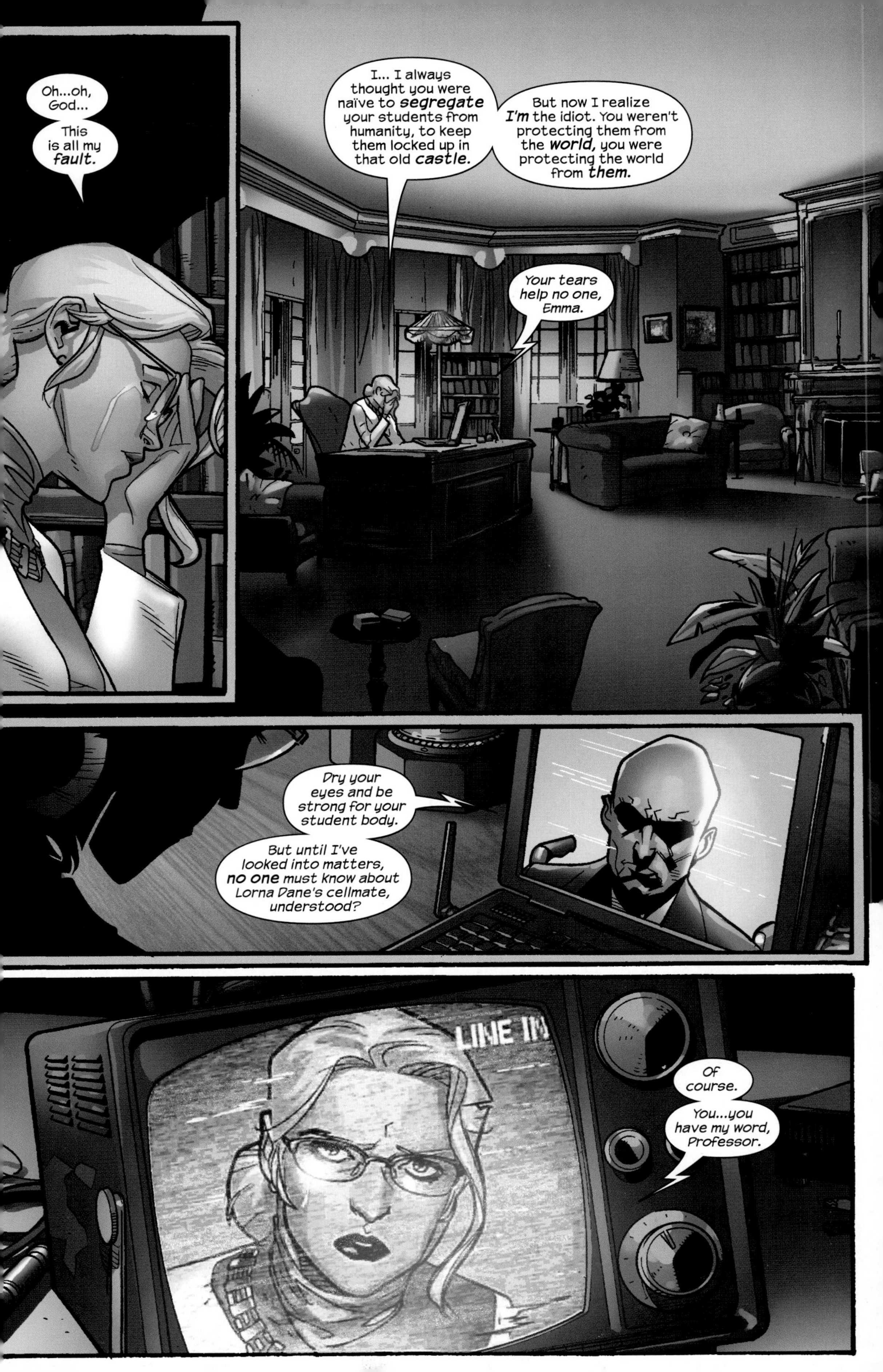
Oh...oh, God...
This is all my fault.
I... I always thought you were naïve to segregate your students from humanity, to keep them locked up in that old castle.
But now I realize I'm the idiot. You weren't protecting them from the world, you were protecting the world from them.
Your tears help no one, Emma.
Dry your eyes and be strong for your student body.
But until I've looked into matters, no one must know about Lorna Dane's cellmate, understood?
LINE IN
Of course.
You...you have my word, Professor.

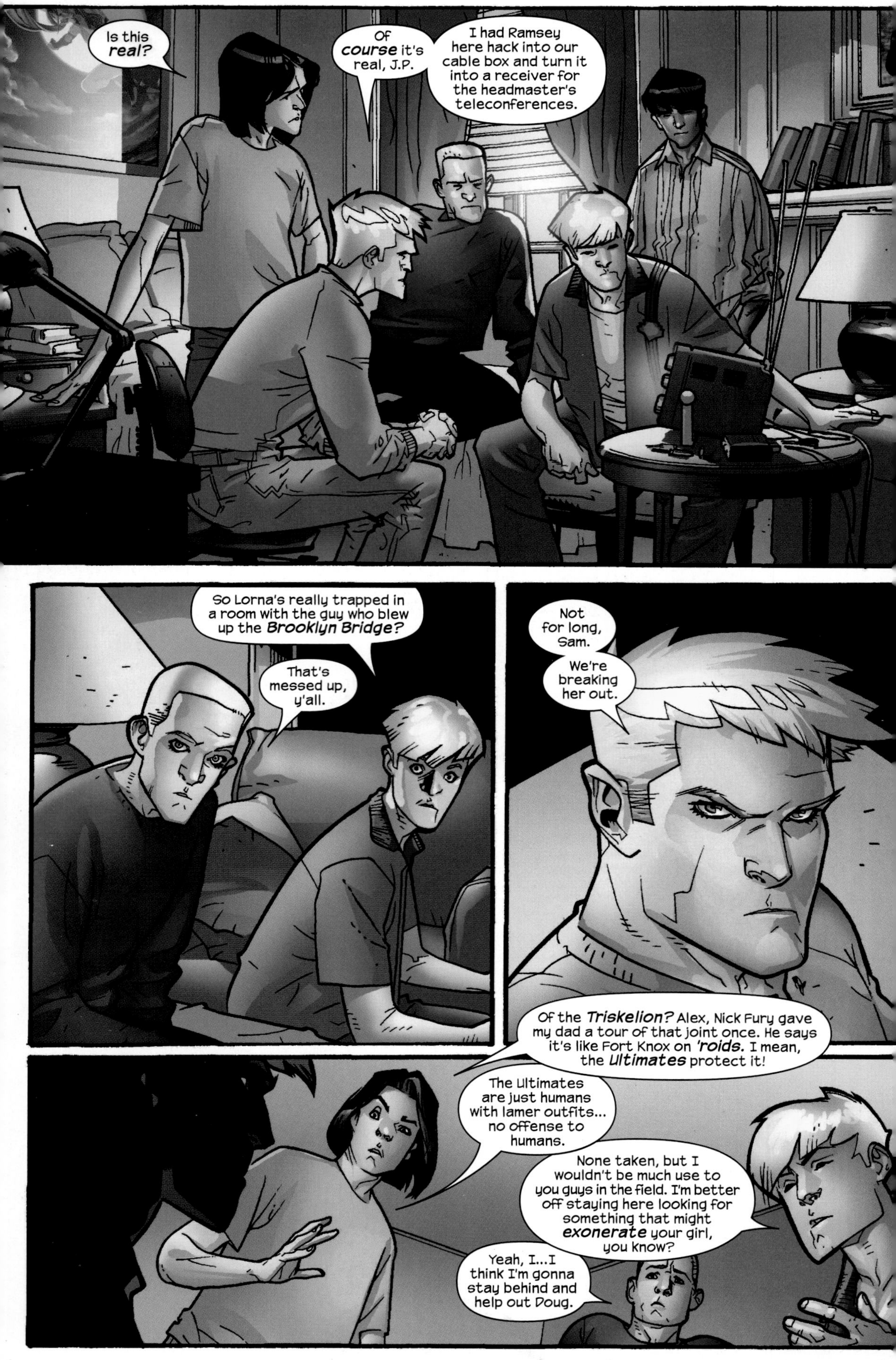

Is this real?
Of course it's real, J.P.
I had Ramsey here hack into our cable box and turn it into a receiver for the headmaster's teleconferences.
So Lorna's really trapped in a room with the guy who blew up the Brooklyn Bridge?
That's messed up, y'all.
Not for long, Sam.
We're breaking her out.
Of the Triskelion? Alex, Nick Fury gave my dad a tour of that joint once. He says it's like Fort Knox on 'roids. I mean, the Ultimates protect it!
The Ultimates are just humans with lamer outfits... no offense to humans.
None taken, but I wouldn't be much use to you guys in the field. I'm better off staying here looking for something that might exonerate your girl, you know?
Yeah, I...I think I'm gonna stay behind and help out Doug.

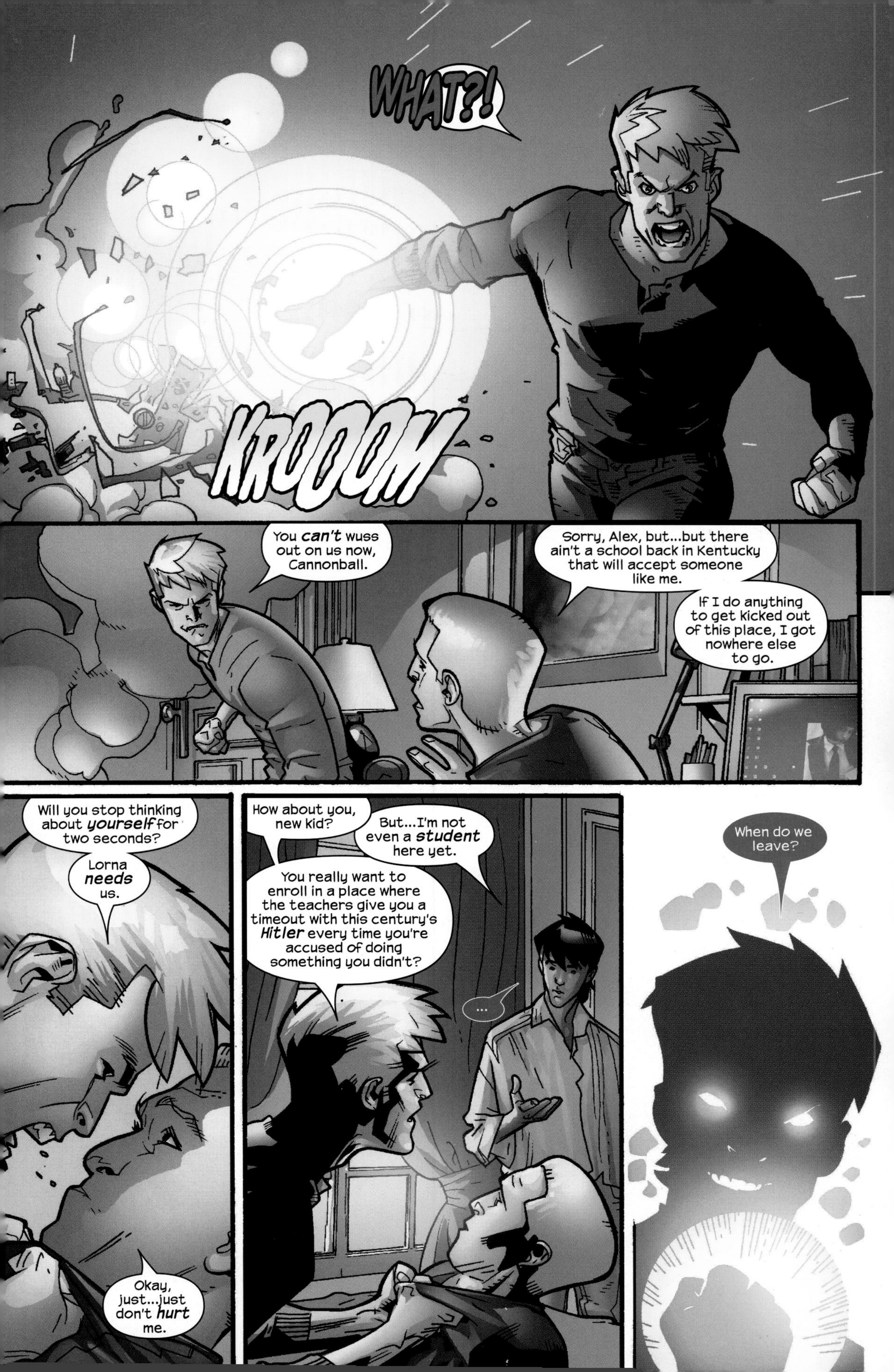
WHAT?!
KROOOM
You can't wuss out on us now, Cannonball.
Sorry, Alex, but...but there ain't a school back in Kentucky that will accept someone like me.
If I do anything to get kicked out of this place, I got nowhere else to go.
Will you stop thinking about yourself for two seconds?
Lorna needs us.
Okay, just...just don't hurt me.
How about you, new kid?
But...I'm not even a student here yet.
You really want to enroll in a place where the teachers give you a timeout with this century's Hitler every time you're accused of doing something you didn't?
...
When do we leave?

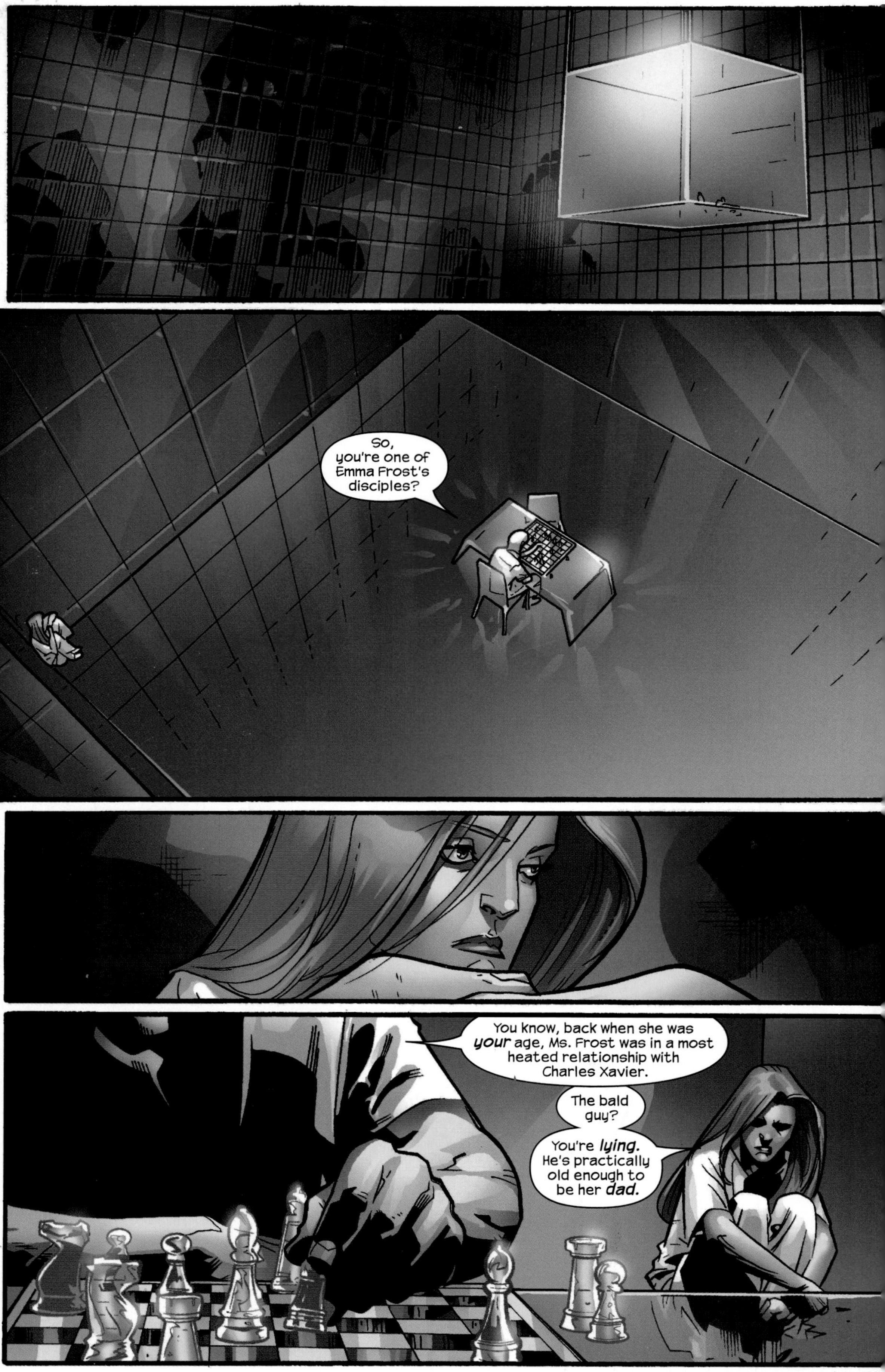
So, you're one of Emma Frost's disciples?
You know, back when she was *your* age, Ms. Frost was in a most heated relationship with Charles Xavier.
The bald guy?
You're *lying.* He's practically old enough to be her *dad.*

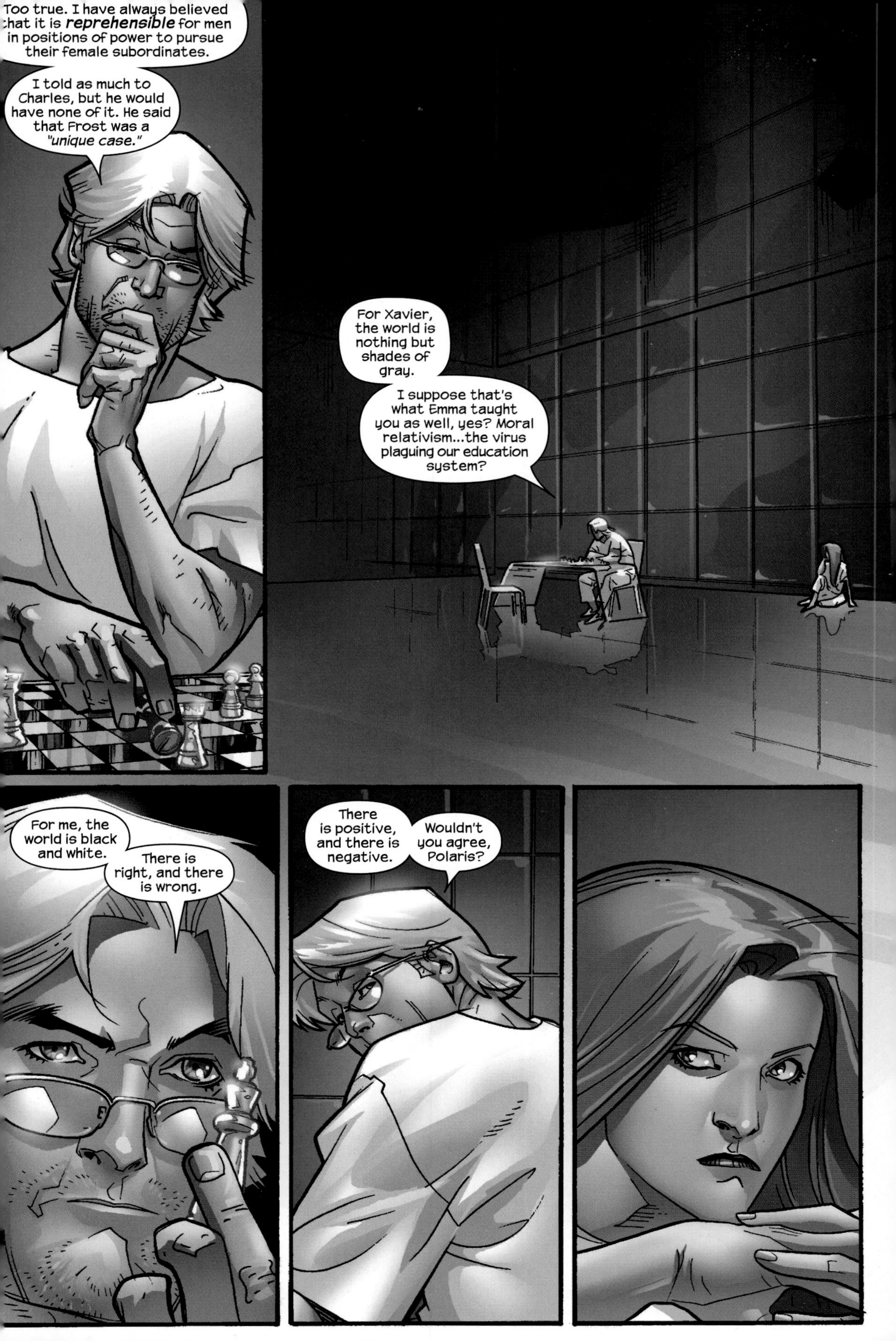
Too true. I have always believed that it is ***reprehensible*** for men in positions of power to pursue their female subordinates.
I told as much to Charles, but he would have none of it. He said that Frost was a *"unique case."*
For Xavier, the world is nothing but shades of gray.
I suppose that's what Emma taught you as well, yes? Moral relativism...the virus plaguing our education system?
For me, the world is black and white.
There is right, and there is wrong.
There is positive, and there is negative.
Wouldn't you agree, Polaris?

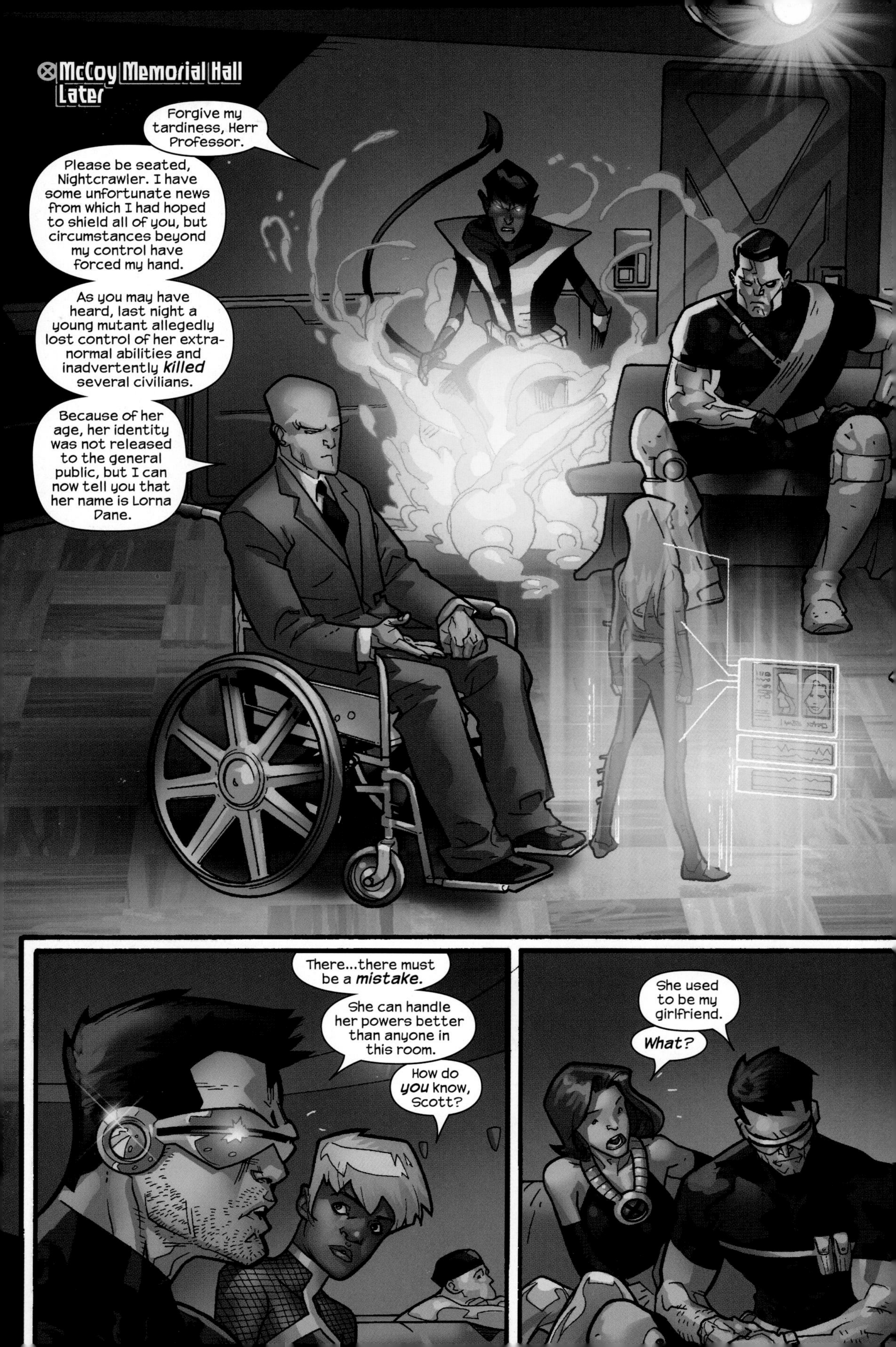
McCoy Memorial Hall
Later
Forgive my tardiness, Herr Professor.
Please be seated, Nightcrawler. I have some unfortunate news from which I had hoped to shield all of you, but circumstances beyond my control have forced my hand.
As you may have heard, last night a young mutant allegedly lost control of her extra-normal abilities and inadvertently *killed* several civilians.
Because of her age, her identity was not released to the general public, but I can now tell you that her name is Lorna Dane.
There...there must be a *mistake.*
She can handle her powers better than anyone in this room.
How do *you* know, Scott?
She used to be my girlfriend.
What?

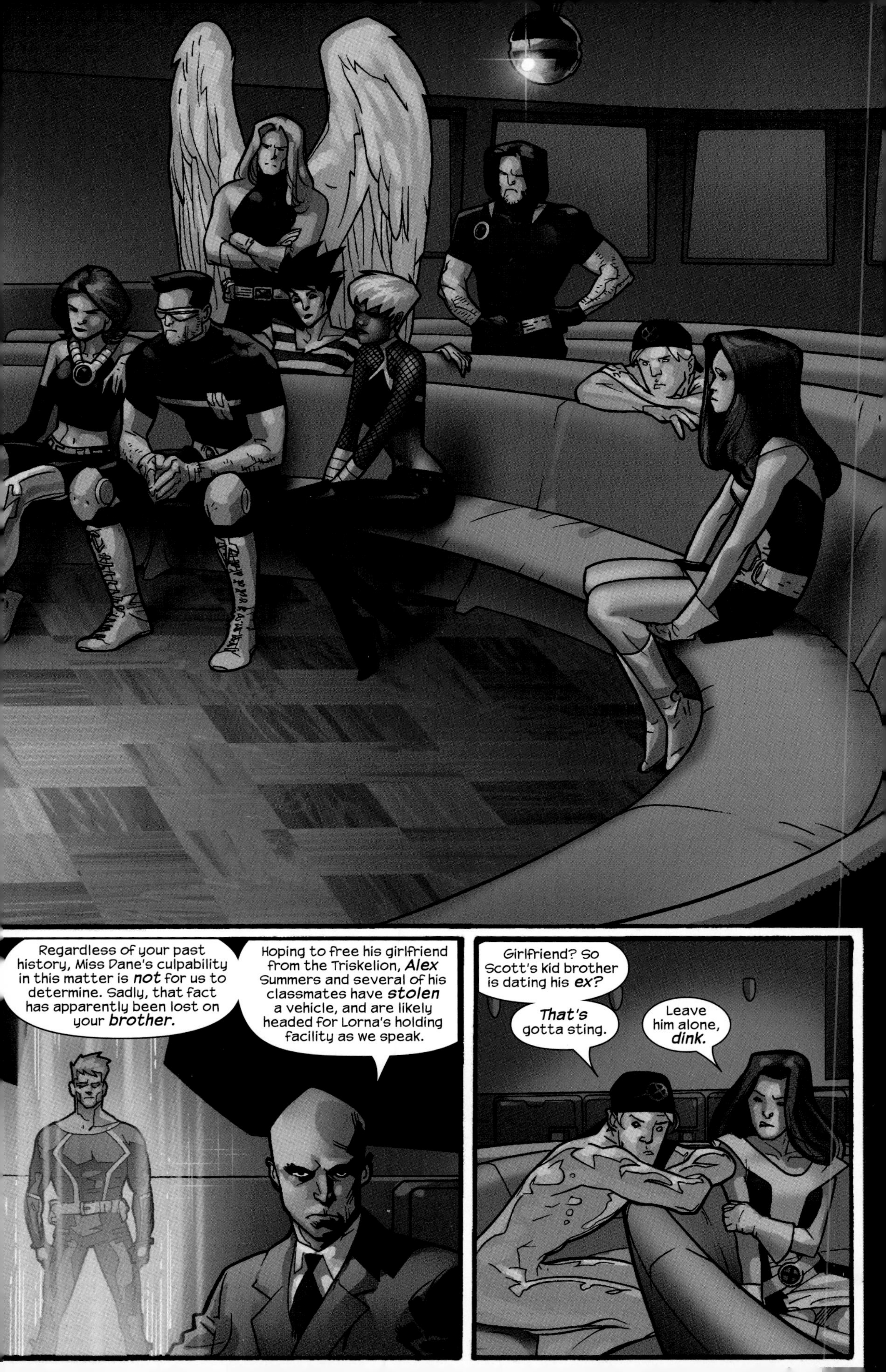
Regardless of your past history, Miss Dane's culpability in this matter is not for us to determine. Sadly, that fact has apparently been lost on your brother.
Hoping to free his girlfriend from the Triskelion, Alex Summers and several of his classmates have stolen a vehicle, and are likely headed for Lorna's holding facility as we speak.
Girlfriend? So Scott's kid brother is dating his ex?
That's gotta sting.
Leave him alone, dink.

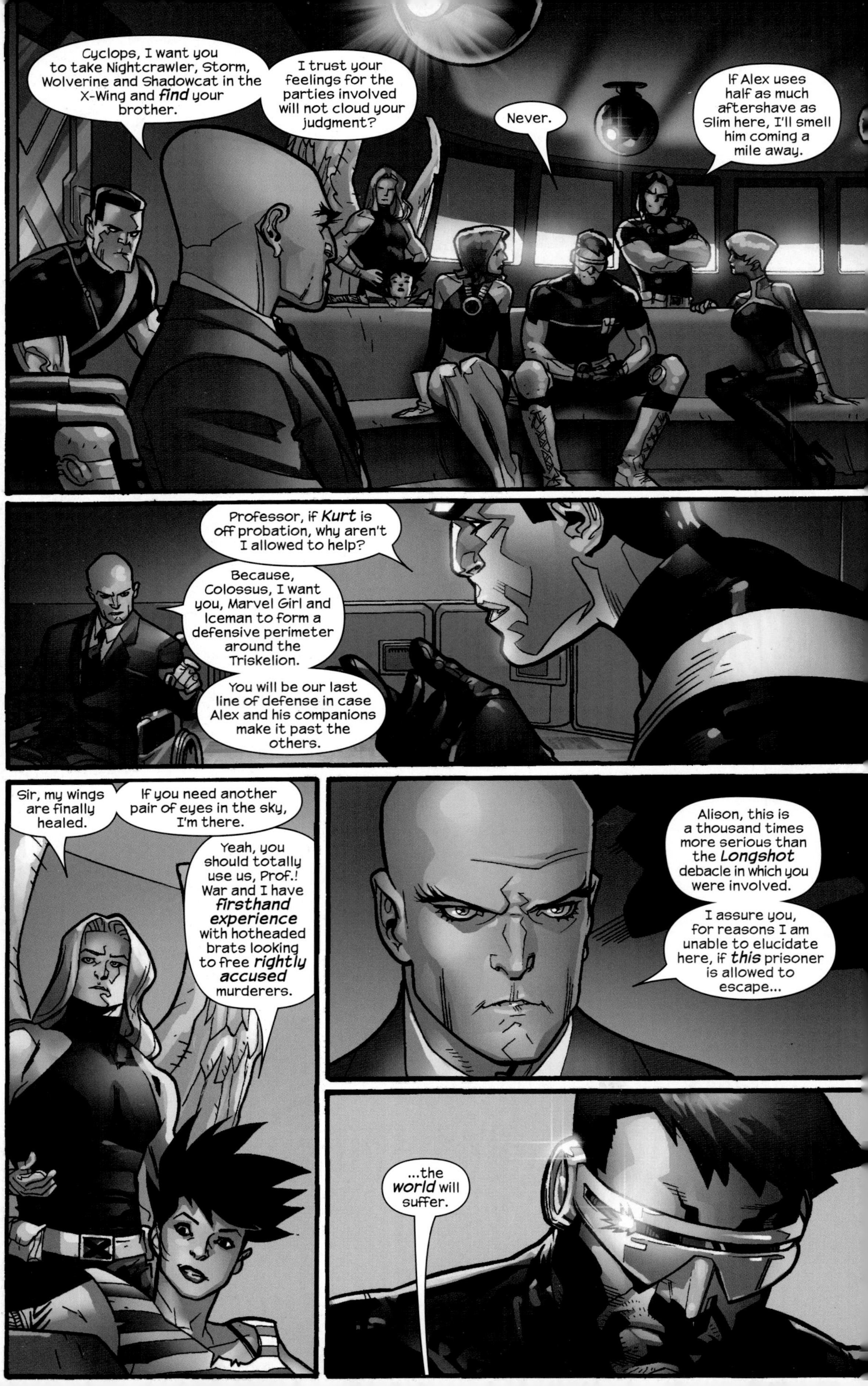

Cyclops, I want you to take Nightcrawler, Storm, Wolverine and Shadowcat in the X-Wing and *find* your brother.
I trust your feelings for the parties involved will not cloud your judgment?
Never.
If Alex uses half as much aftershave as Slim here, I'll smell him coming a mile away.
Professor, if *Kurt* is off probation, why aren't I allowed to help?
Because, Colossus, I want you, Marvel Girl and Iceman to form a defensive perimeter around the Triskelion.
You will be our last line of defense in case Alex and his companions make it past the others.
Sir, my wings are finally healed.
If you need another pair of eyes in the sky, I'm there.
Yeah, you should totally use us, Prof.! War and I have *firsthand experience* with hotheaded brats looking to free *rightly accused* murderers.
Alison, this is a thousand times more serious than the *Longshot* debacle in which you were involved.
I assure you, for reasons I am unable to elucidate here, if *this* prisoner is allowed to escape...
...the *world* will suffer.

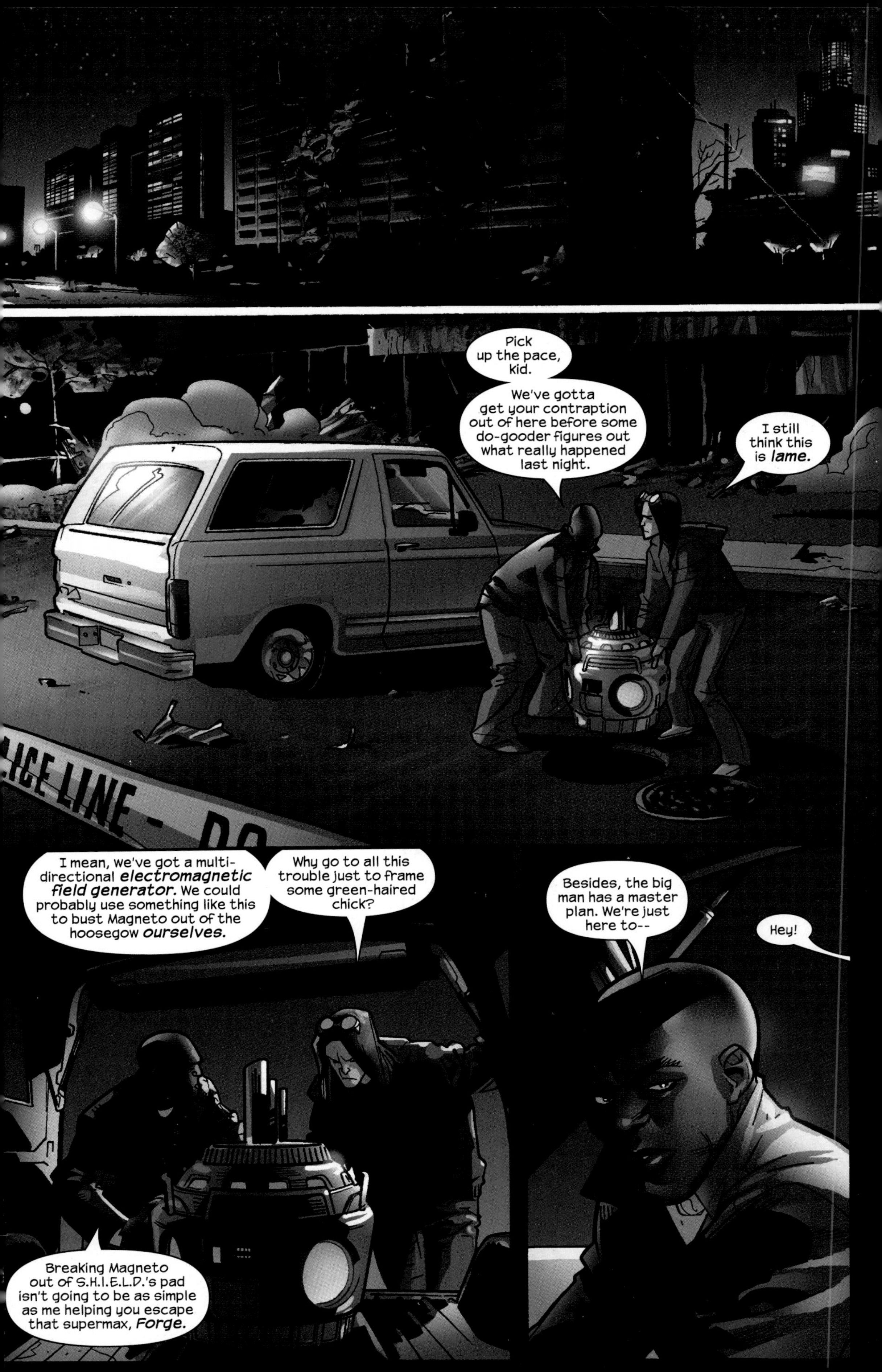

Pick up the pace, kid.
We've gotta get your contraption out of here before some do-gooder figures out what really happened last night.
I still think this is *lame.*
ICE LINE - DO
I mean, we've got a multi-directional *electromagnetic field generator.* We could probably use something like this to bust Magneto out of the hoosegow *ourselves.*
Why go to all this trouble just to frame some green-haired chick?
Breaking Magneto out of S.H.I.E.L.D.'s pad isn't going to be as simple as me helping you escape that supermax, *Forge.*
Besides, the big man has a master plan. We're just here to--
Hey!

You guys can't be here!

This is an active *crime scene!*

Truer words...

KRACK

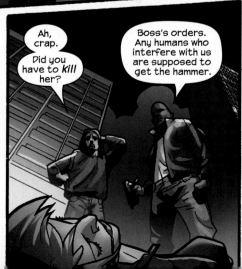

Ah, crap.

Did you have to *kill* her?

Boss's orders. Any humans who interfere with us are supposed to get the hammer.

Anyway, a healthy body count is kinda Magneto's *calling card,* you know?

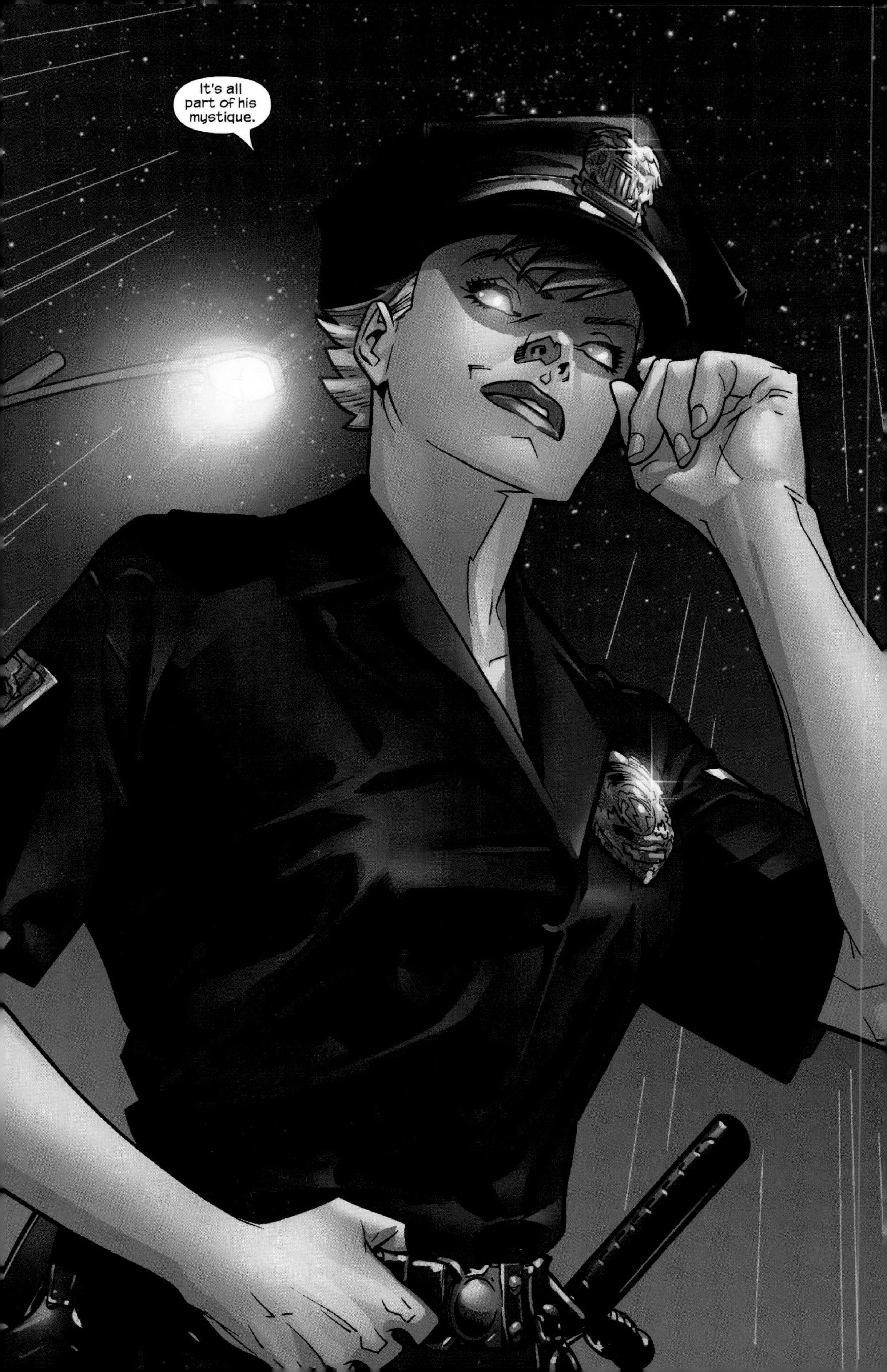
It's all part of his mystique.

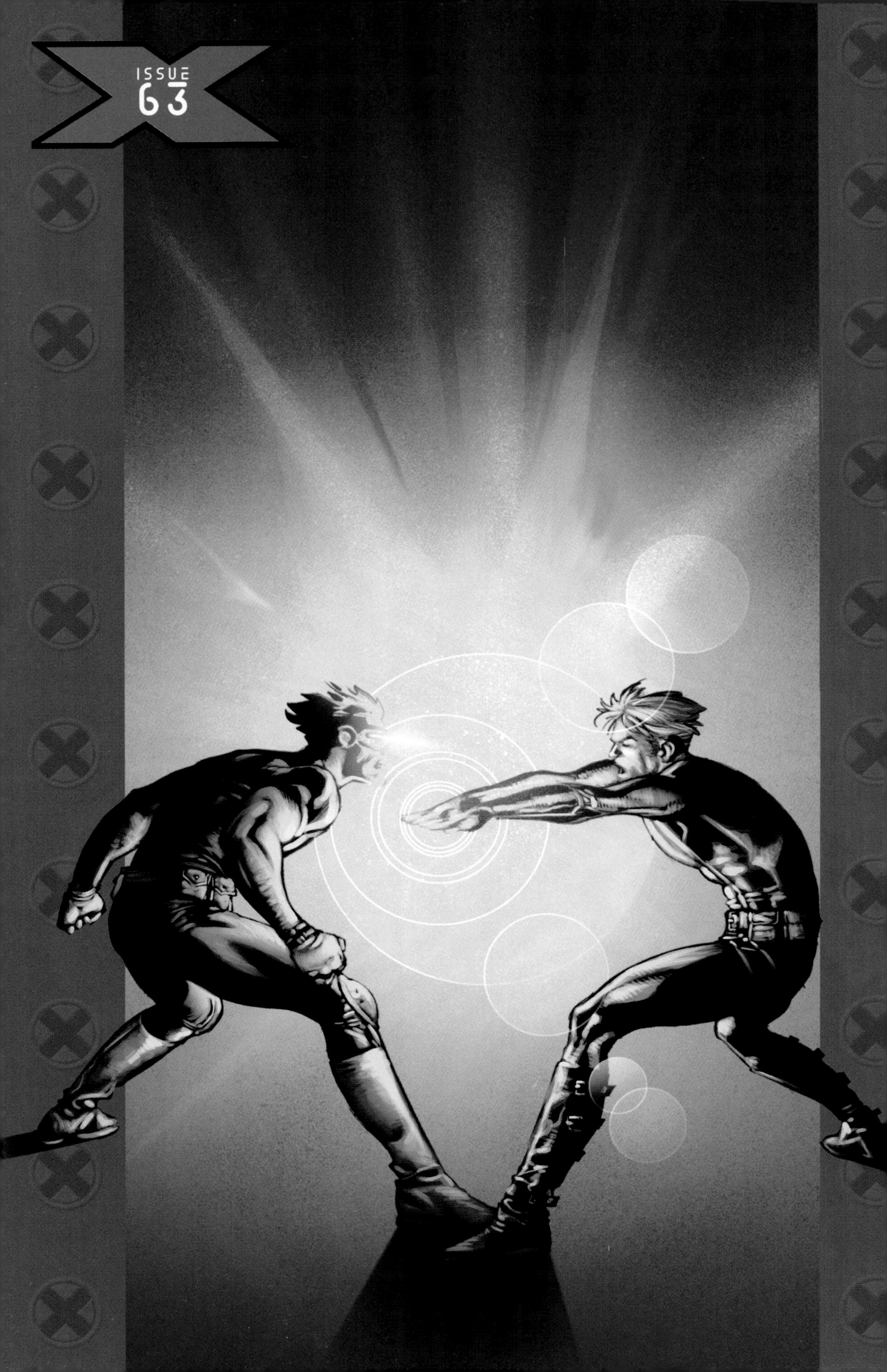
ISSUE
63

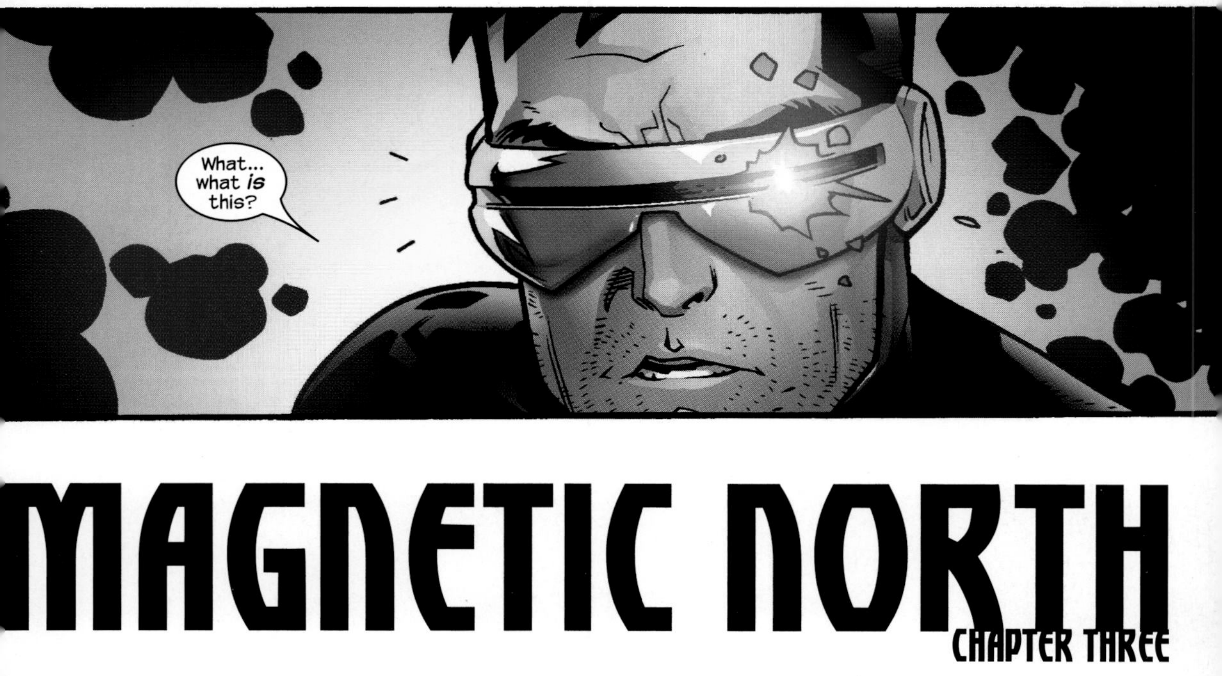
What... what *is* this?

MAGNETIC NORTH

CHAPTER THREE

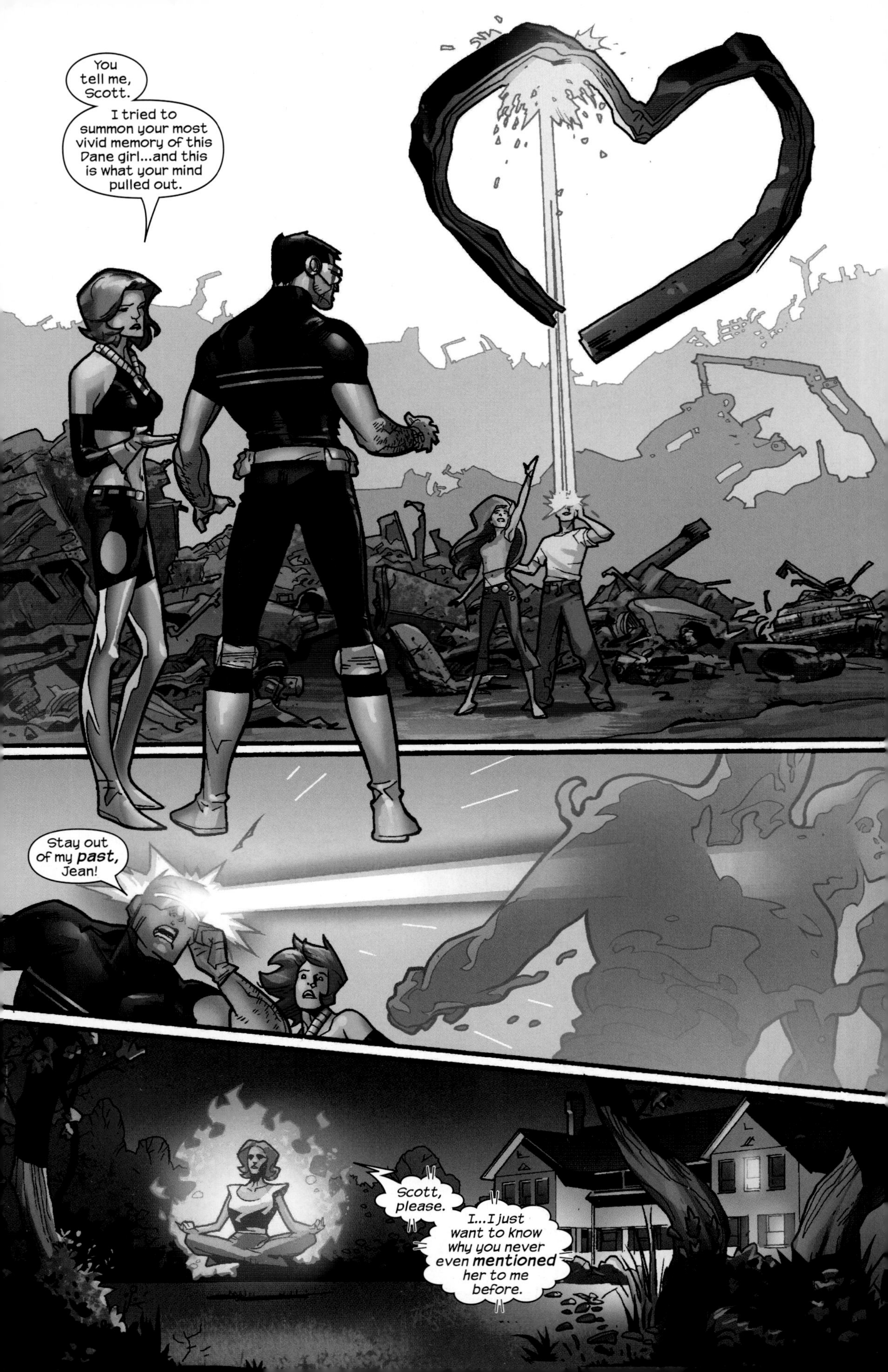
You tell me, Scott.
I tried to summon your most vivid memory of this Dane girl...and this is what your mind pulled out.
Stay out of my past, Jean!
Scott, please.
I...I just want to know why you never even mentioned her to me before.

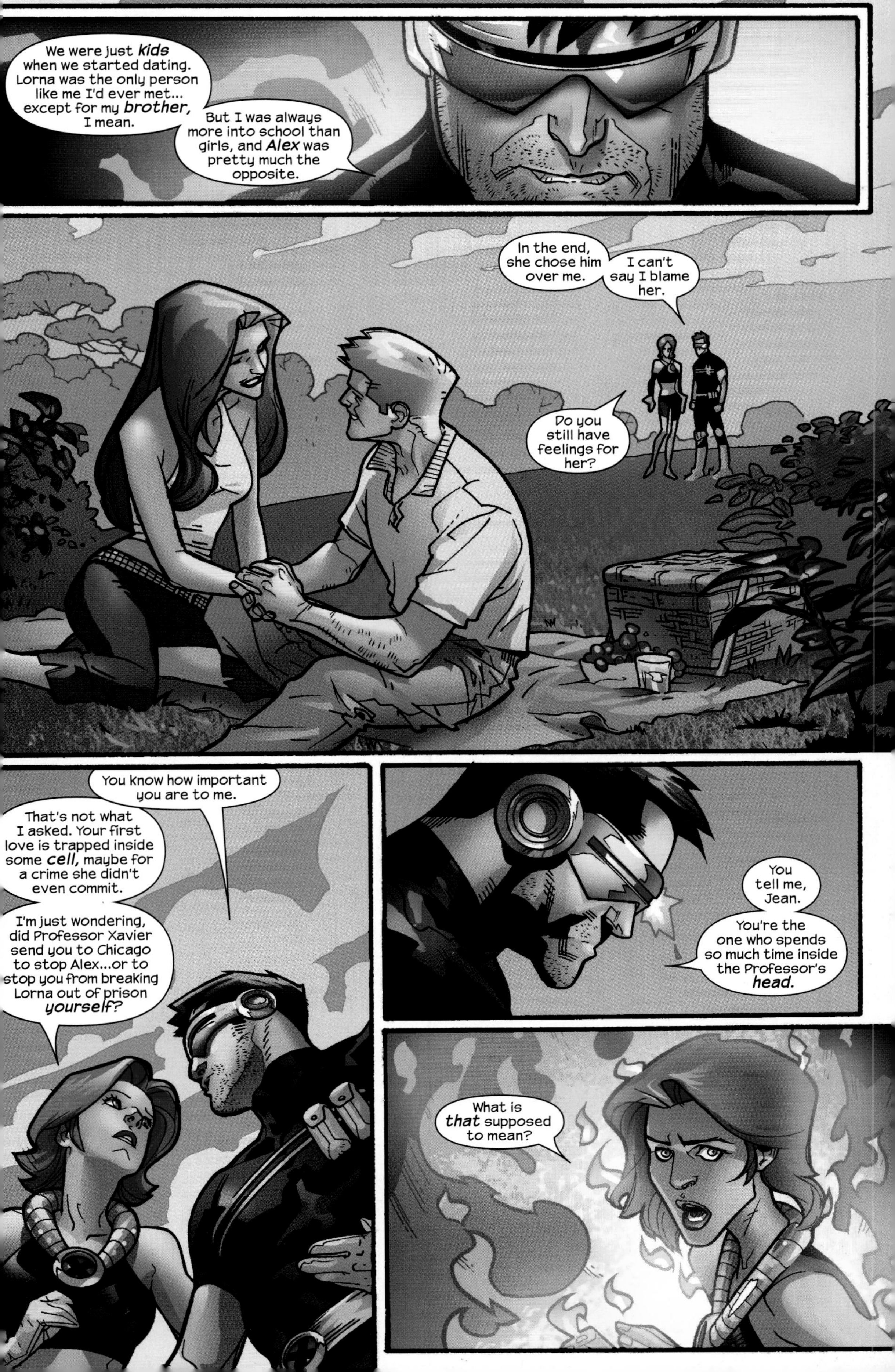

We were just kids when we started dating. Lorna was the only person like me I'd ever met... except for my brother, I mean.
But I was always more into school than girls, and Alex was pretty much the opposite.
In the end, she chose him over me.
I can't say I blame her.
Do you still have feelings for her?
You know how important you are to me.
That's not what I asked. Your first love is trapped inside some cell, maybe for a crime she didn't even commit.
I'm just wondering, did Professor Xavier send you to Chicago to stop Alex...or to stop you from breaking Lorna out of prison yourself?
You tell me, Jean.
You're the one who spends so much time inside the Professor's head.
What is that supposed to mean?

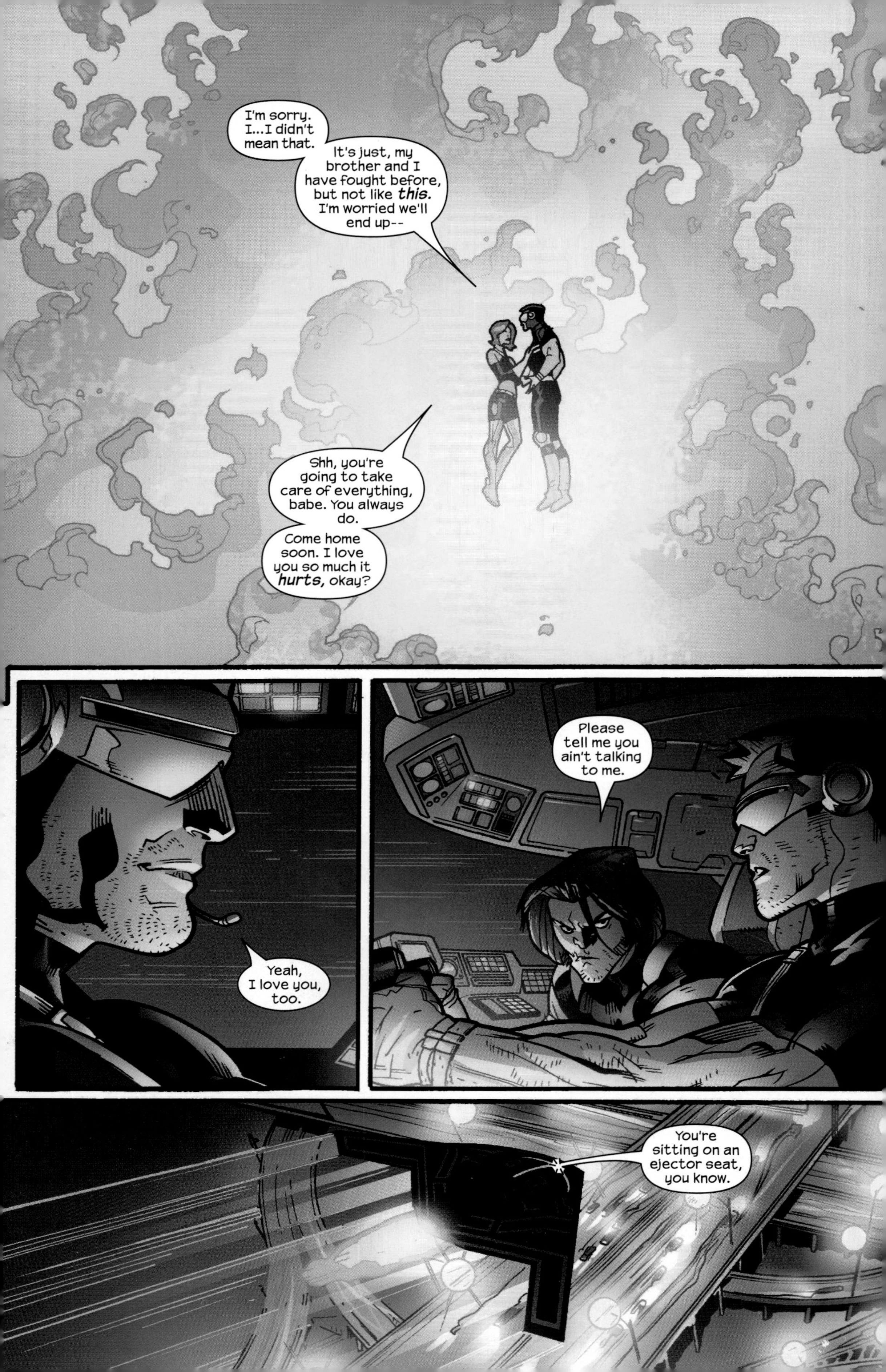
I'm sorry. I...I didn't mean that.
It's just, my brother and I have fought before, but not like *this.* I'm worried we'll end up--
Shh, you're going to take care of everything, babe. You always do.
Come home soon. I love you so much it *hurts,* okay?
Yeah, I love you, too.
Please tell me you ain't talking to me.
You're sitting on an ejector seat, you know.

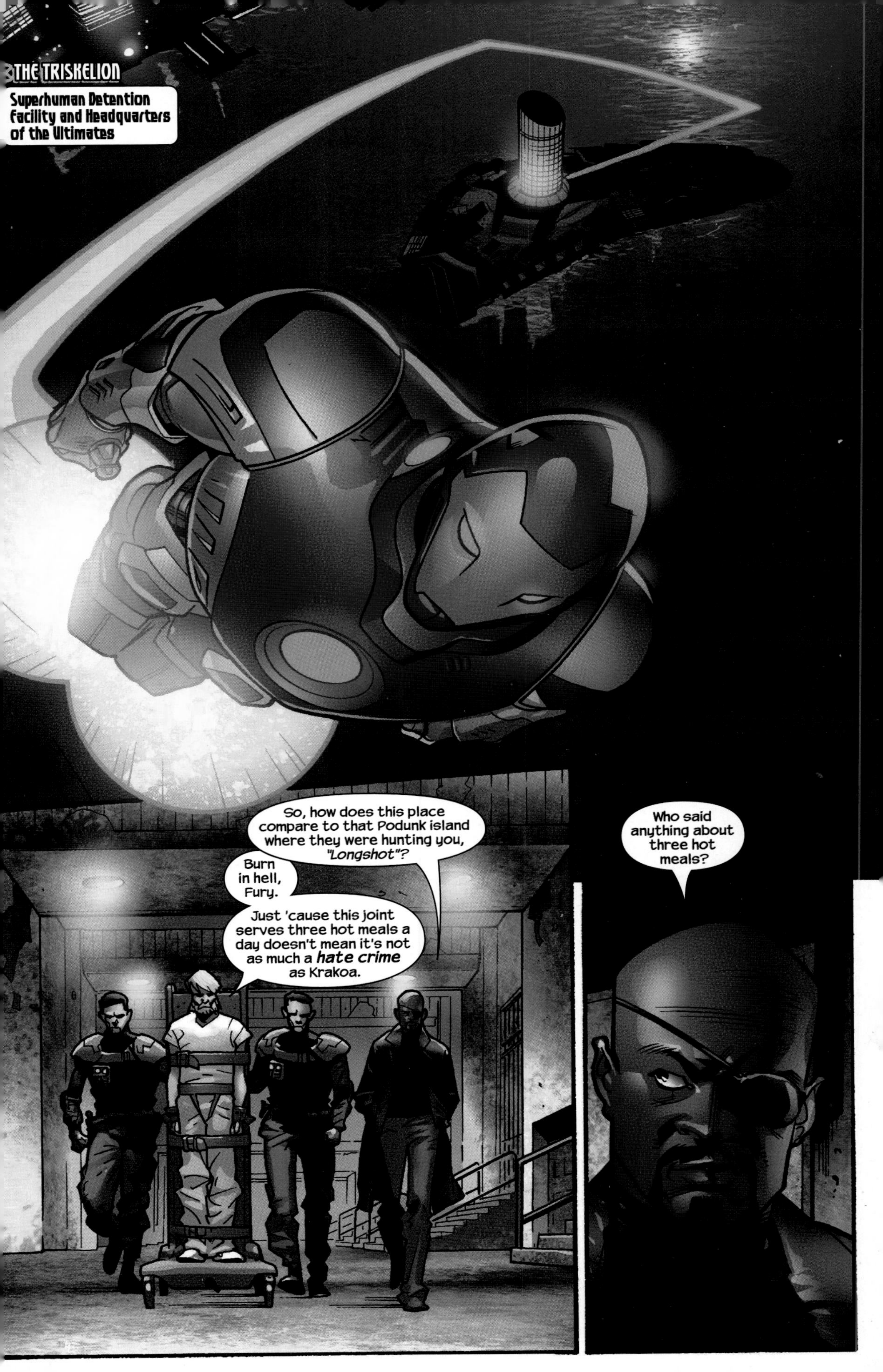
THE TRISKELION
Superhuman Detention Facility and Headquarters of the Ultimates
So, how does this place compare to that Podunk island where they were hunting you, "Longshot"?
Burn in hell, Fury.
Just 'cause this joint serves three hot meals a day doesn't mean it's not as much a *hate crime* as Krakoa.
Who said anything about three hot meals?

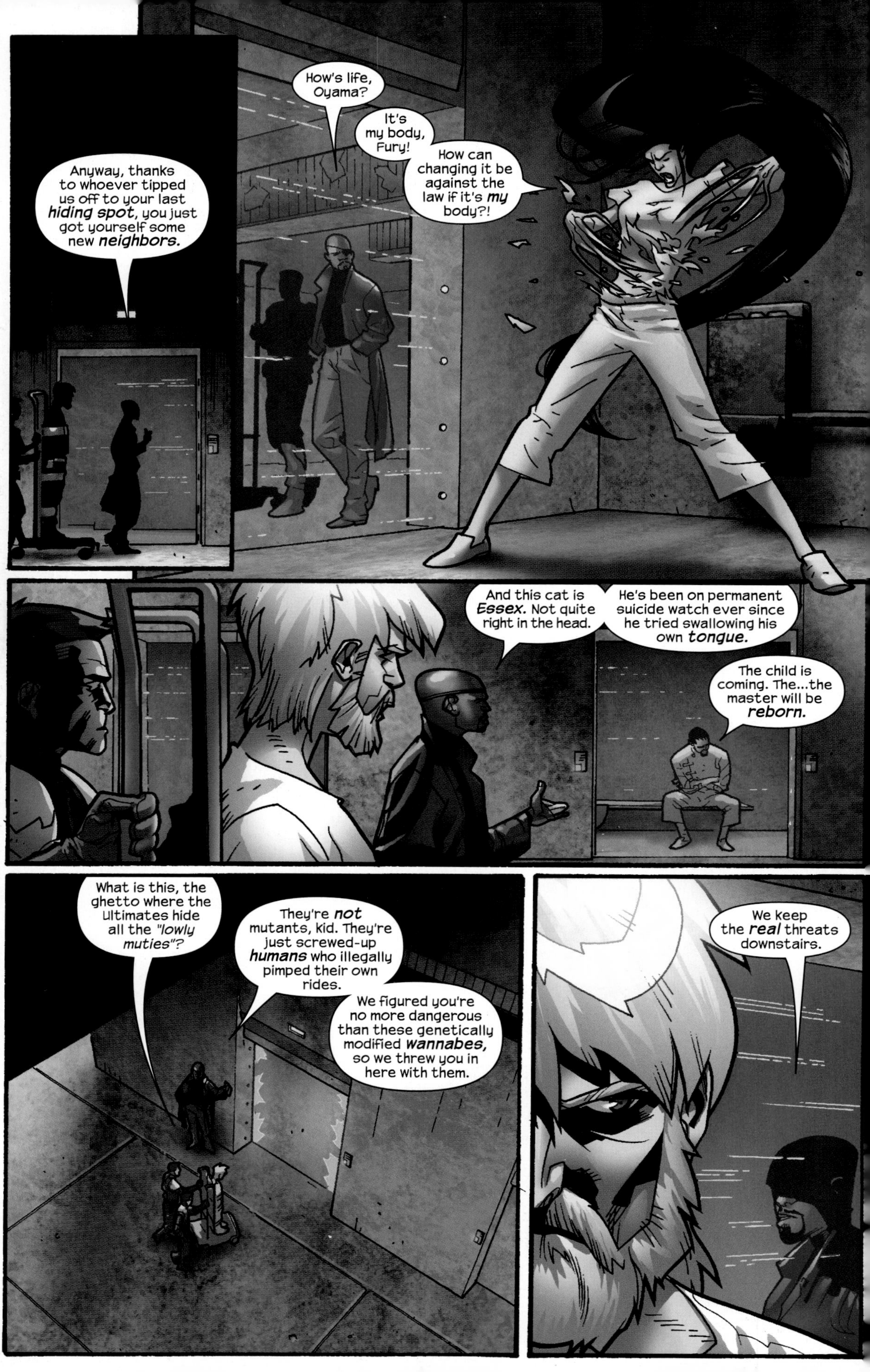
Anyway, thanks to whoever tipped us off to your last hiding spot, you just got yourself some new neighbors.
How's life, Oyama?
It's my body, Fury!
How can changing it be against the law if it's my body?!
And this cat is Essex. Not quite right in the head.
He's been on permanent suicide watch ever since he tried swallowing his own tongue.
The child is coming. The...the master will be reborn.
What is this, the ghetto where the Ultimates hide all the "lowly muties"?
They're not mutants, kid. They're just screwed-up humans who illegally pimped their own rides.
We figured you're no more dangerous than these genetically modified wannabes, so we threw you in here with them.
We keep the real threats downstairs.

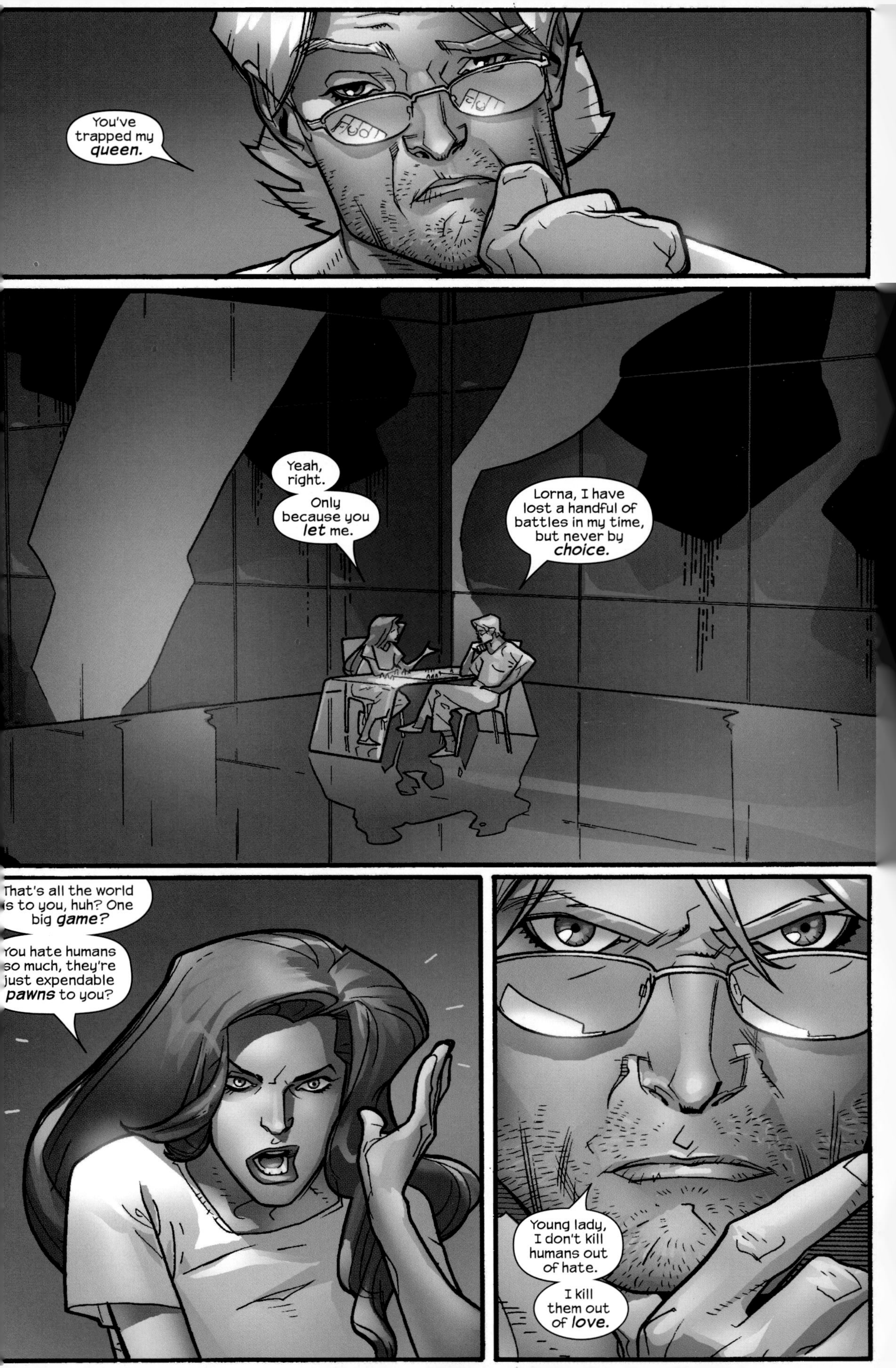
You've trapped my queen.
Yeah, right.
Only because you let me.
Lorna, I have lost a handful of battles in my time, but never by choice.
That's all the world is to you, huh? One big game?
You hate humans so much, they're just expendable pawns to you?
Young lady, I don't kill humans out of hate.
I kill them out of love.

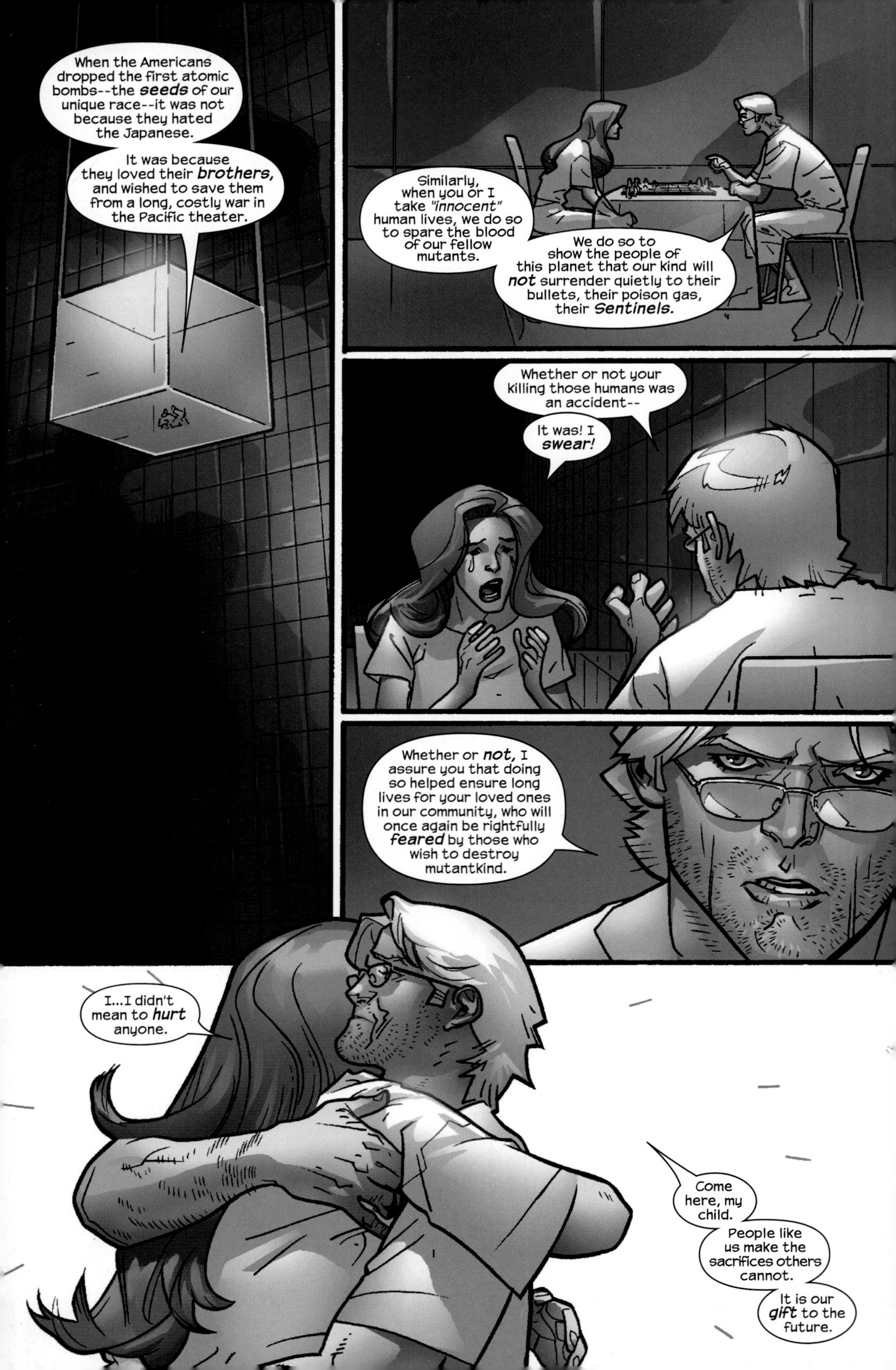
When the Americans dropped the first atomic bombs--the ***seeds*** of our unique race--it was not because they hated the Japanese.
It was because they loved their ***brothers,*** and wished to save them from a long, costly war in the Pacific theater.
Similarly, when you or I take *"innocent"* human lives, we do so to spare the blood of our fellow mutants.
We do so to show the people of this planet that our kind will ***not*** surrender quietly to their bullets, their poison gas, their ***Sentinels.***
Whether or not your killing those humans was an accident--
It was! I ***swear!***
Whether or ***not,*** I assure you that doing so helped ensure long lives for your loved ones in our community, who will once again be rightfully ***feared*** by those who wish to destroy mutantkind.
I...I didn't mean to ***hurt*** anyone.
Come here, my child.
People like us make the sacrifices others cannot.
It is our ***gift*** to the future.

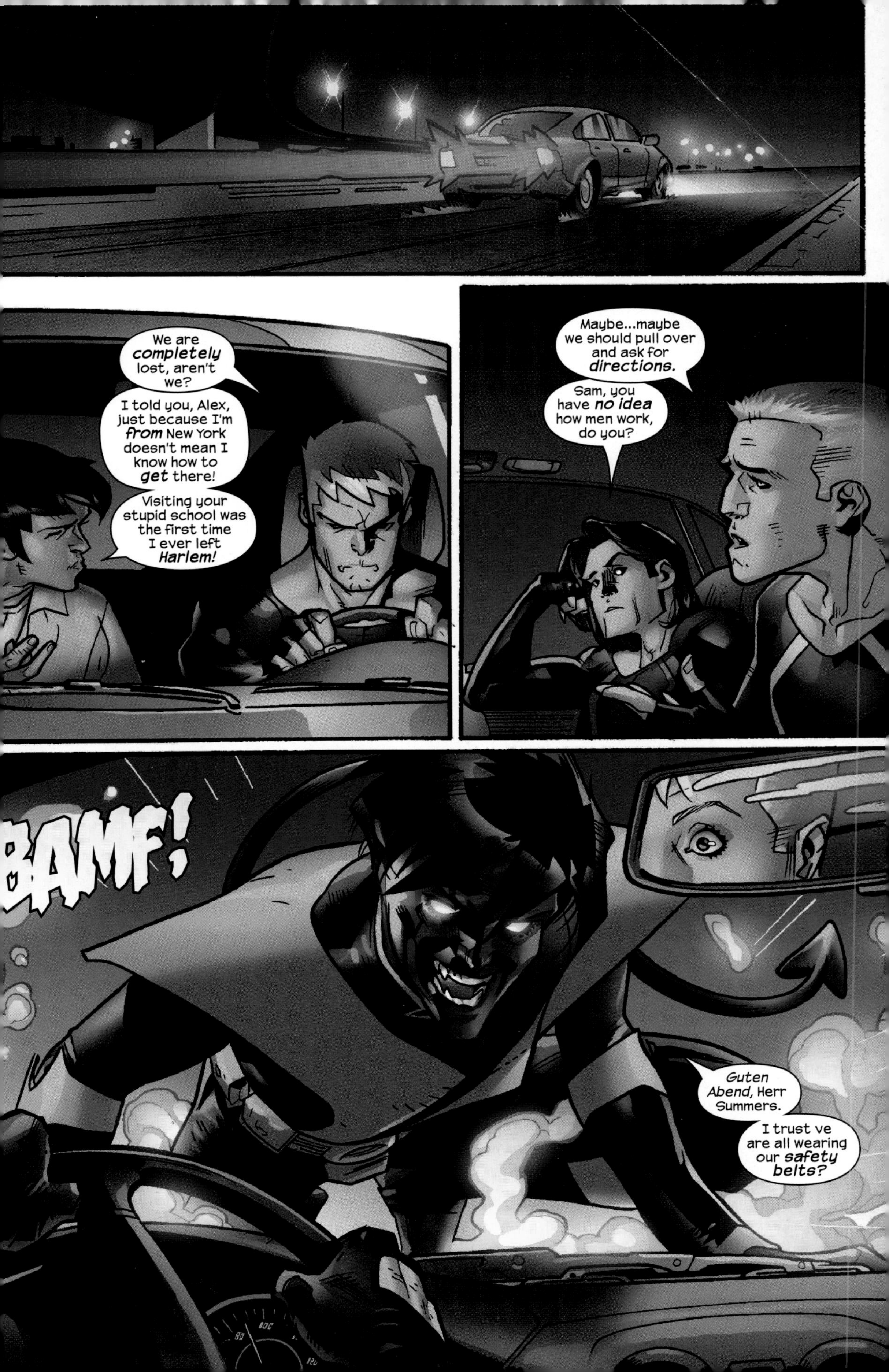
We are completely lost, aren't we?
I told you, Alex, just because I'm from New York doesn't mean I know how to get there!
Visiting your stupid school was the first time I ever left Harlem!
Maybe...maybe we should pull over and ask for directions.
Sam, you have no idea how men work, do you?
BAMF!
Guten Abend, Herr Summers.
I trust ve are all wearing our safety belts?

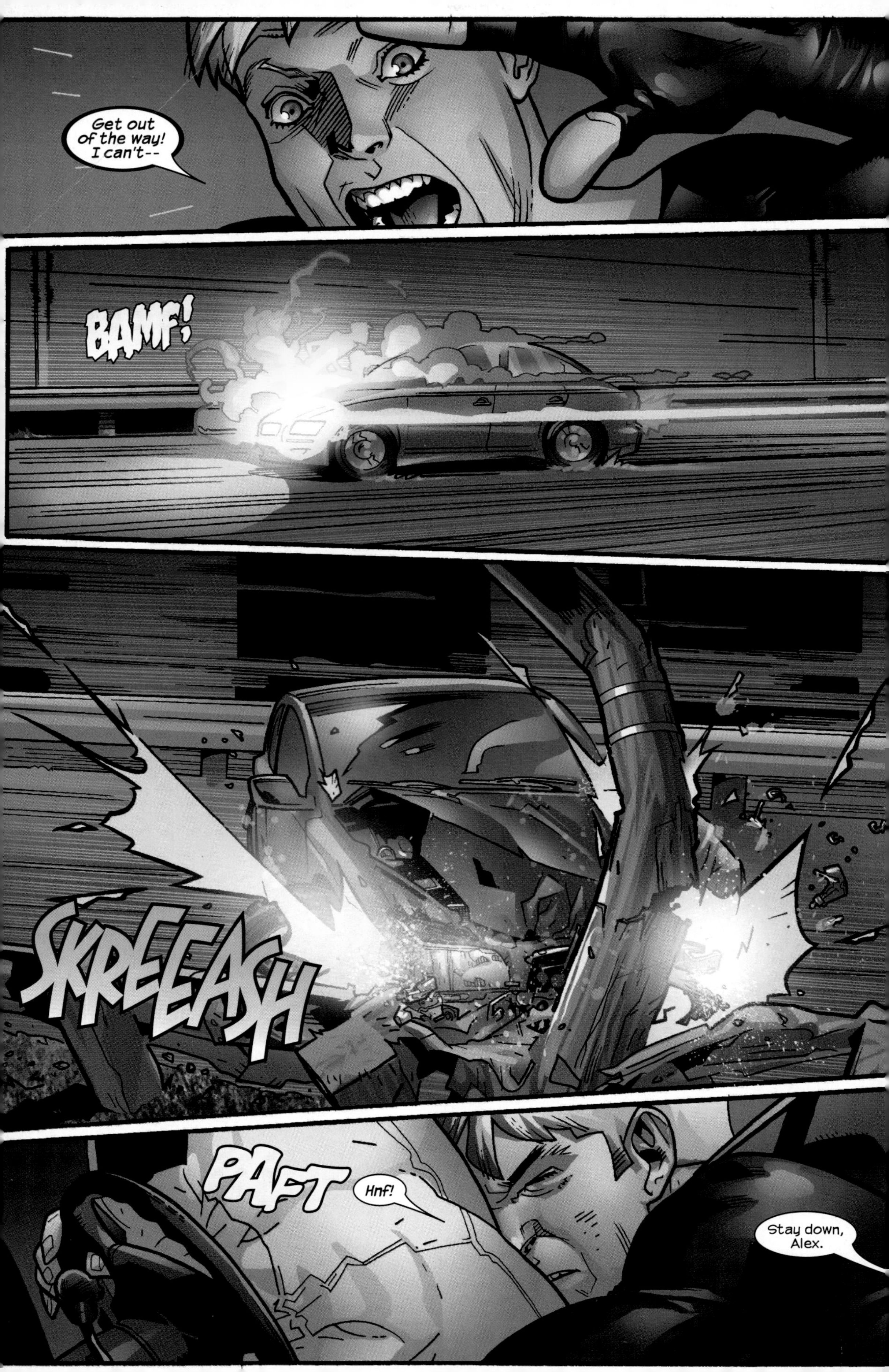
Get out of the way! I can't--
BAMF!
SKREEEASH
PAFT
Hnf!
Stay down, Alex.

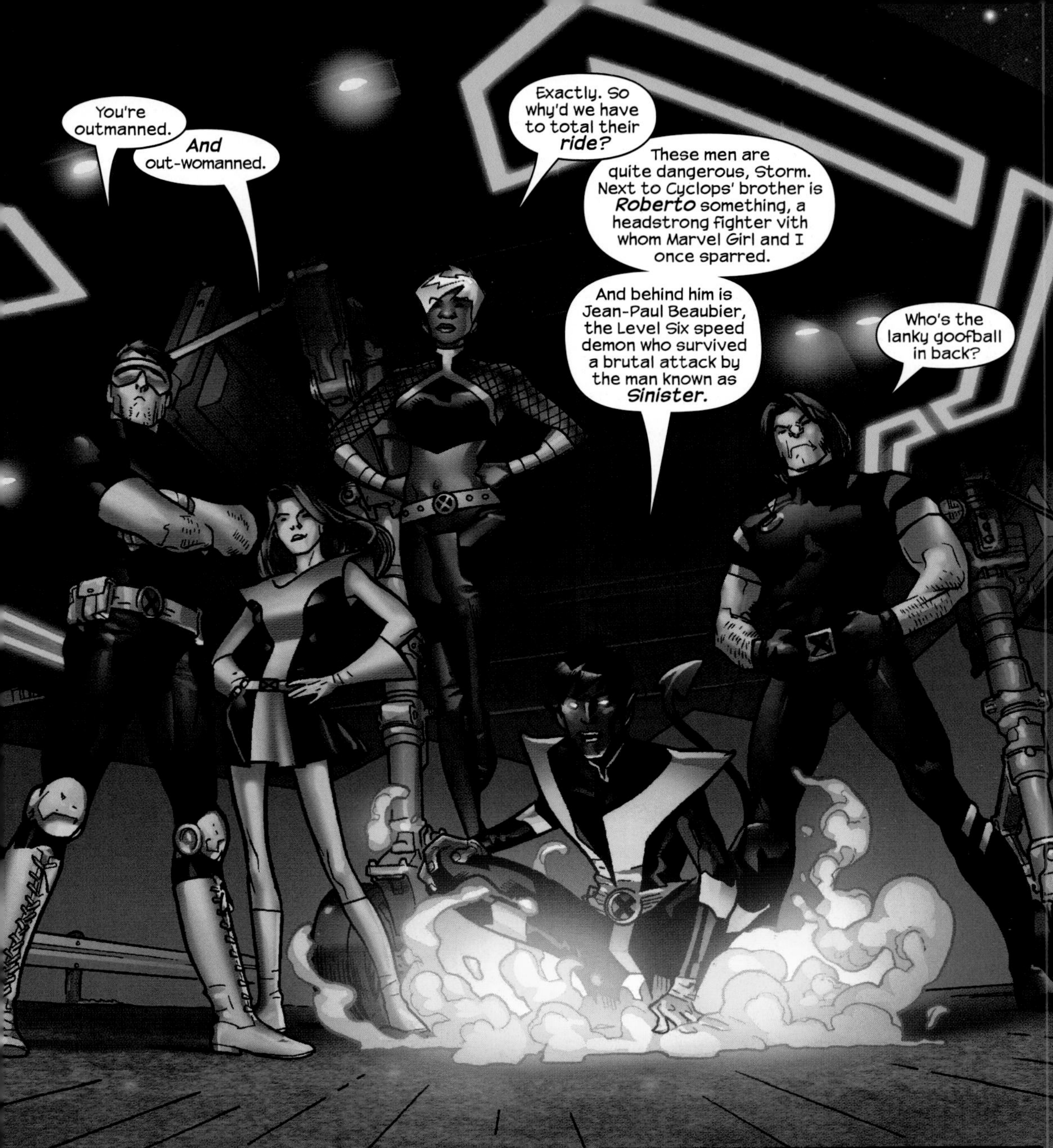
You're outmanned.
And out-womanned.
Exactly. So why'd we have to total their ride?
These men are quite dangerous, Storm. Next to Cyclops' brother is Roberto something, a headstrong fighter vith whom Marvel Girl and I once sparred.
And behind him is Jean-Paul Beaubier, the Level Six speed demon who survived a brutal attack by the man known as Sinister.
Who's the lanky goofball in back?

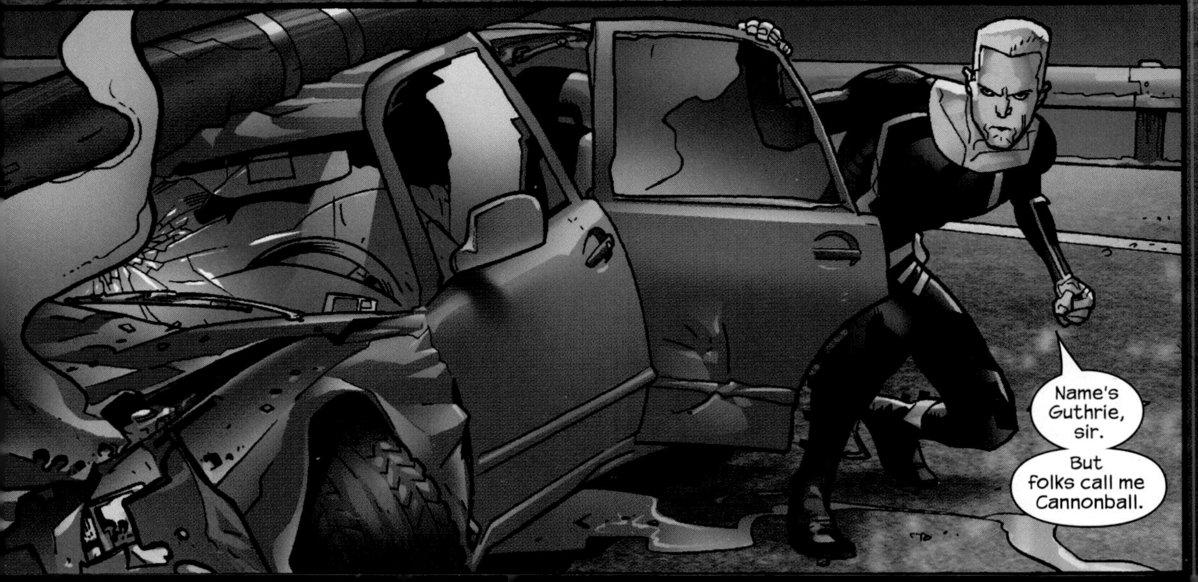
Name's Guthrie, sir.
But folks call me Cannonball.

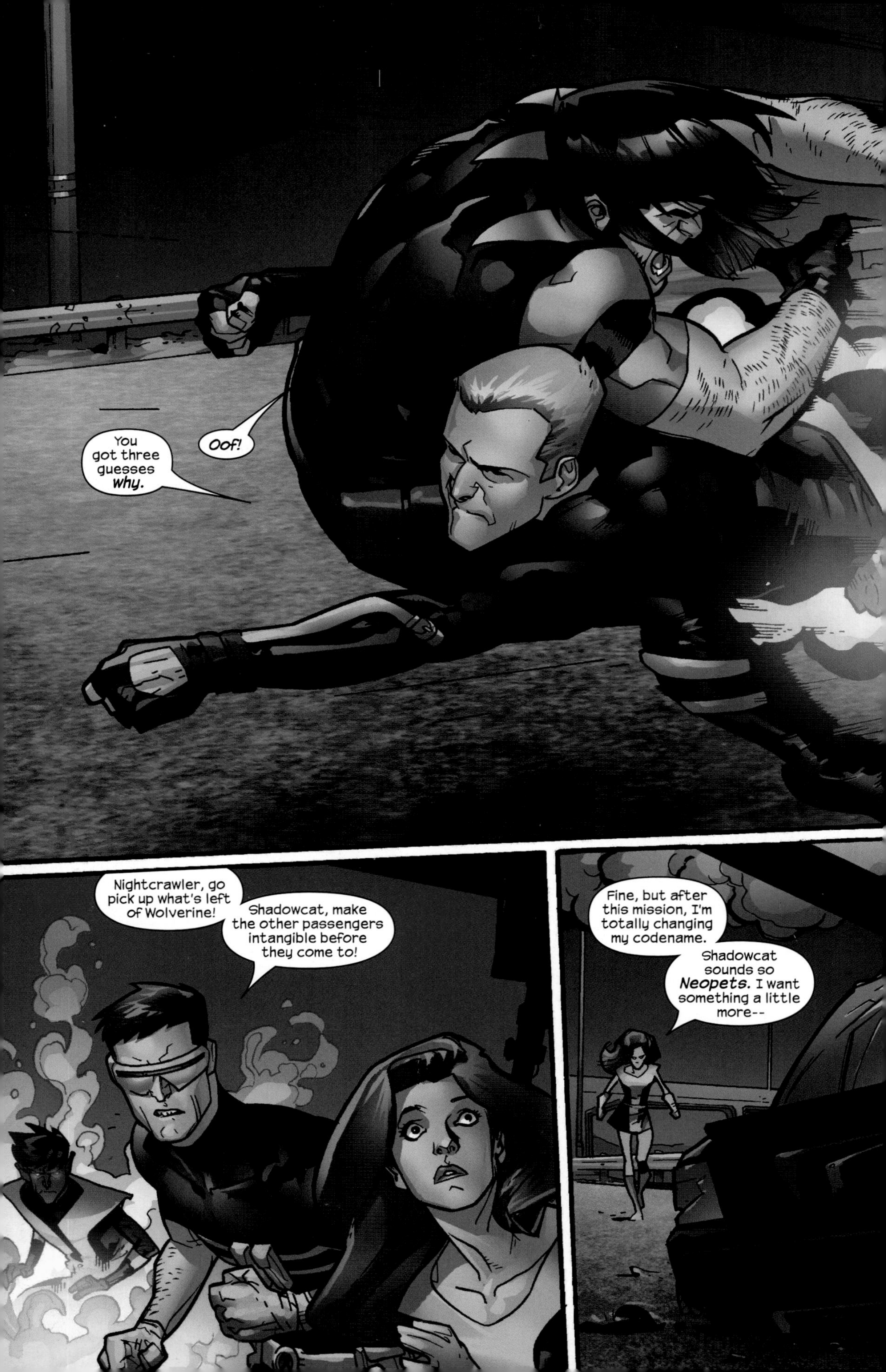
Oof!
You got three guesses *why.*
Nightcrawler, go pick up what's left of Wolverine!
Shadowcat, make the other passengers intangible before they come to!
Fine, but after this mission, I'm totally changing my codename.
Shadowcat sounds so *Neopets.* I want something a little more--

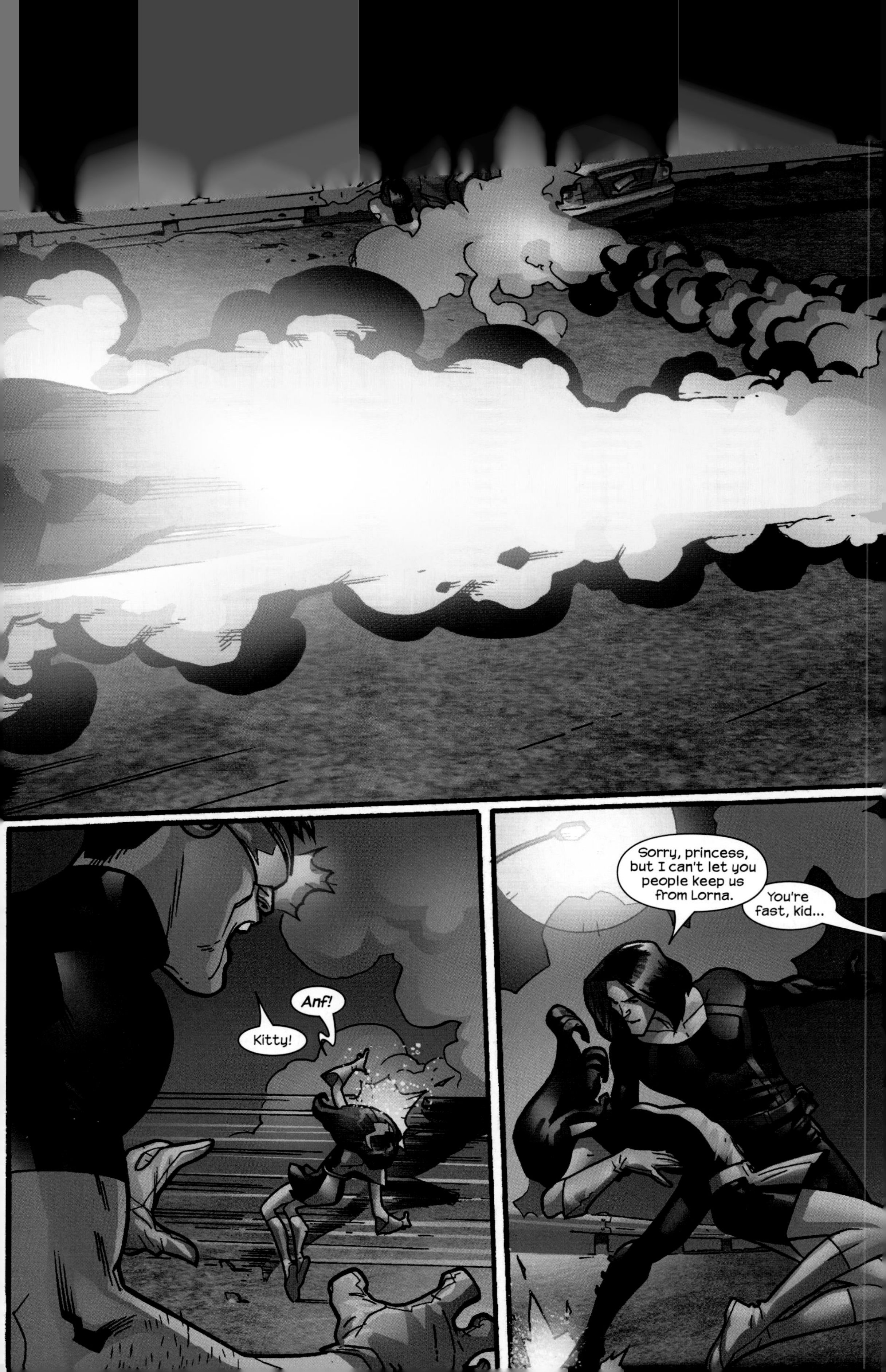
Kitty!
Anf!
Sorry, princess, but I can't let you people keep us from Lorna.
You're fast, kid...

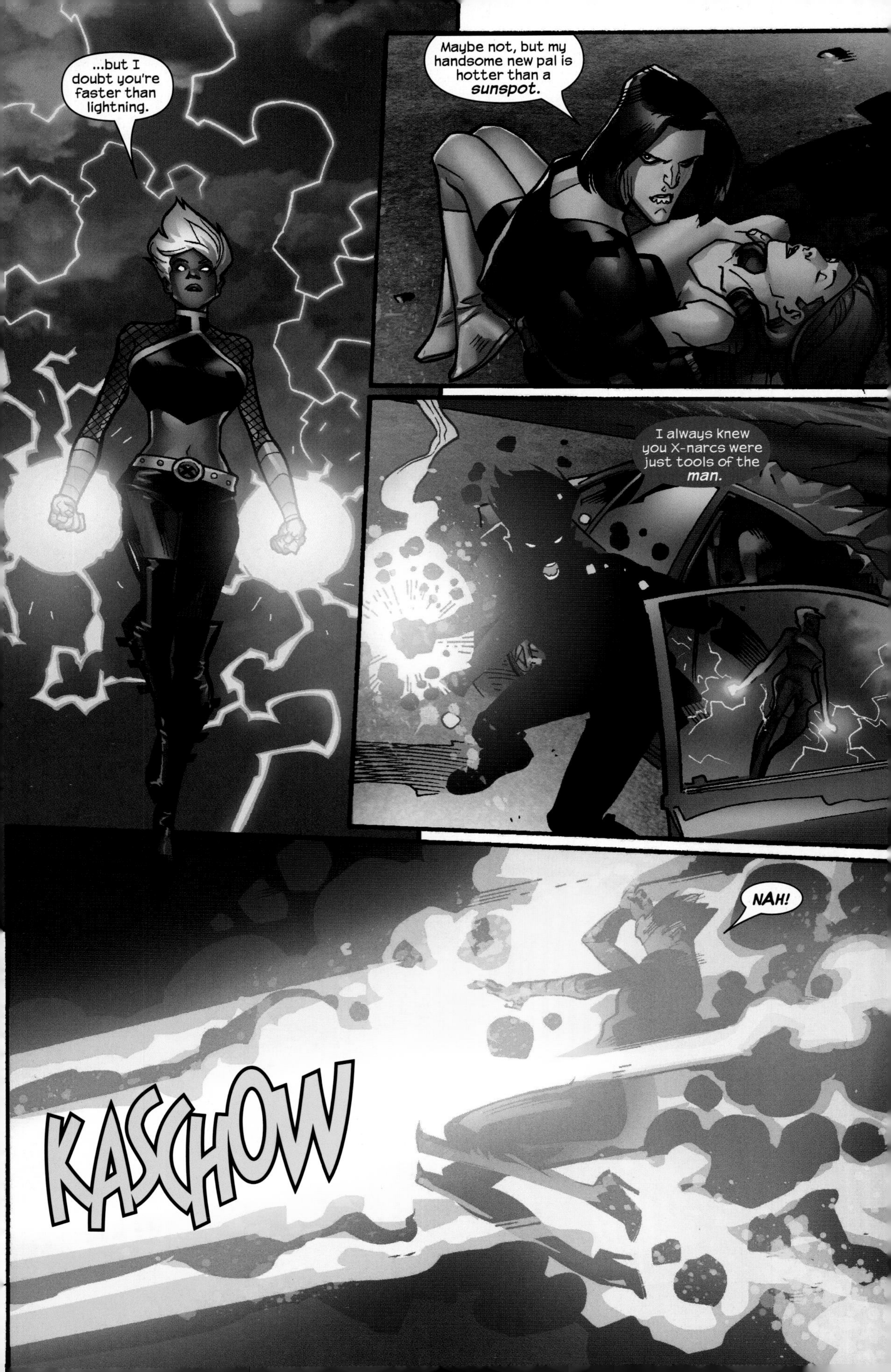
...but I doubt you're faster than lightning.
Maybe not, but my handsome new pal is hotter than a *sunspot*.
I always knew you X-narcs were just tools of the *man*.
NAH!
KASCHOW

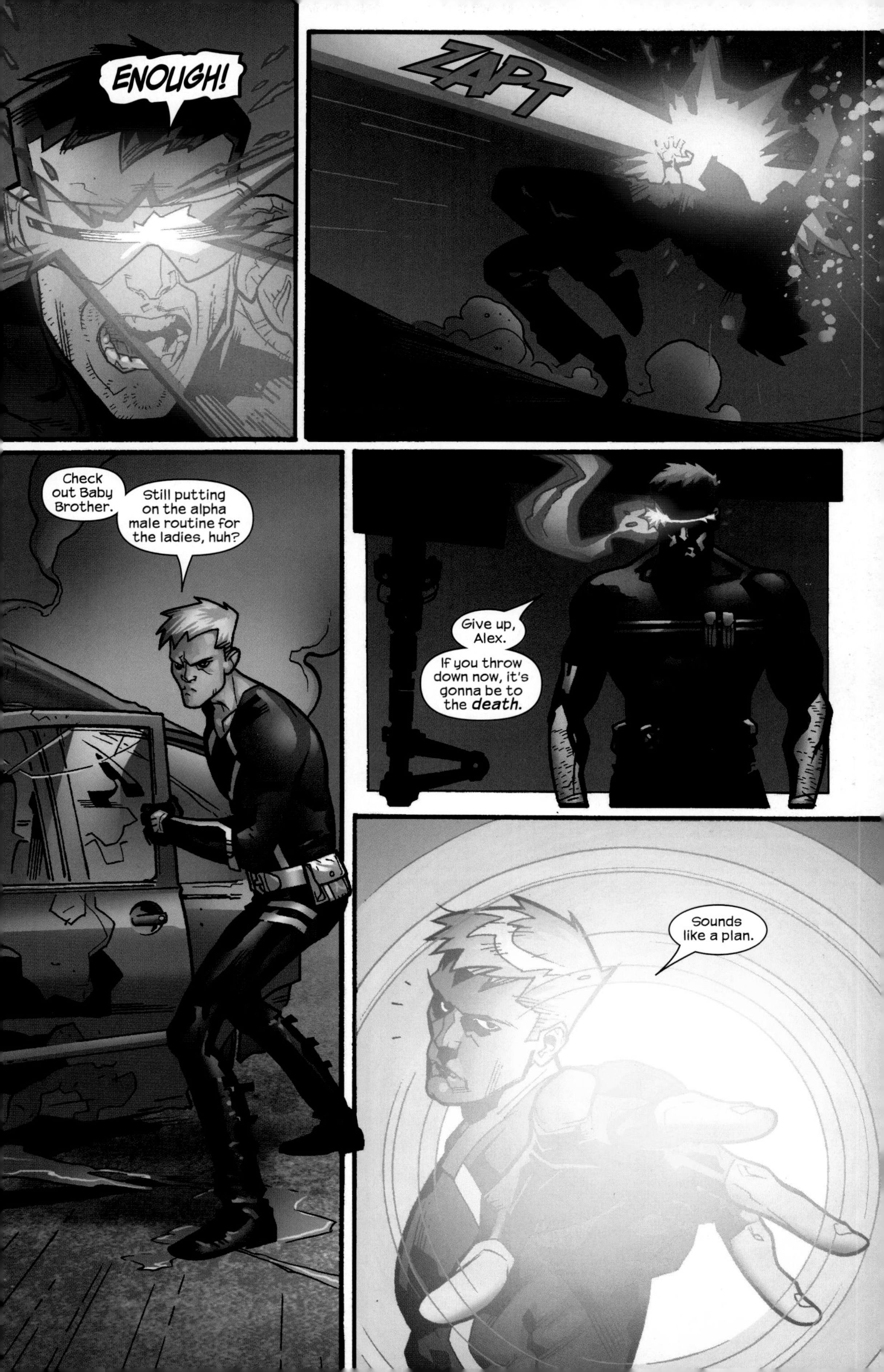
ENOUGH!
ZAPT
Check out Baby Brother.
Still putting on the alpha male routine for the ladies, huh?
Give up, Alex.
If you throw down now, it's gonna be to the *death.*
Sounds like a plan.

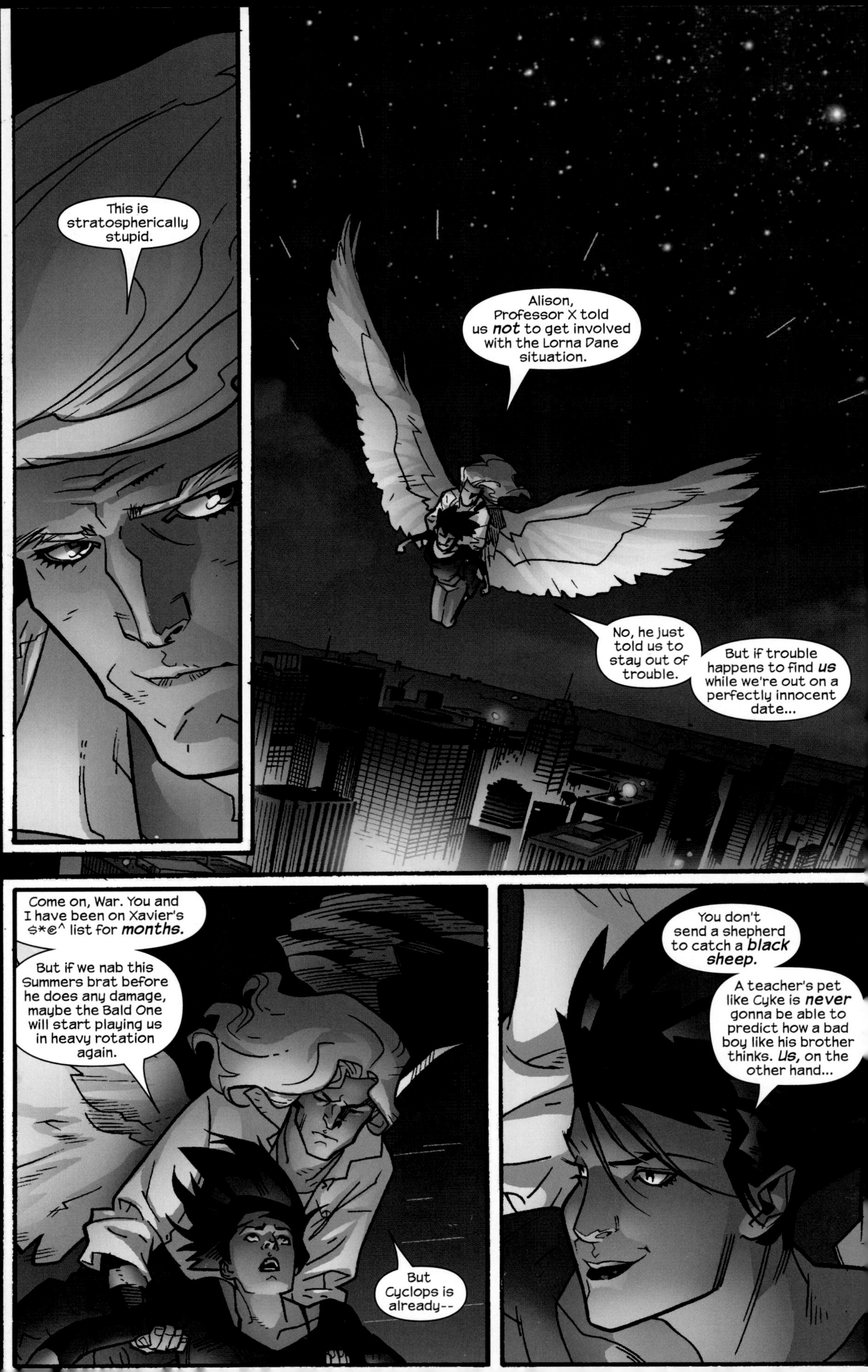

This is stratospherically stupid.
Alison, Professor X told us *not* to get involved with the Lorna Dane situation.
No, he just told us to stay out of trouble.
But if trouble happens to find *us* while we're out on a perfectly innocent date...
Come on, War. You and I have been on Xavier's $*@^ list for *months.*
But if we nab this Summers brat before he does any damage, maybe the Bald One will start playing us in heavy rotation again.
But Cyclops is already--
You don't send a shepherd to catch a *black sheep.*
A teacher's pet like Cyke is *never* gonna be able to predict how a bad boy like his brother thinks. *Us,* on the other hand...

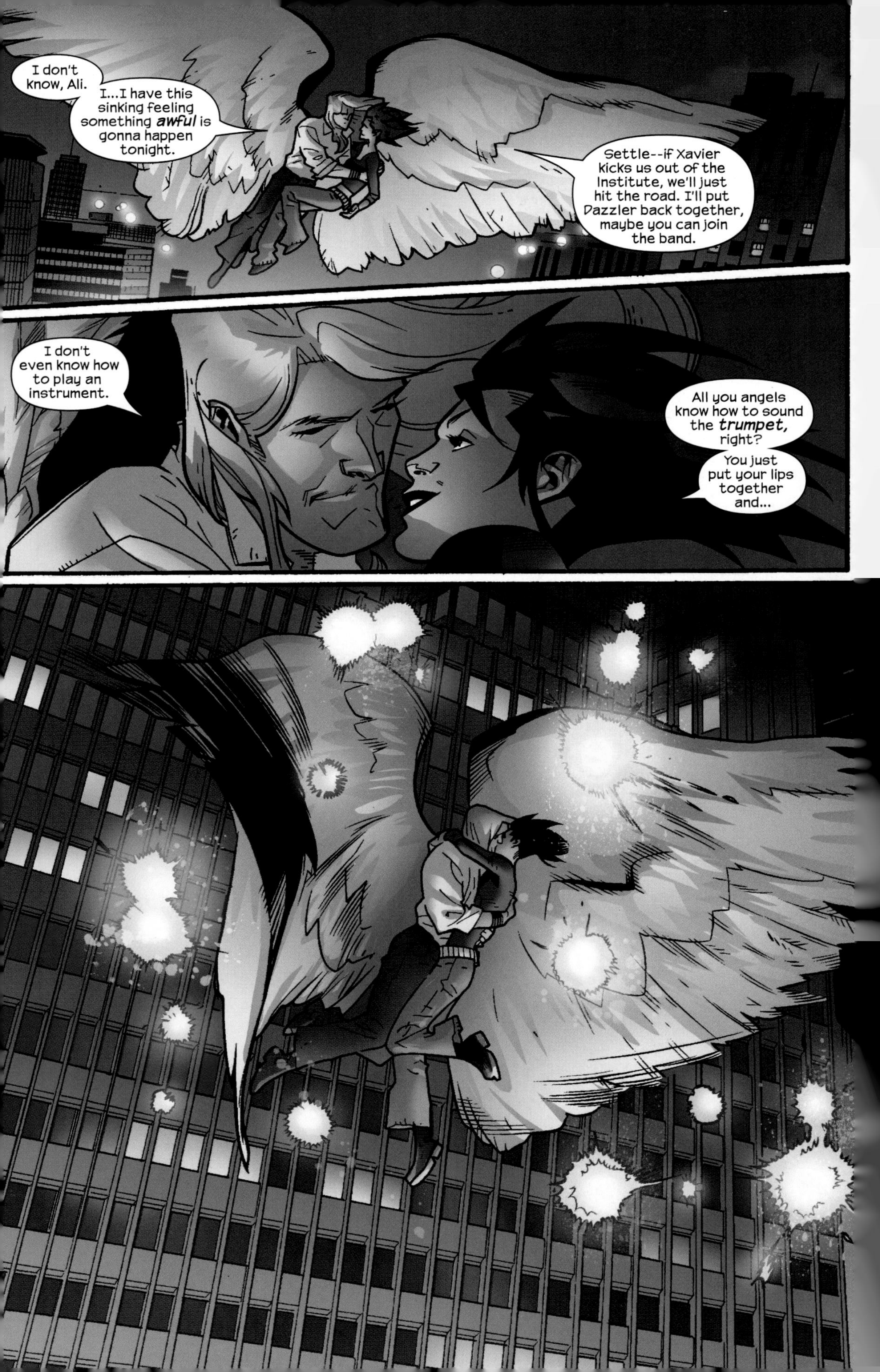
I don't know, Ali.
I...I have this sinking feeling something *awful* is gonna happen tonight.
Settle--if Xavier kicks us out of the Institute, we'll just hit the road. I'll put Dazzler back together, maybe you can join the band.
I don't even know how to play an instrument.
All you angels know how to sound the *trumpet,* right?
You just put your lips together and...

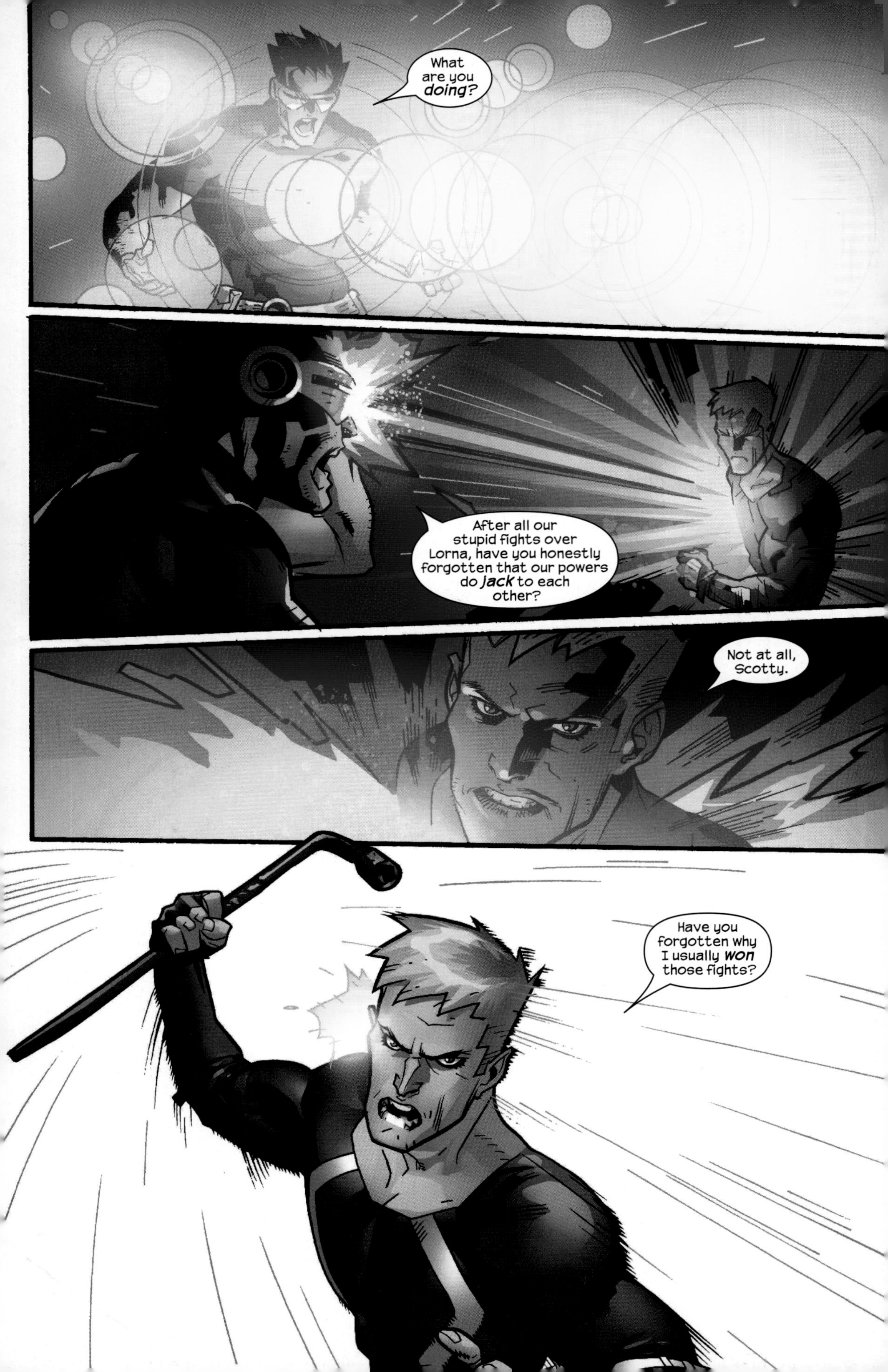
What are you *doing?*
After all our stupid fights over Lorna, have you honestly forgotten that our powers do *jack* to each other?
Not at all, Scotty.
Have you forgotten why I usually *won* those fights?

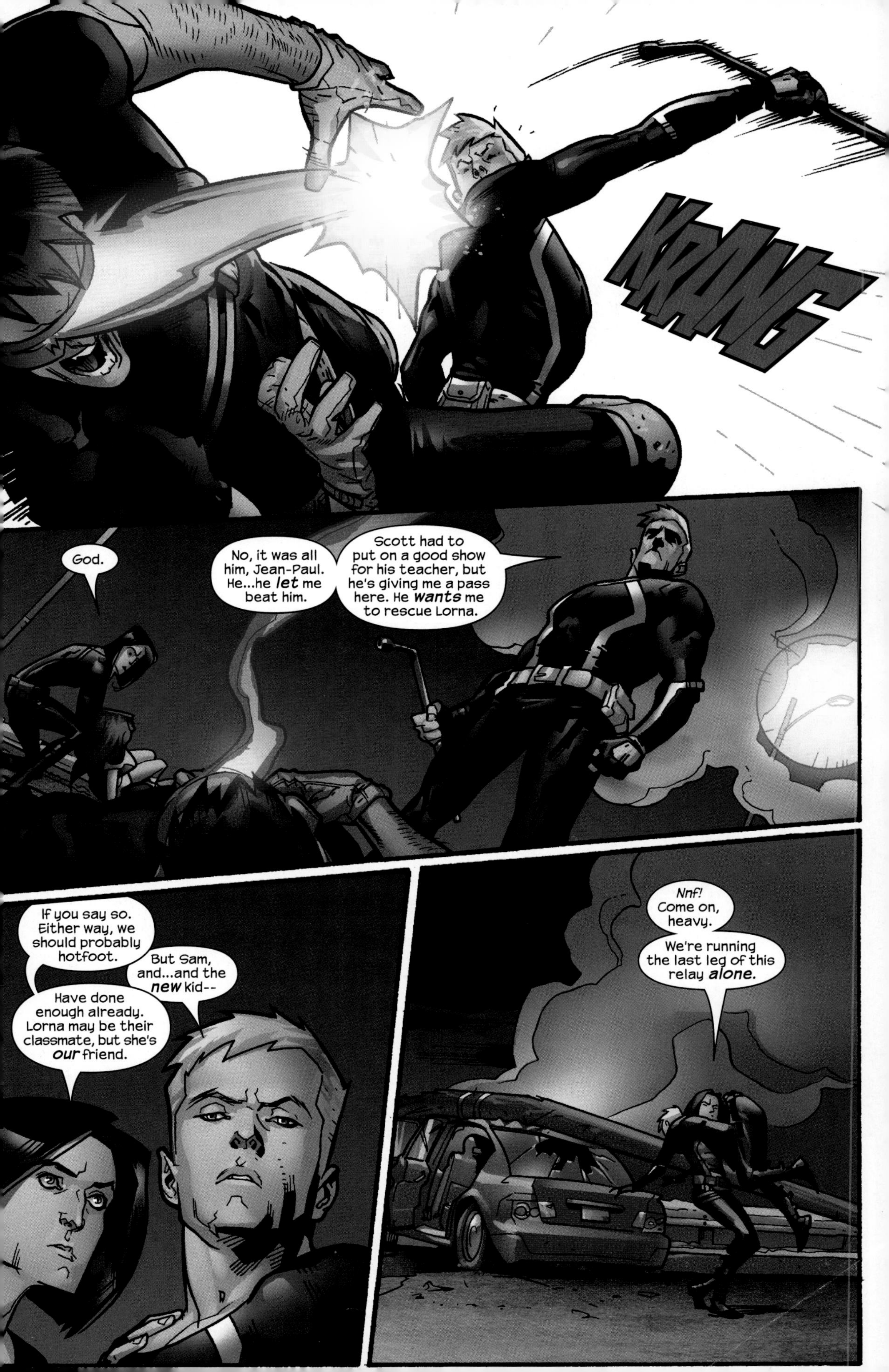
KRANG
God.
No, it was all him, Jean-Paul. He...he *let* me beat him.
Scott had to put on a good show for his teacher, but he's giving me a pass here. He *wants* me to rescue Lorna.
If you say so. Either way, we should probably hotfoot.
But Sam, and...and the *new* kid--
Have done enough already. Lorna may be their classmate, but she's *our* friend.
Nnf! Come on, heavy.
We're running the last leg of this relay *alone.*

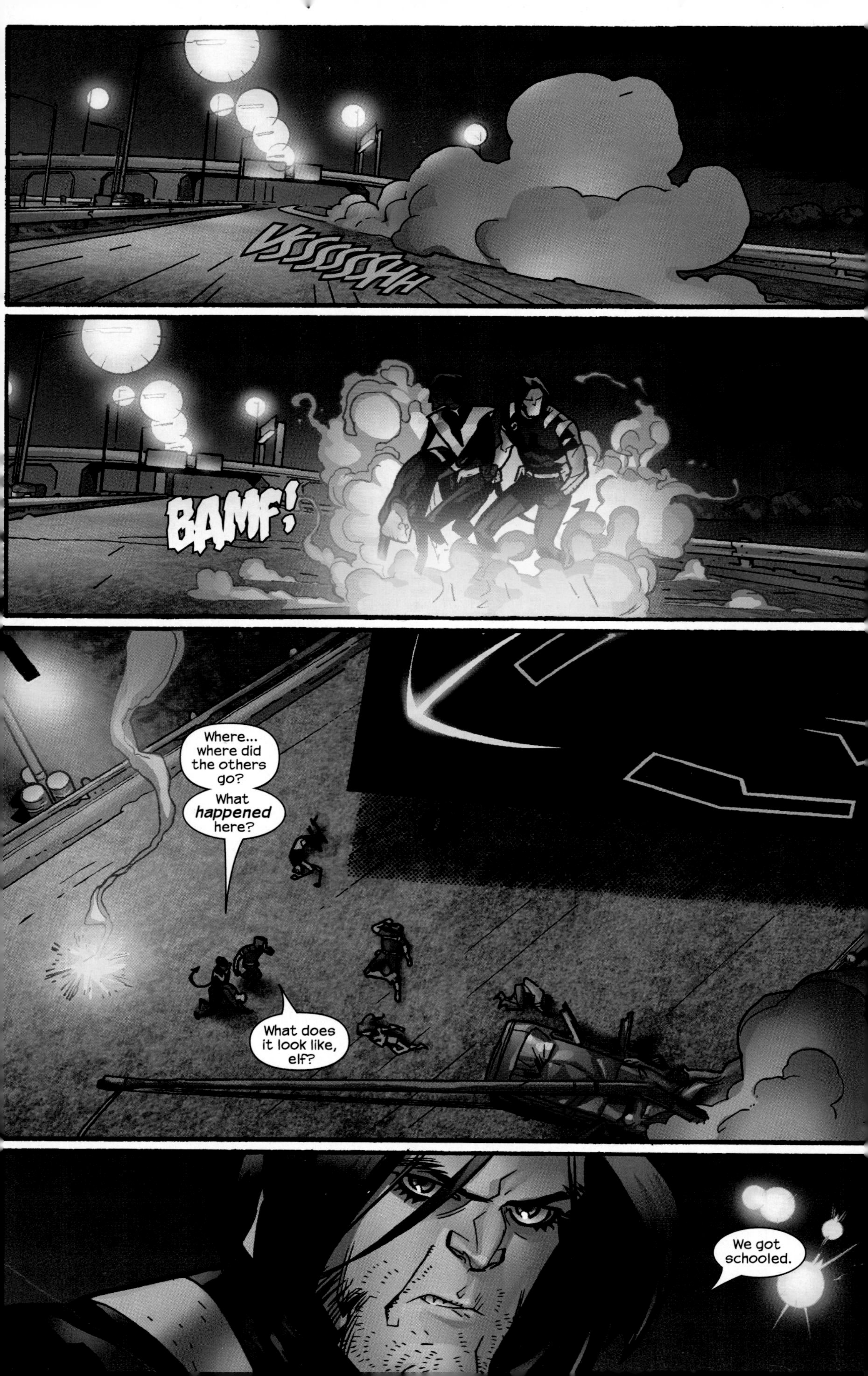
VSSSSSHH
BAMF!
Where... where did the others go?
What *happened* here?
What does it look like, elf?
We got schooled.

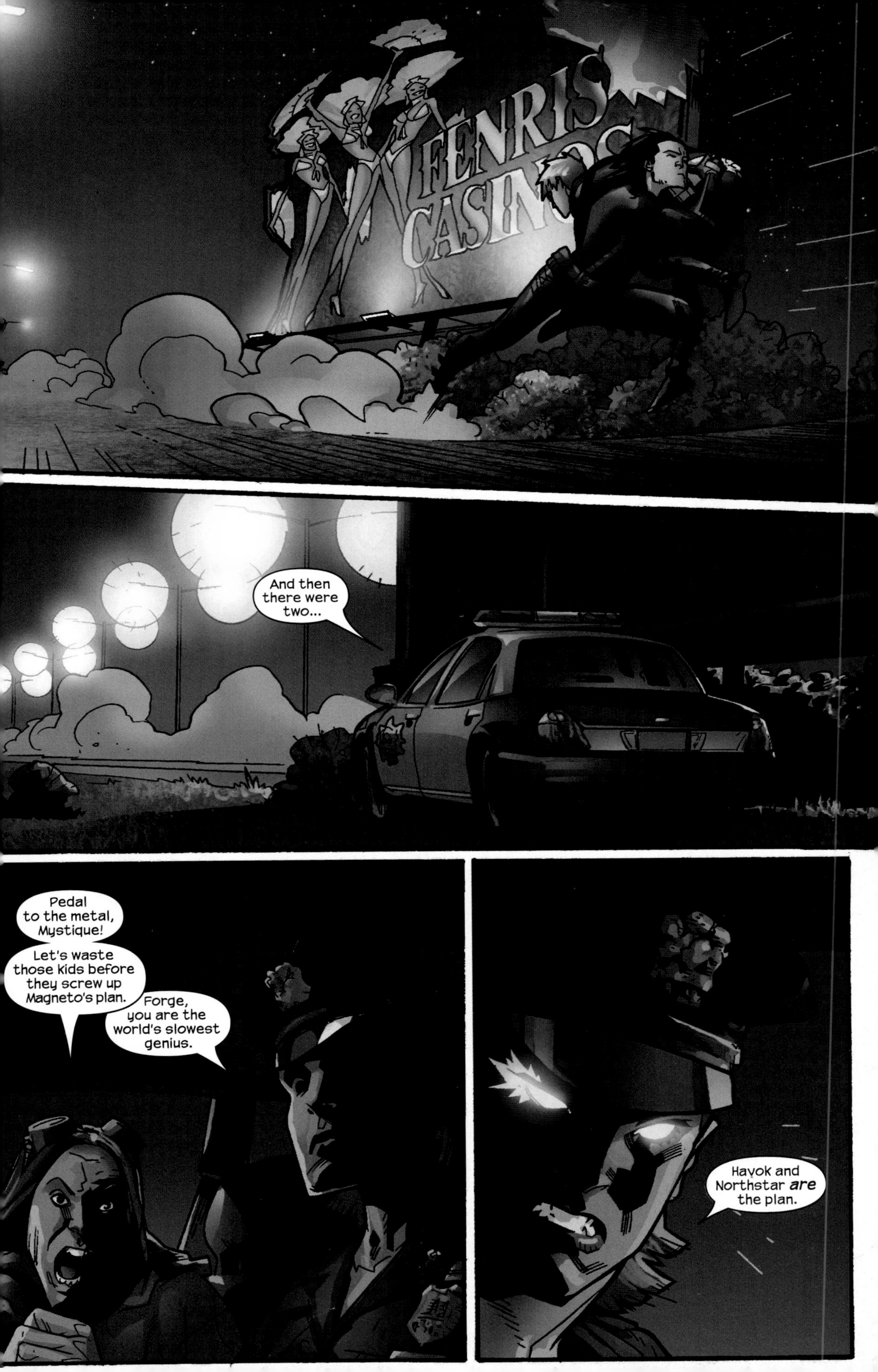
FENRIS CASINOS
And then there were two...
Pedal to the metal, Mystique!
Let's waste those kids before they screw up Magneto's plan.
Forge, you are the world's slowest genius.
Havok and Northstar *are* the plan.

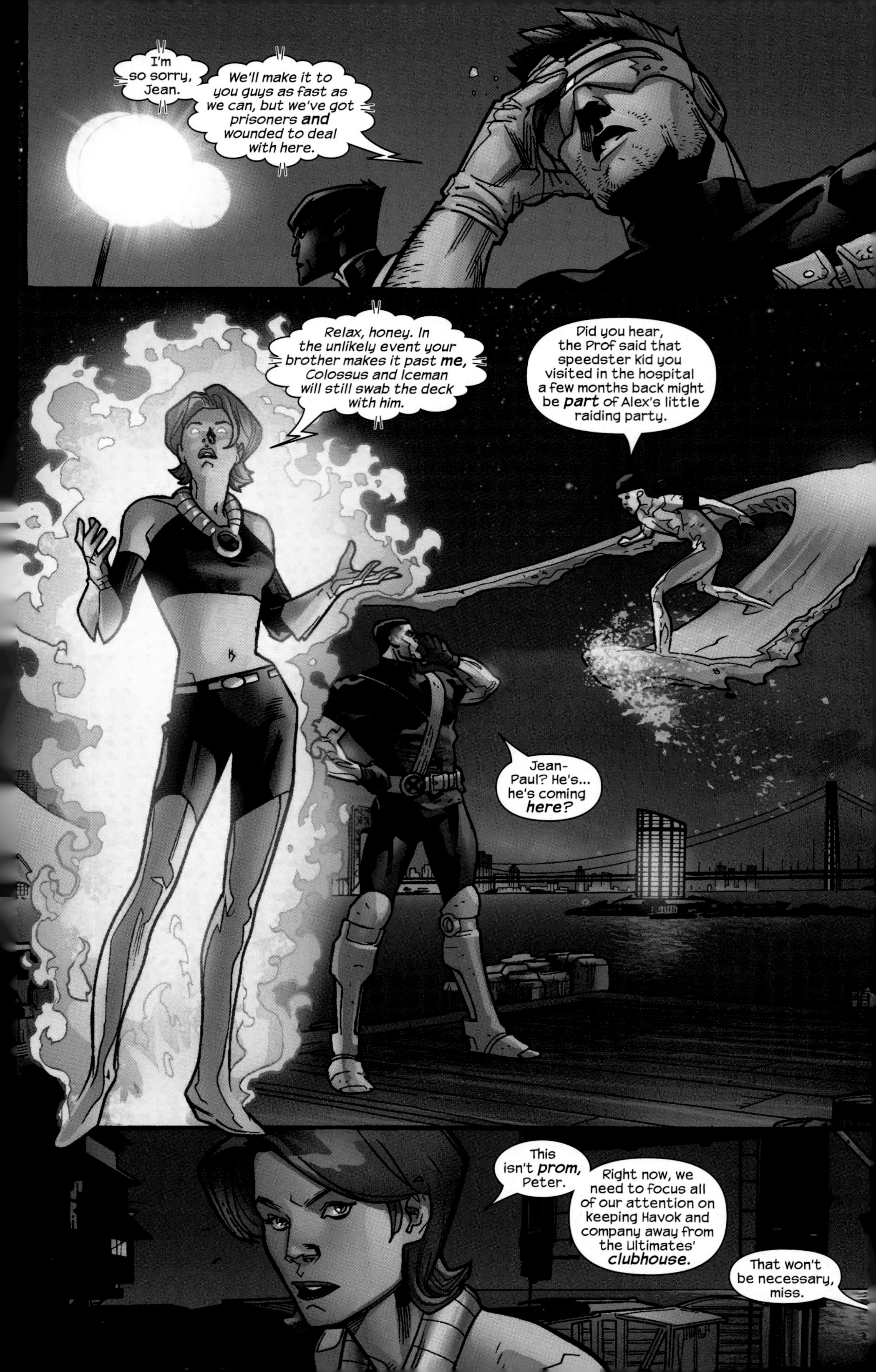
I'm so sorry, Jean.
We'll make it to you guys as fast as we can, but we've got prisoners **and** wounded to deal with here.
Relax, honey. In the unlikely event your brother makes it past **me,** Colossus and Iceman will still swab the deck with him.
Did you hear, the Prof said that speedster kid you visited in the hospital a few months back might be **part** of Alex's little raiding party.
Jean-Paul? He's... he's coming **here?**
This isn't **prom,** Peter.
Right now, we need to focus all of our attention on keeping Havok and company away from the Ultimates' **clubhouse.**
That won't be necessary, miss.

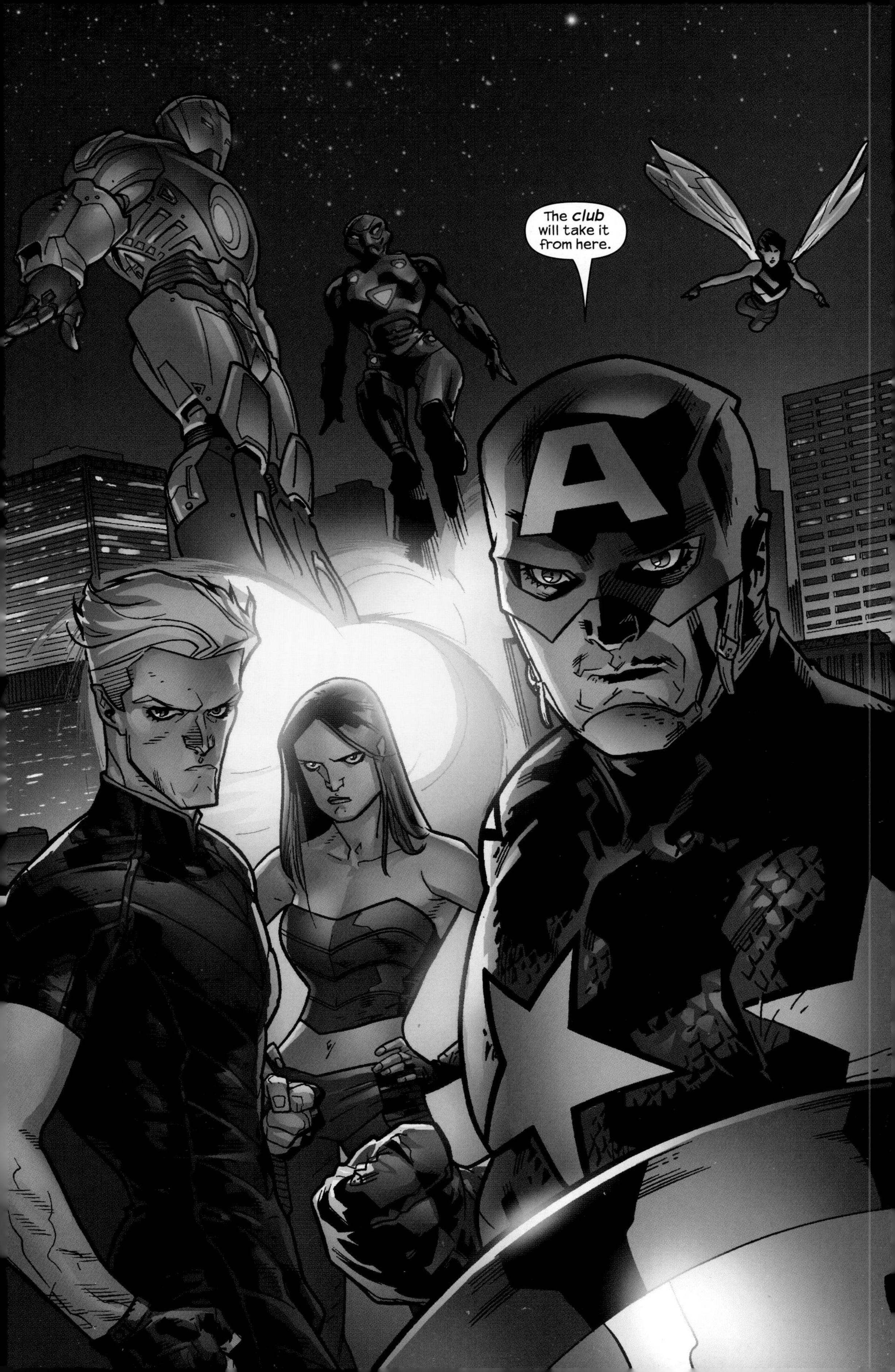
The club will take it from here.

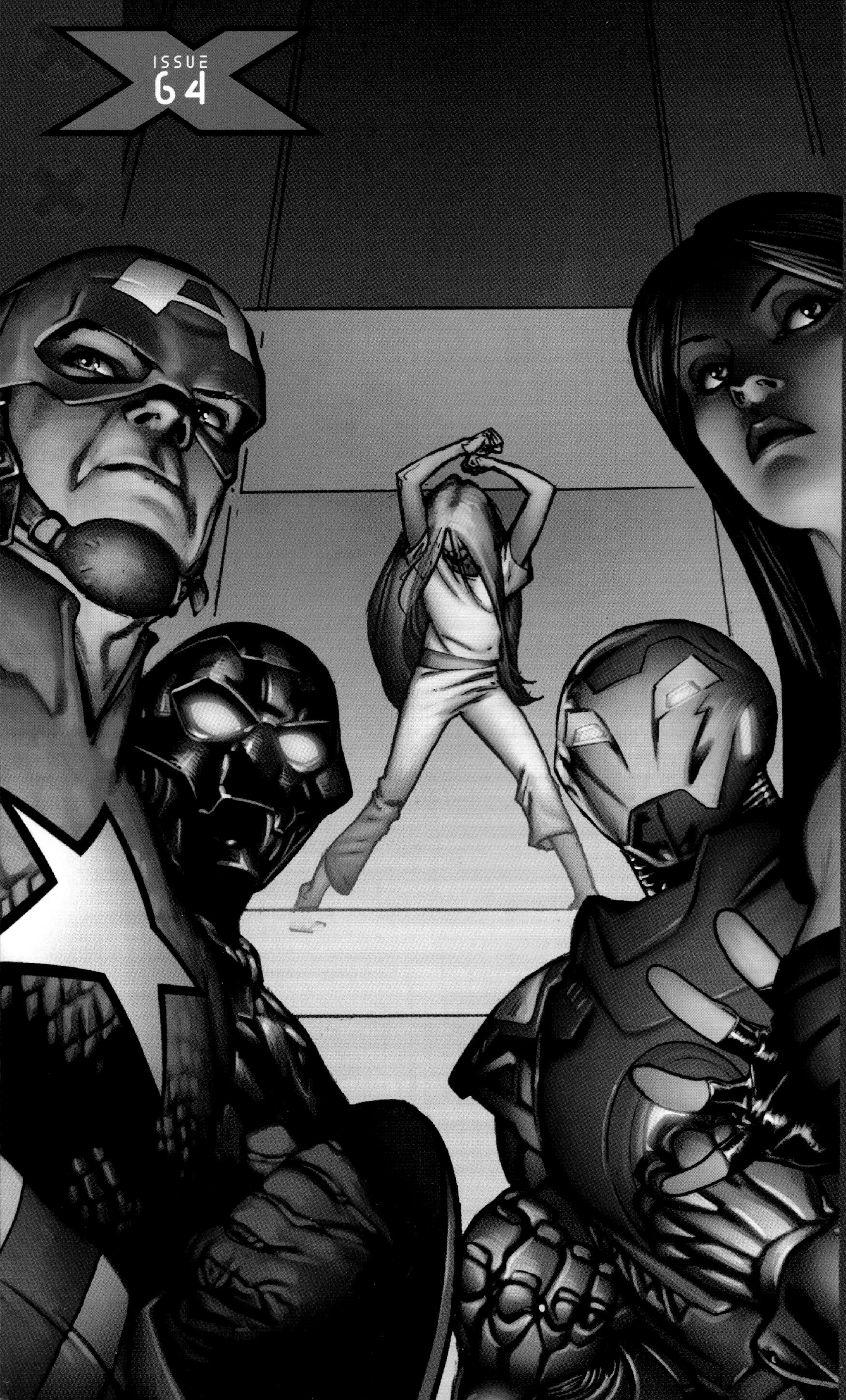
ISSUE
64

The Academy of Tomorrow
Chicago, Illinois
Now

I rock.

I rock
so hard.

MAGNETIC NORTH

CHAPTER FOUR

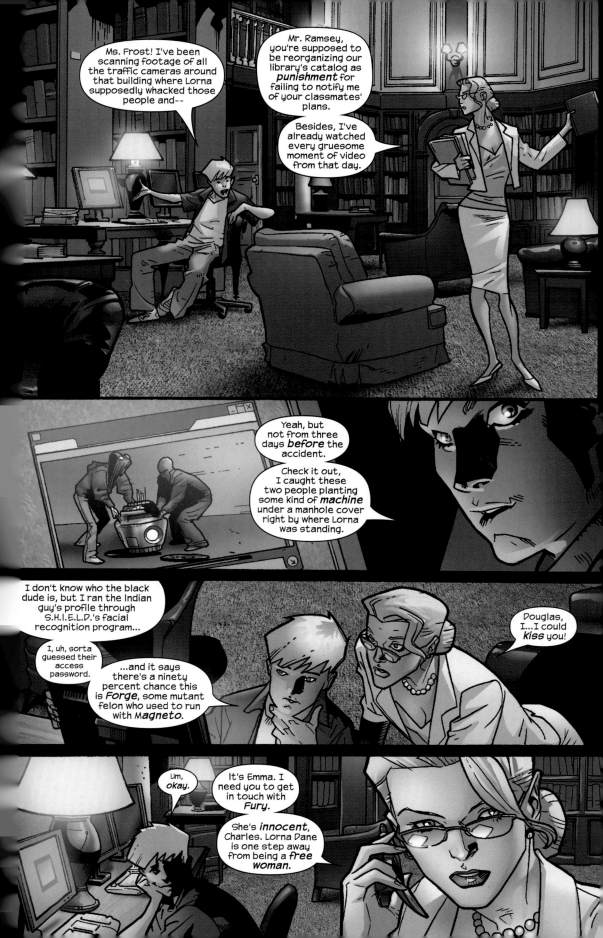

Ms. Frost! I've been scanning footage of all the traffic cameras around that building where Lorna supposedly whacked those people and--

Mr. Ramsey, you're supposed to be reorganizing our library's catalog as *punishment* for failing to notify me of your classmates' plans.

Besides, I've already watched every gruesome moment of video from that day.

Yeah, but not from three days *before* the accident.

Check it out, I caught these two people planting some kind of *machine* under a manhole cover right by where Lorna was standing.

I don't know who the black dude is, but I ran the Indian guy's profile through S.H.I.E.L.D.'s facial recognition program...

I, uh, sorta guessed their access password.

...and it says there's a ninety percent chance this is *Forge,* some mutant felon who used to run with *Magneto.*

Douglas, I...I could *kiss* you!

Um, *okay.*

It's Emma. I need you to get in touch with *Fury.*

She's *innocent,* Charles. Lorna Dane is one step away from being a *free woman.*

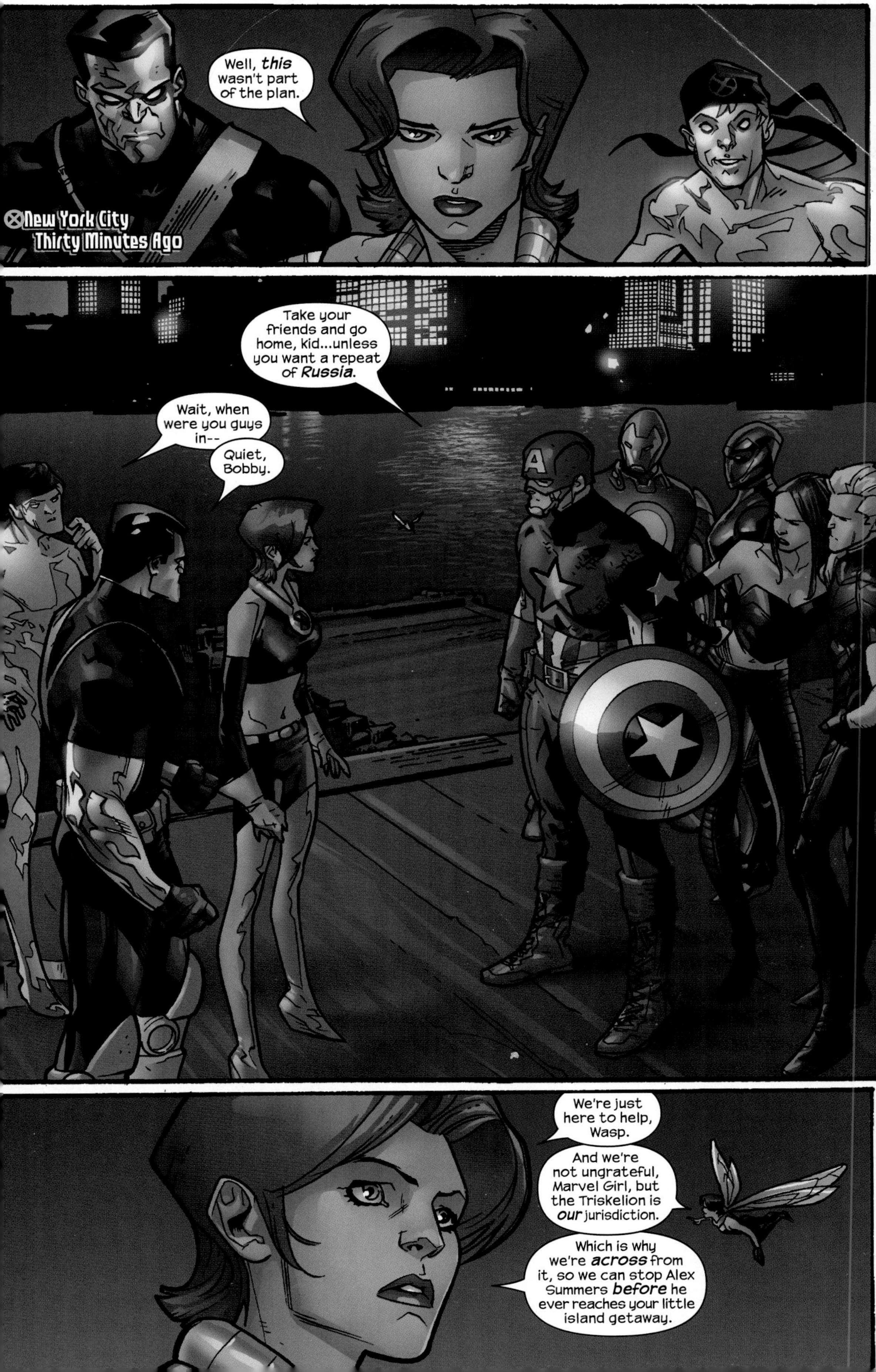
Well, *this* wasn't part of the plan.
New York City
Thirty Minutes Ago
Take your friends and go home, kid...unless you want a repeat of *Russia*.
Wait, when were you guys in--
Quiet, Bobby.
We're just here to help, Wasp.
And we're not ungrateful, Marvel Girl, but the Triskelion is *our* jurisdiction.
Which is why we're *across* from it, so we can stop Alex Summers *before* he ever reaches your little island getaway.

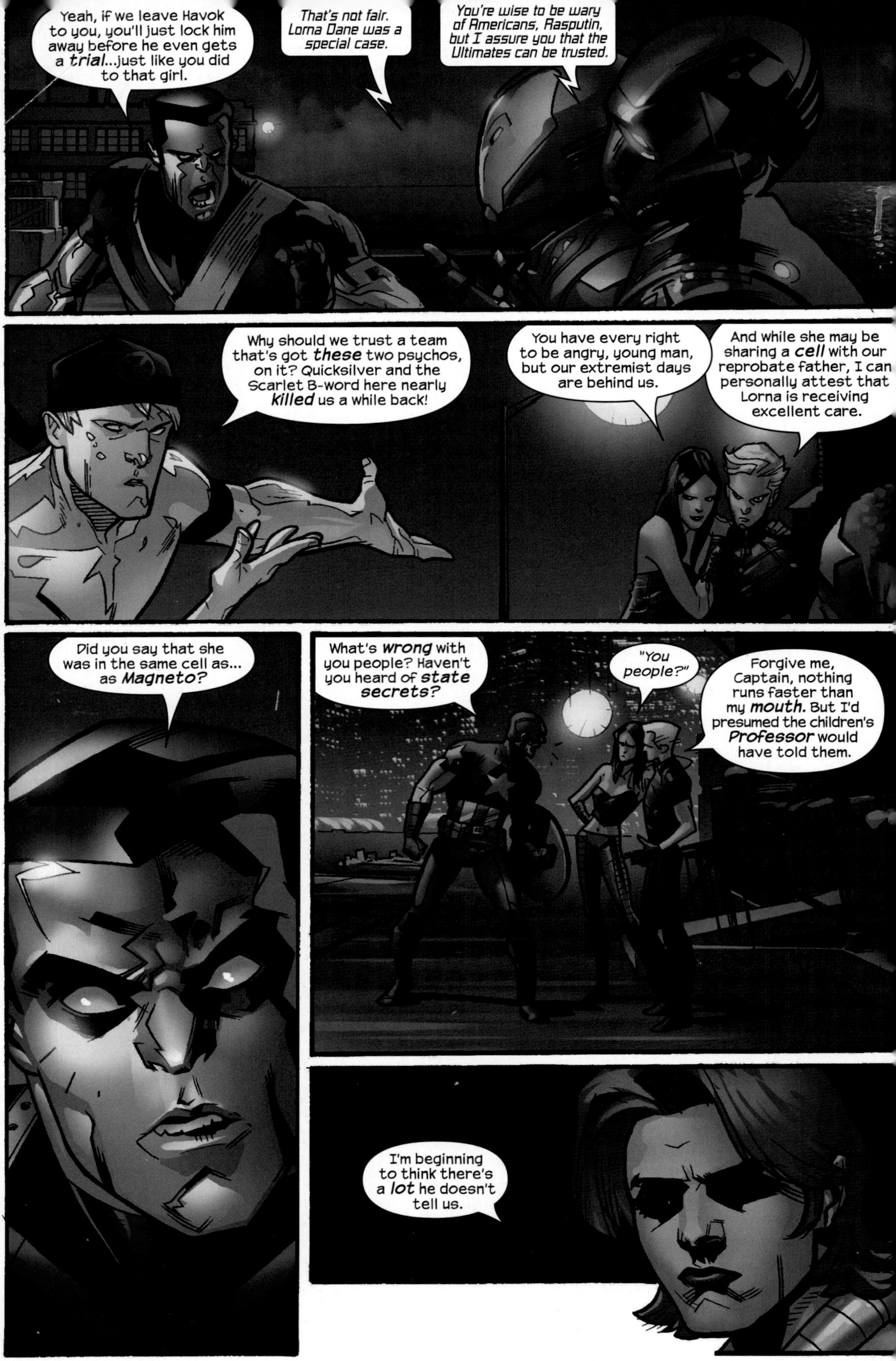
Yeah, if we leave Havok to you, you'll just lock him away before he even gets a trial...just like you did to that girl.
That's not fair. Lorna Dane was a special case.
You're wise to be wary of Americans, Rasputin, but I assure you that the Ultimates can be trusted.
Why should we trust a team that's got these two psychos, on it? Quicksilver and the Scarlet B-word here nearly killed us a while back!
You have every right to be angry, young man, but our extremist days are behind us.
And while she may be sharing a cell with our reprobate father, I can personally attest that Lorna is receiving excellent care.
Did you say that she was in the same cell as... as Magneto?
What's wrong with you people? Haven't you heard of state secrets?
"You people?"
Forgive me, Captain, nothing runs faster than my mouth. But I'd presumed the children's Professor would have told them.
I'm beginning to think there's a lot he doesn't tell us.

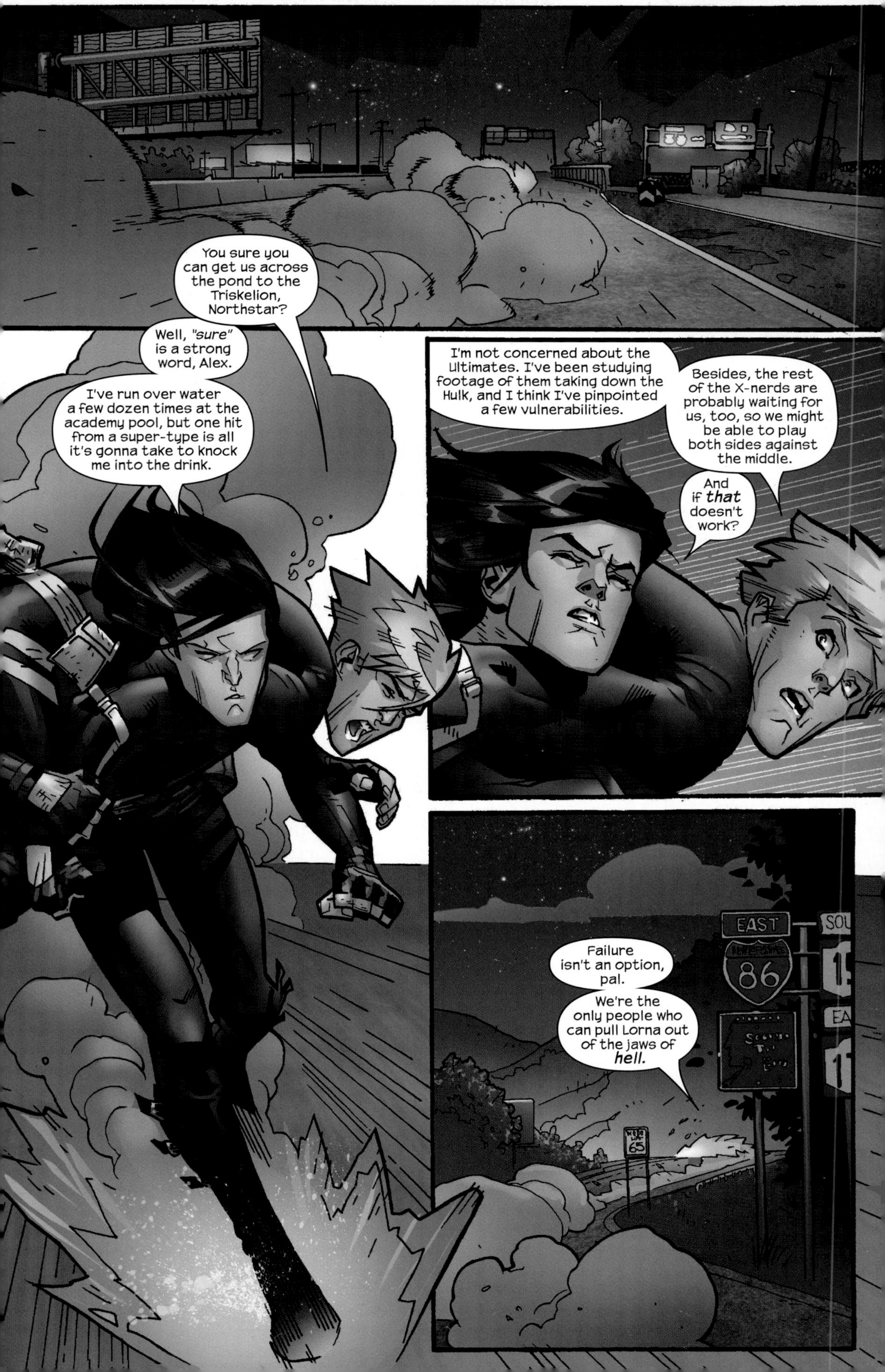
You sure you can get us across the pond to the Triskelion, Northstar?
Well, "*sure*" is a strong word, Alex.
I've run over water a few dozen times at the academy pool, but one hit from a super-type is all it's gonna take to knock me into the drink.
I'm not concerned about the Ultimates. I've been studying footage of them taking down the Hulk, and I think I've pinpointed a few vulnerabilities.
Besides, the rest of the X-nerds are probably waiting for us, too, so we might be able to play both sides against the middle.
And if ***that*** doesn't work?
EAST
86
Failure isn't an option, pal.
We're the only people who can pull Lorna out of the jaws of ***hell.***
65

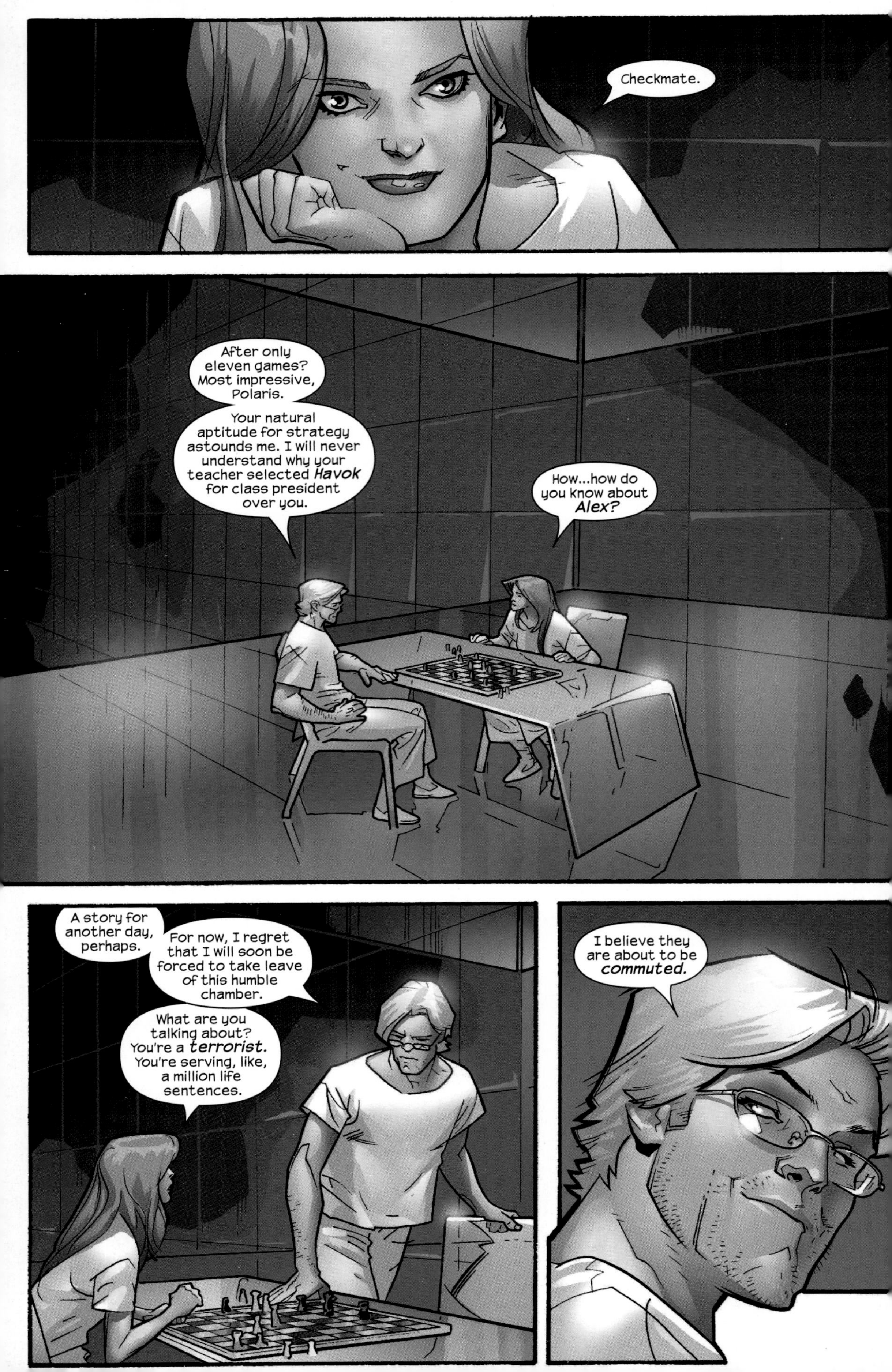
Checkmate.
After only eleven games? Most impressive, Polaris.
Your natural aptitude for strategy astounds me. I will never understand why your teacher selected *Havok* for class president over you.
How...how do you know about *Alex?*
A story for another day, perhaps.
For now, I regret that I will soon be forced to take leave of this humble chamber.
What are you talking about? You're a *terrorist.* You're serving, like, a million life sentences.
I believe they are about to be *commuted.*

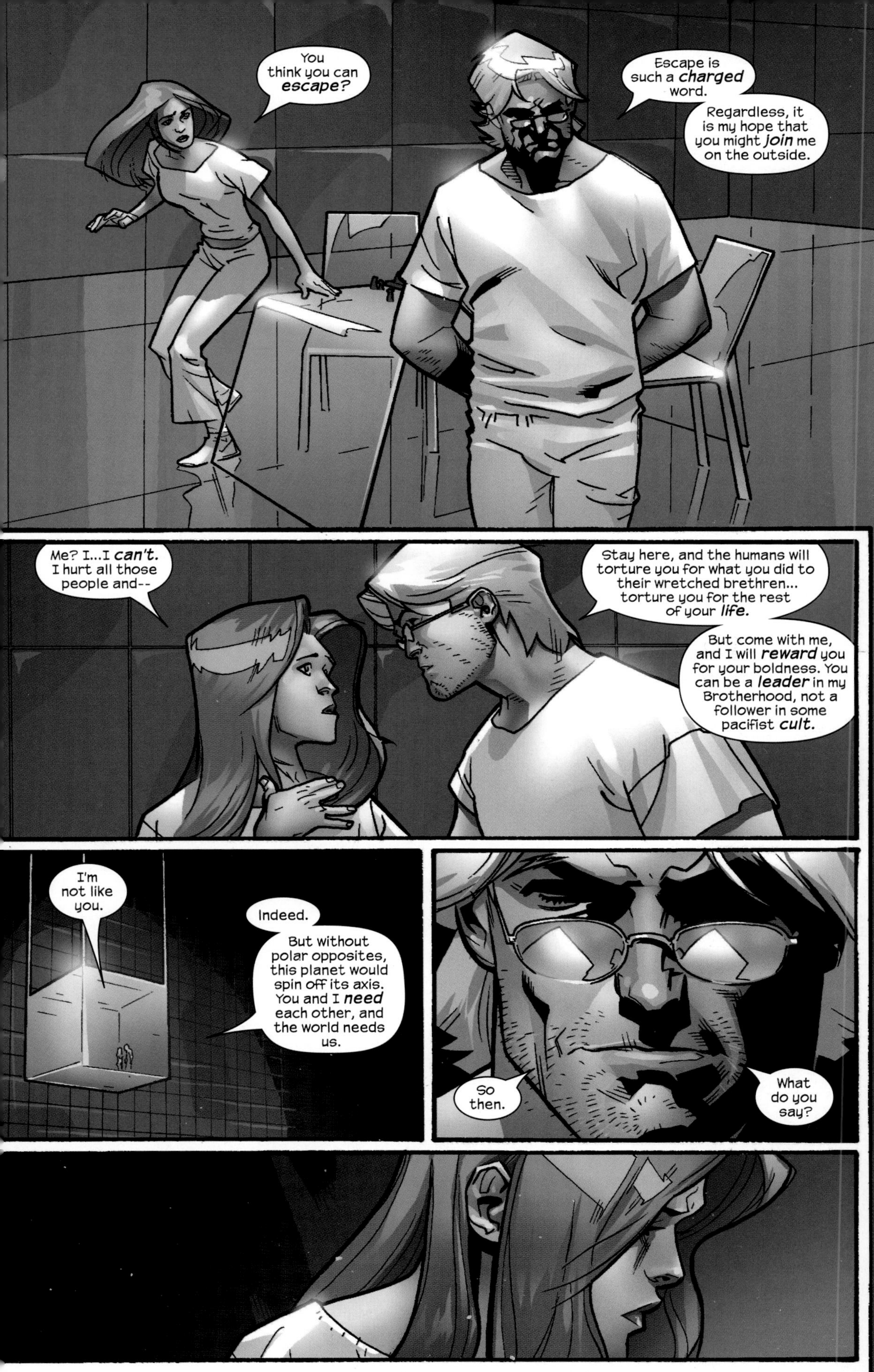
You think you can escape?
Escape is such a charged word.
Regardless, it is my hope that you might join me on the outside.
Me? I...I can't. I hurt all those people and--
Stay here, and the humans will torture you for what you did to their wretched brethren... torture you for the rest of your life.
But come with me, and I will reward you for your boldness. You can be a leader in my Brotherhood, not a follower in some pacifist cult.
I'm not like you.
Indeed.
But without polar opposites, this planet would spin off its axis. You and I need each other, and the world needs us.
So then.
What do you say?

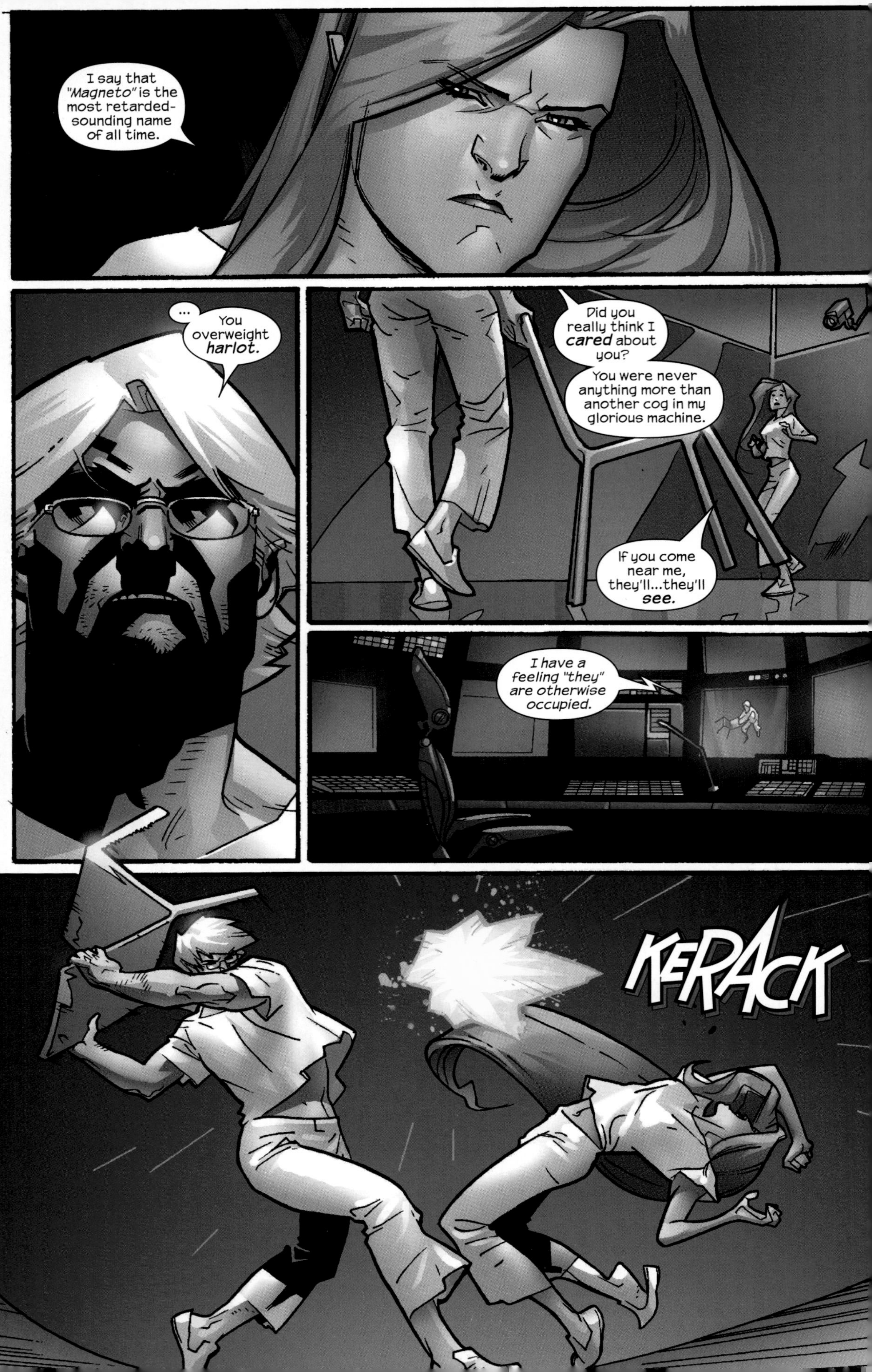
I say that "Magneto" is the most retarded-sounding name of all time.
... You overweight harlot.
Did you really think I cared about you?
You were never anything more than another cog in my glorious machine.
If you come near me, they'll...they'll see.
I have a feeling "they" are otherwise occupied.
KERACK

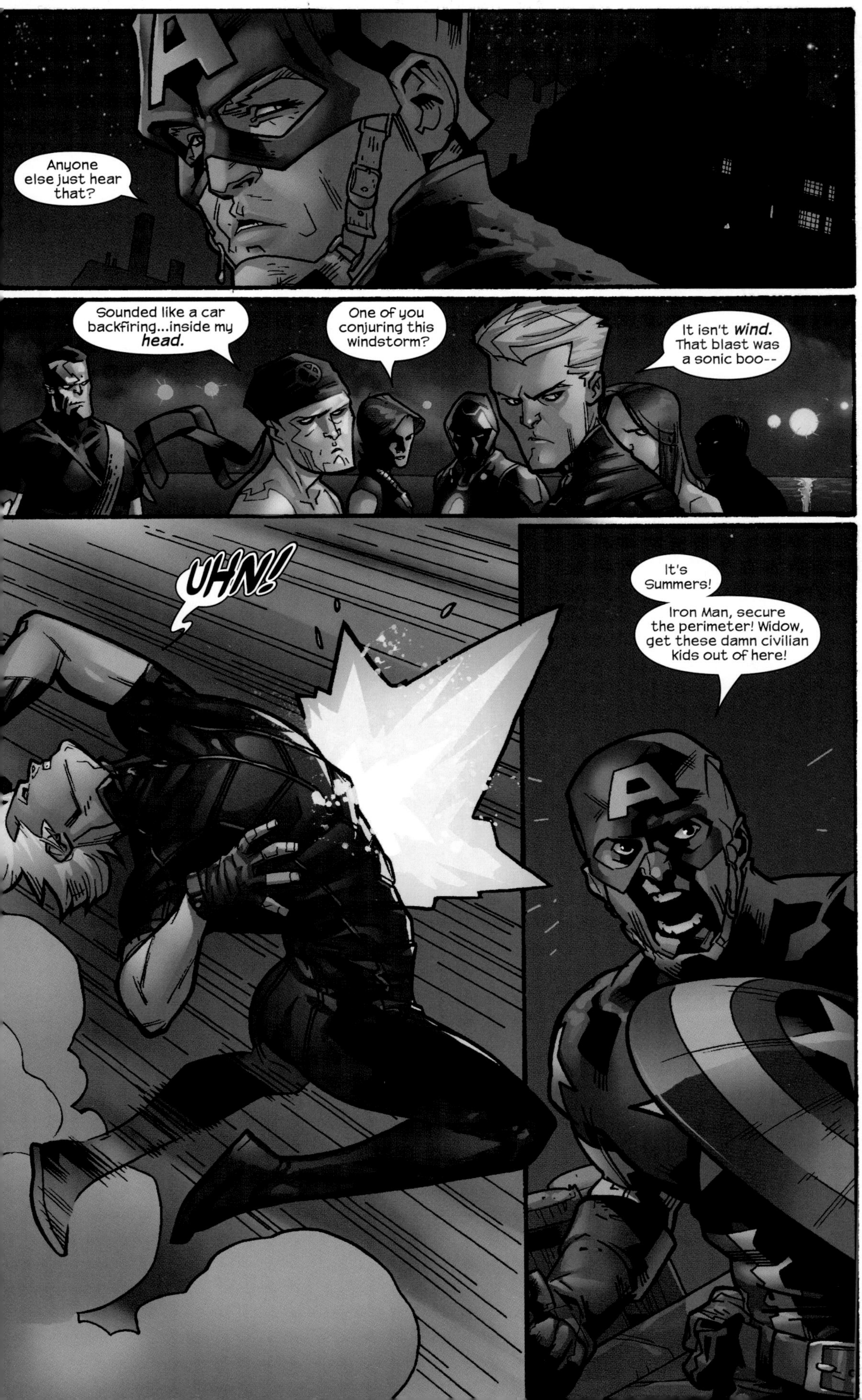

Anyone else just hear that?
Sounded like a car backfiring...inside my *head.*
One of you conjuring this windstorm?
It isn't *wind.* That blast was a sonic boo--
UHN!
It's Summers!
Iron Man, secure the perimeter! Widow, get these damn civilian kids out of here!

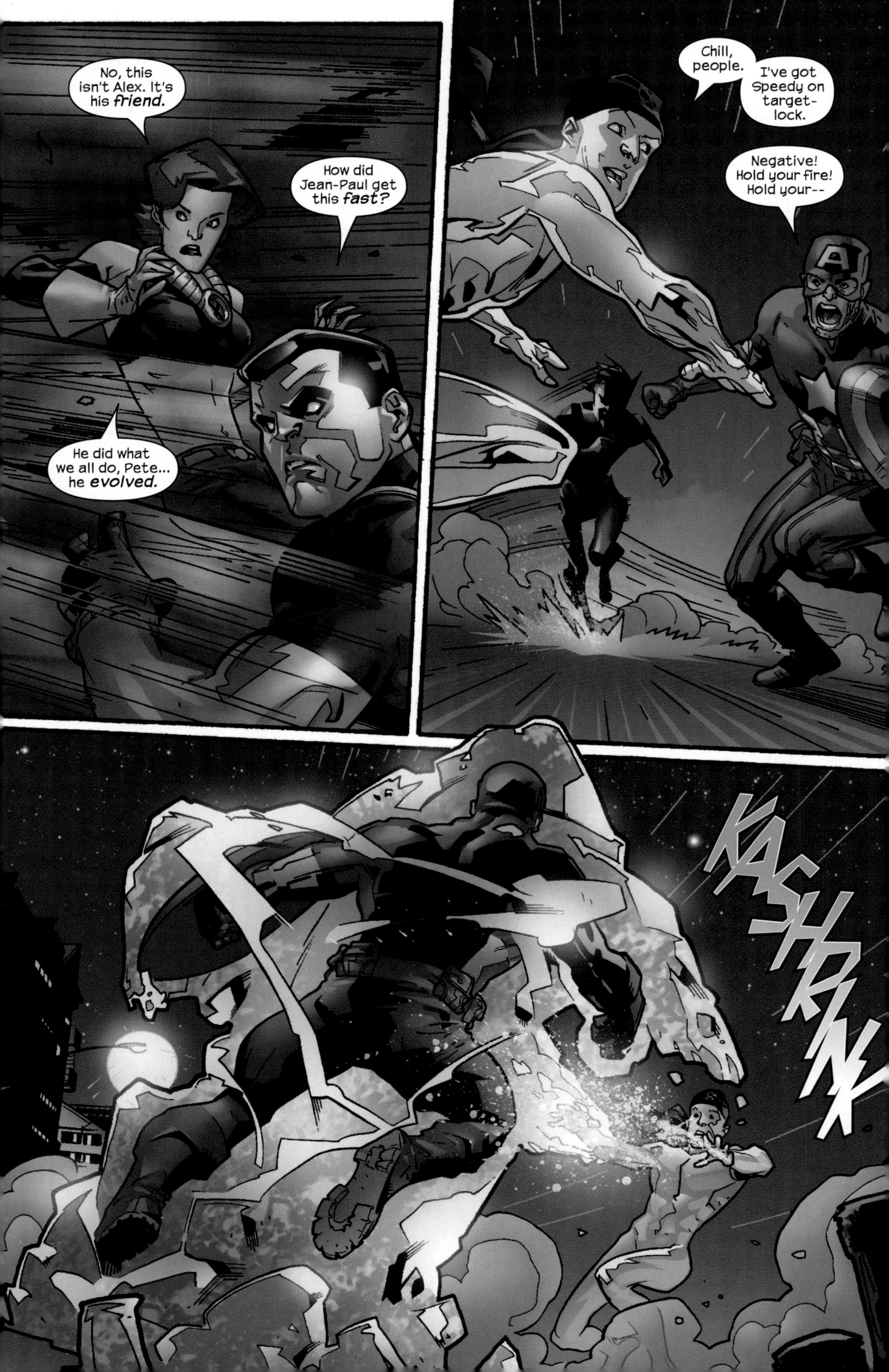
No, this isn't Alex. It's his *friend.*
How did Jean-Paul get this *fast?*
He did what we all do, Pete... he *evolved.*
Chill, people.
I've got Speedy on target-lock.
Negative! Hold your fire! Hold your--
KASHRINK

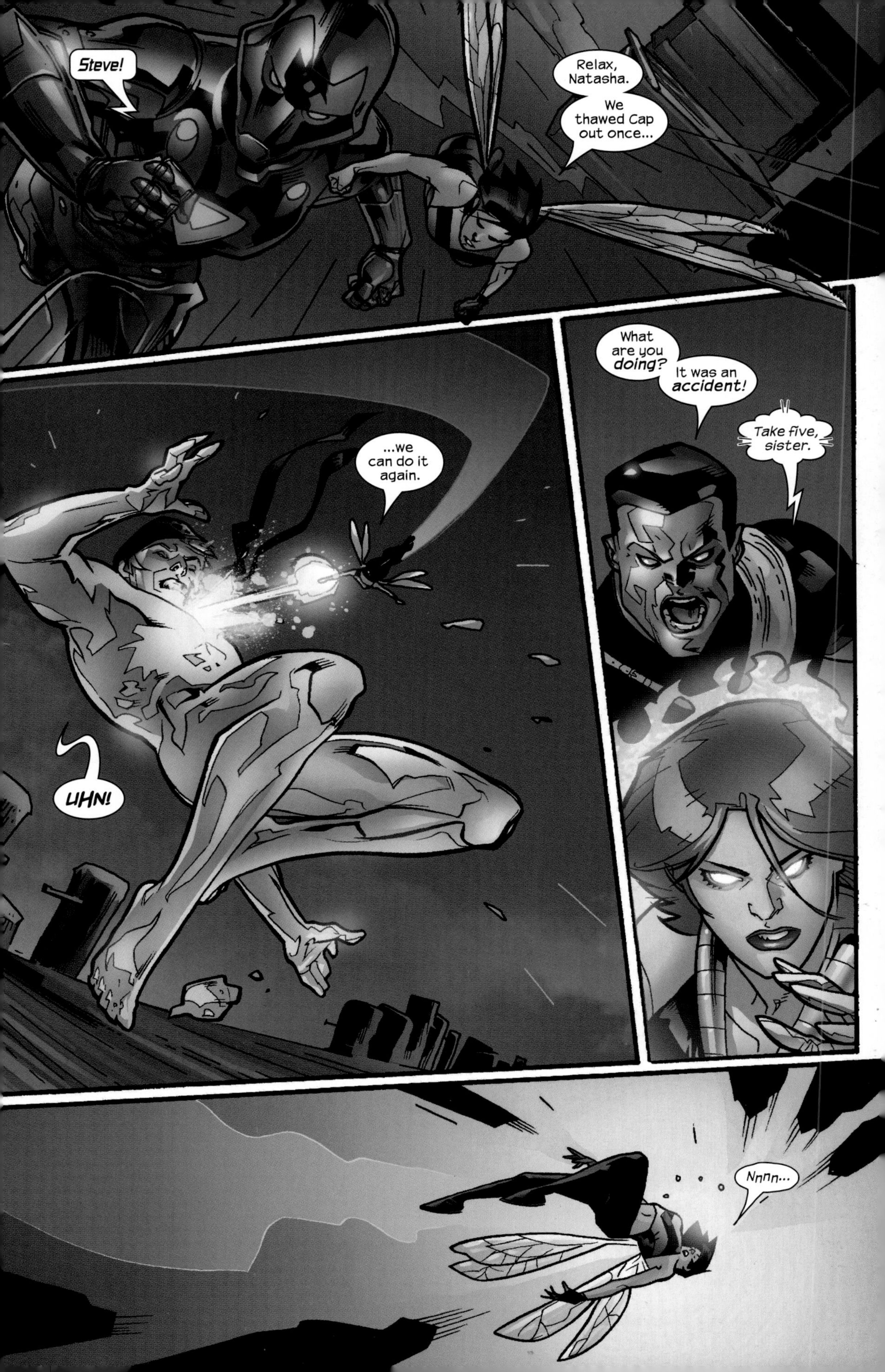
Steve!
Relax, Natasha.
We thawed Cap out once...
...we can do it again.
UHN!
What are you doing?
It was an accident!
Take five, sister.
Nnnn...

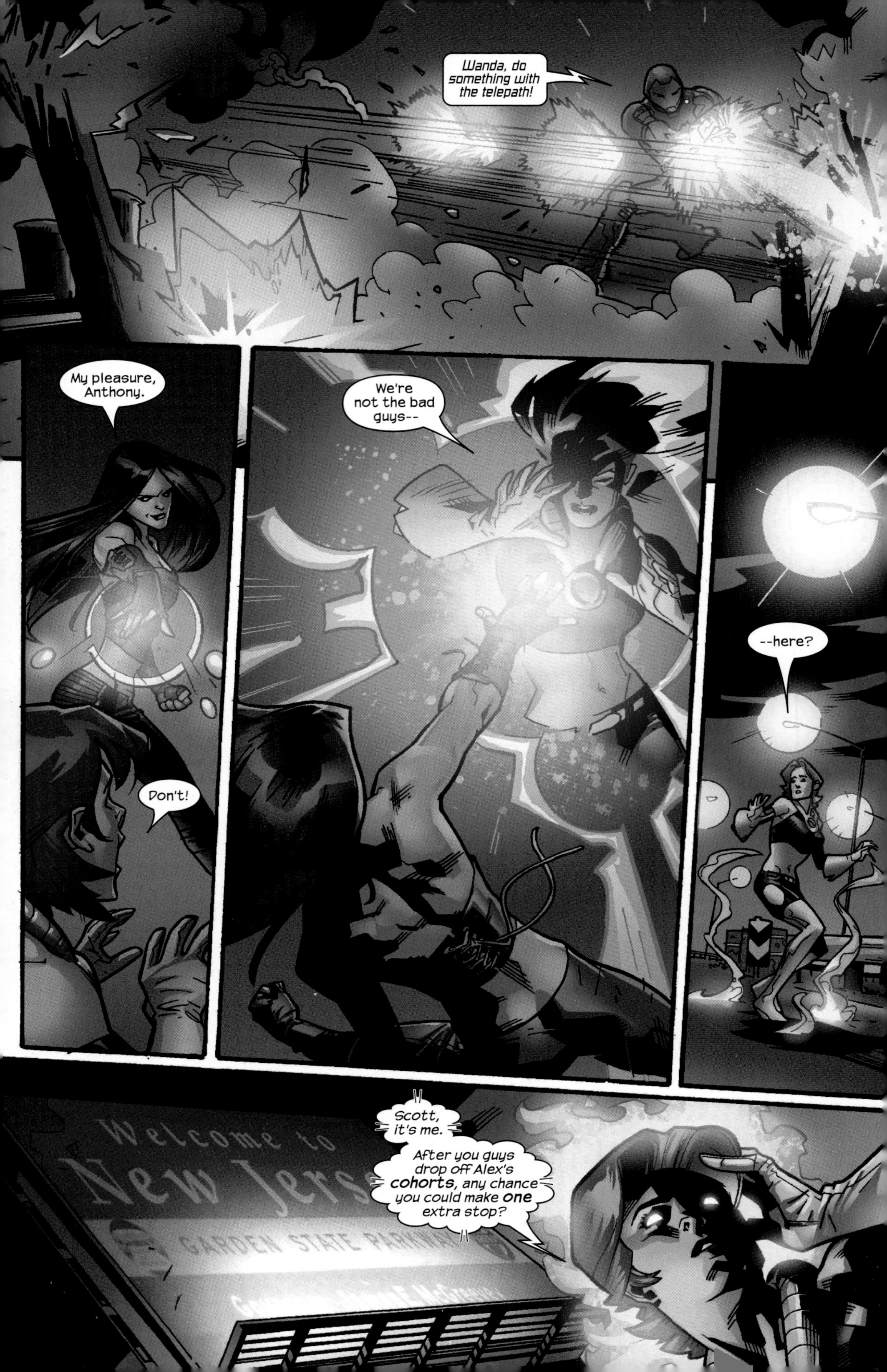
Wanda, do something with the telepath!
My pleasure, Anthony.
Don't!
We're not the bad guys--
--here?
Welcome to New Jers
GARDEN STATE PARKWAY
Scott, it's me.
After you guys drop off Alex's cohorts, any chance you could make one extra stop?

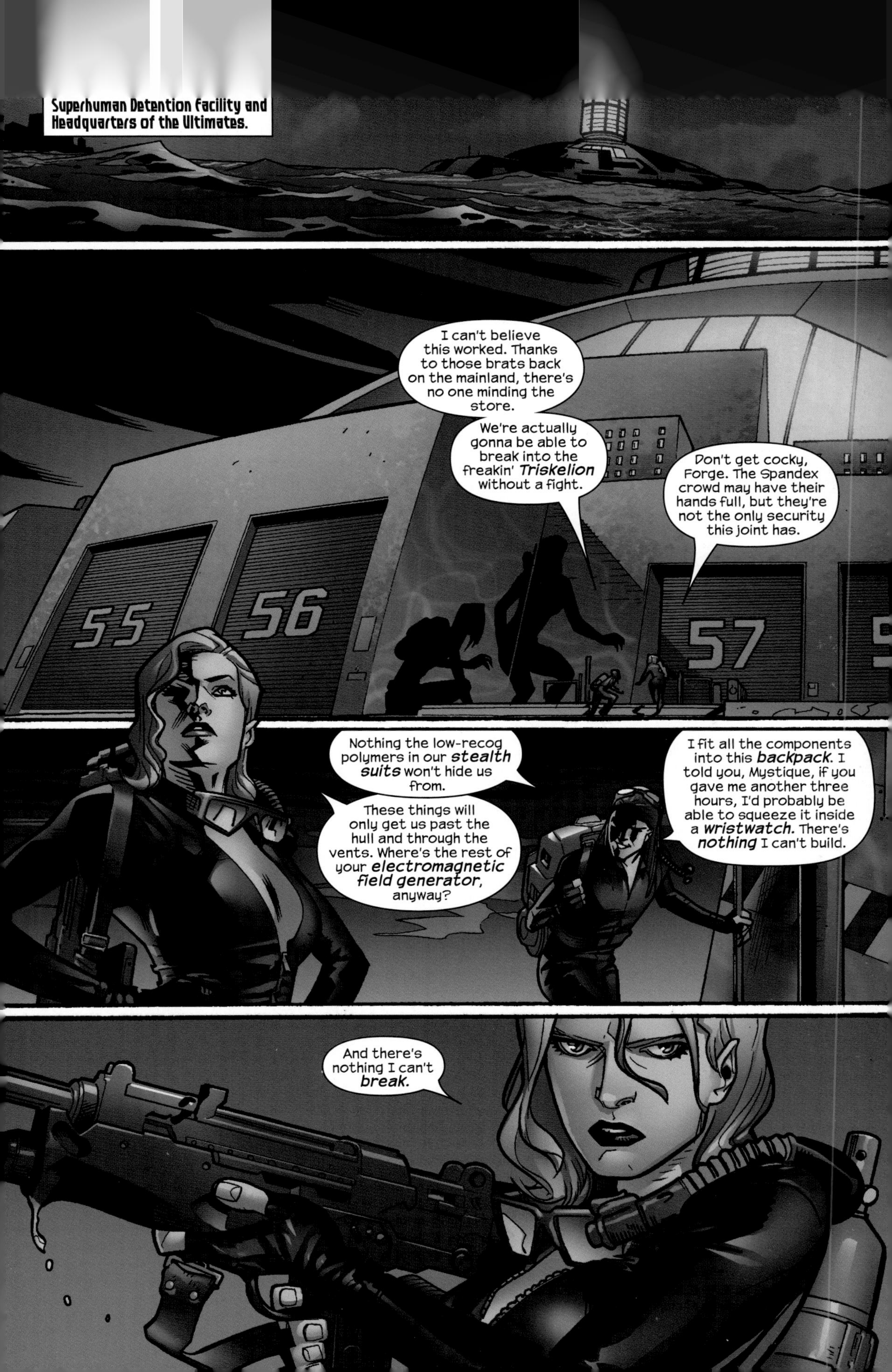
Superhuman Detention Facility and Headquarters of the Ultimates.
I can't believe this worked. Thanks to those brats back on the mainland, there's no one minding the store.
We're actually gonna be able to break into the freakin' Triskelion without a fight.
Don't get cocky, Forge. The Spandex crowd may have their hands full, but they're not the only security this joint has.
55
56
57
Nothing the low-recog polymers in our stealth suits won't hide us from.
These things will only get us past the hull and through the vents. Where's the rest of your electromagnetic field generator, anyway?
I fit all the components into this backpack. I told you, Mystique, if you gave me another three hours, I'd probably be able to squeeze it inside a wristwatch. There's nothing I can't build.
And there's nothing I can't break.

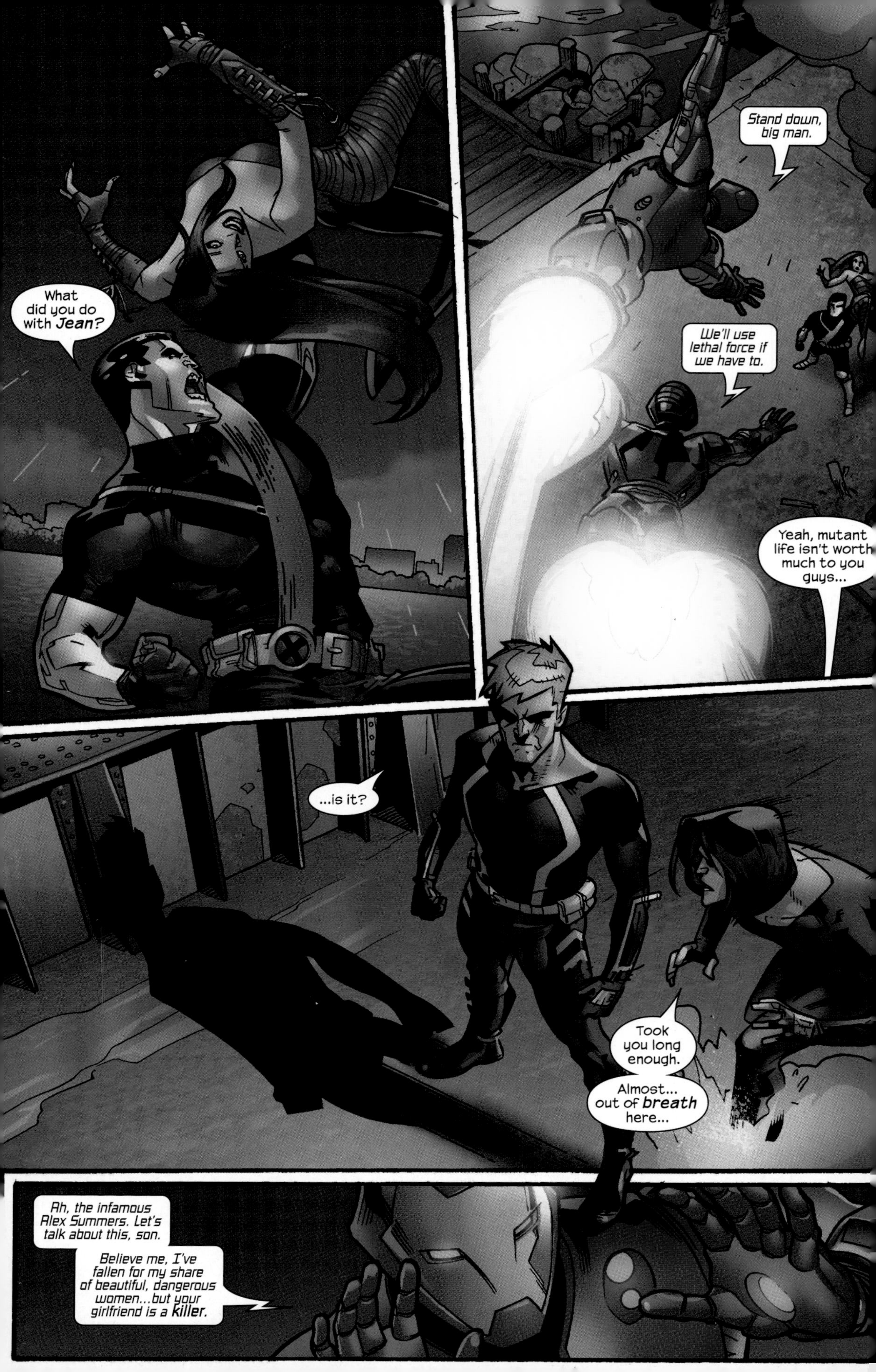
What did you do with *Jean?*
Stand down, big man.
We'll use lethal force if we have to.
Yeah, mutant life isn't worth much to you guys...
...is it?
Took you long enough.
Almost... out of *breath* here...
Ah, the infamous Alex Summers. Let's talk about this, son.
Believe me, I've fallen for my share of beautiful, dangerous women...but your girlfriend is a *killer*.

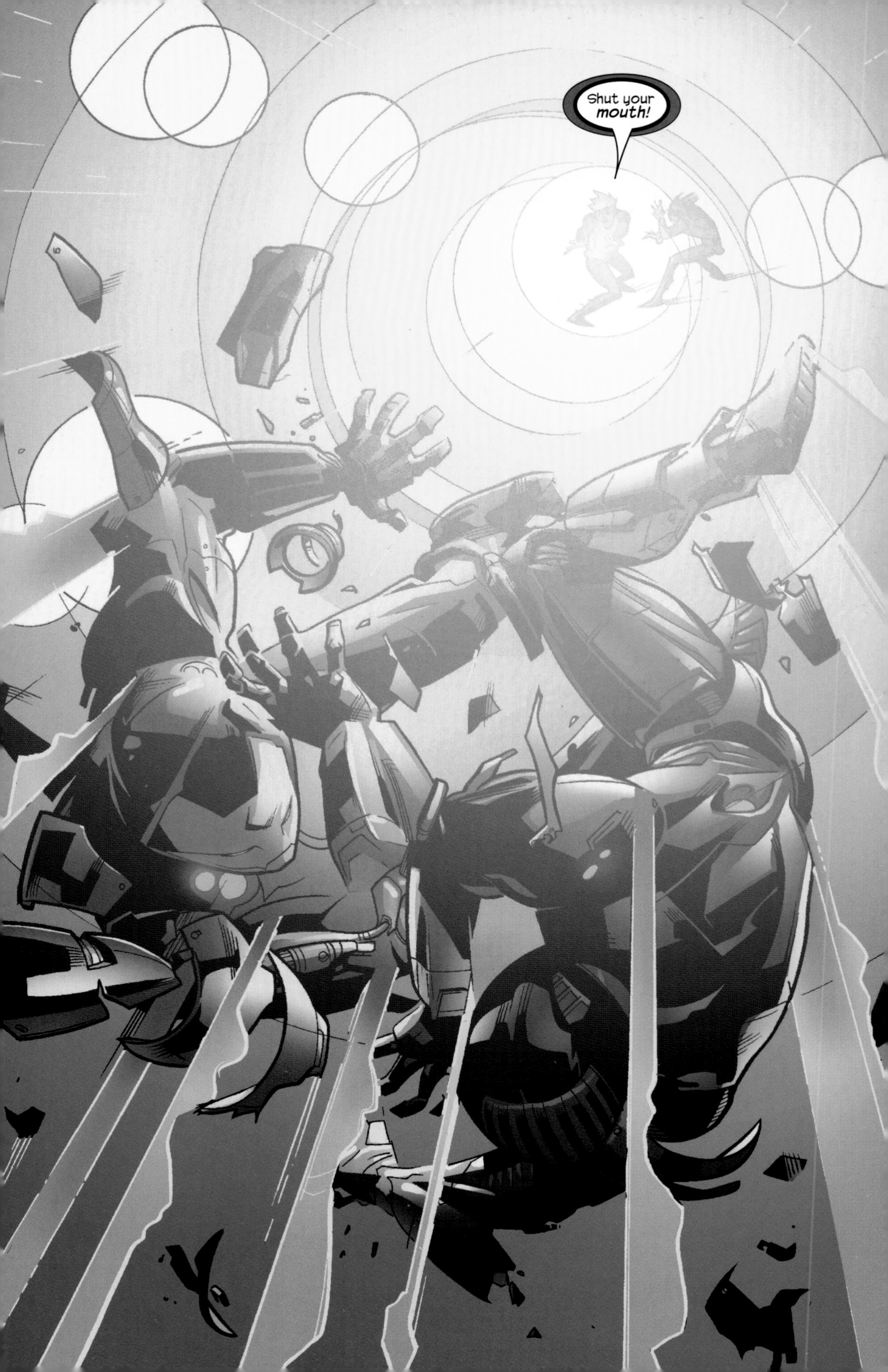
Shut your mouth!

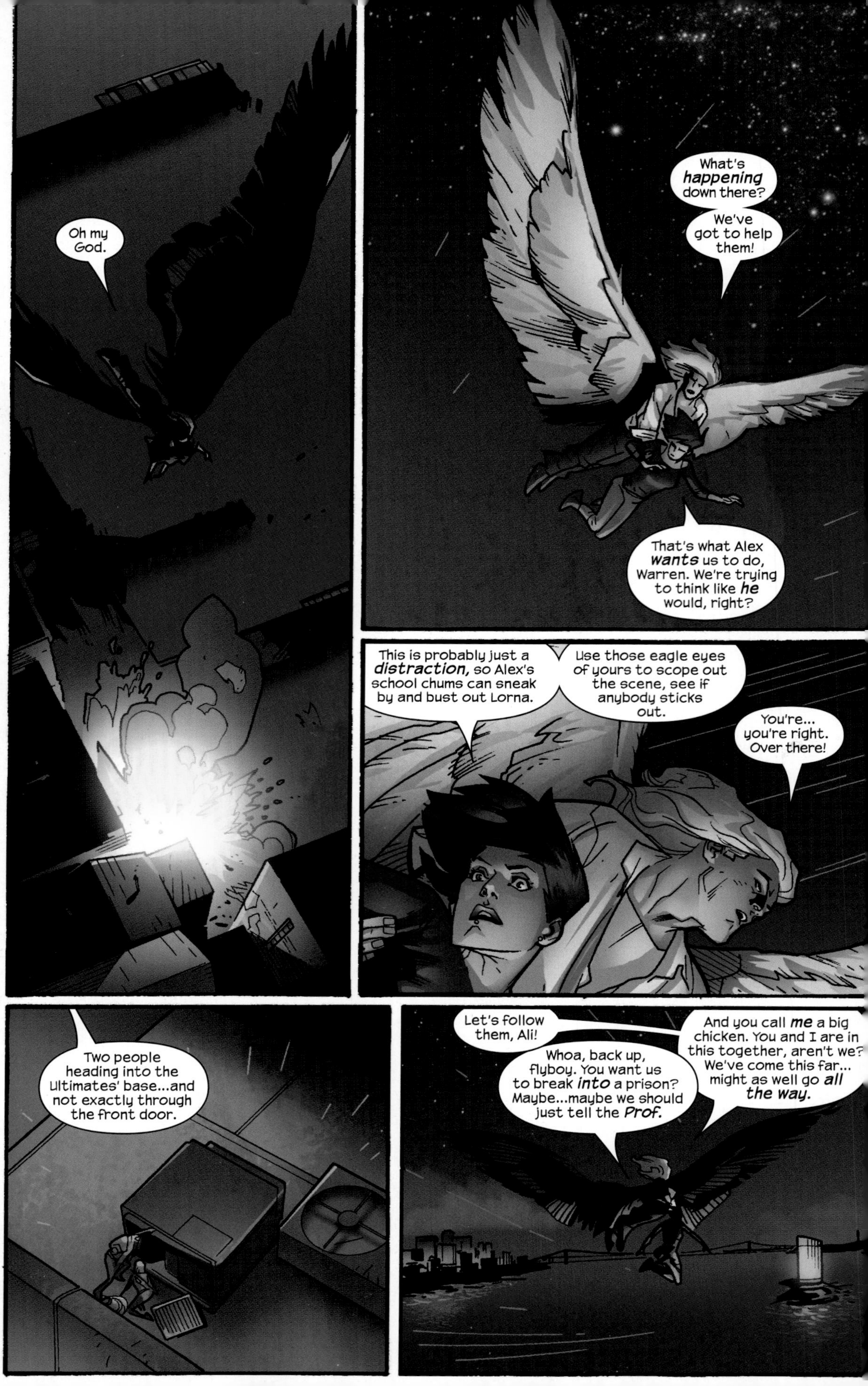
Oh my God.
What's happening down there?
We've got to help them!
That's what Alex wants us to do, Warren. We're trying to think like he would, right?
This is probably just a distraction, so Alex's school chums can sneak by and bust out Lorna.
Use those eagle eyes of yours to scope out the scene, see if anybody sticks out.
You're... you're right. Over there!
Two people heading into the Ultimates' base...and not exactly through the front door.
Let's follow them, Ali!
Whoa, back up, flyboy. You want us to break into a prison? Maybe...maybe we should just tell the Prof.
And you call me a big chicken. You and I are in this together, aren't we? We've come this far... might as well go all the way.

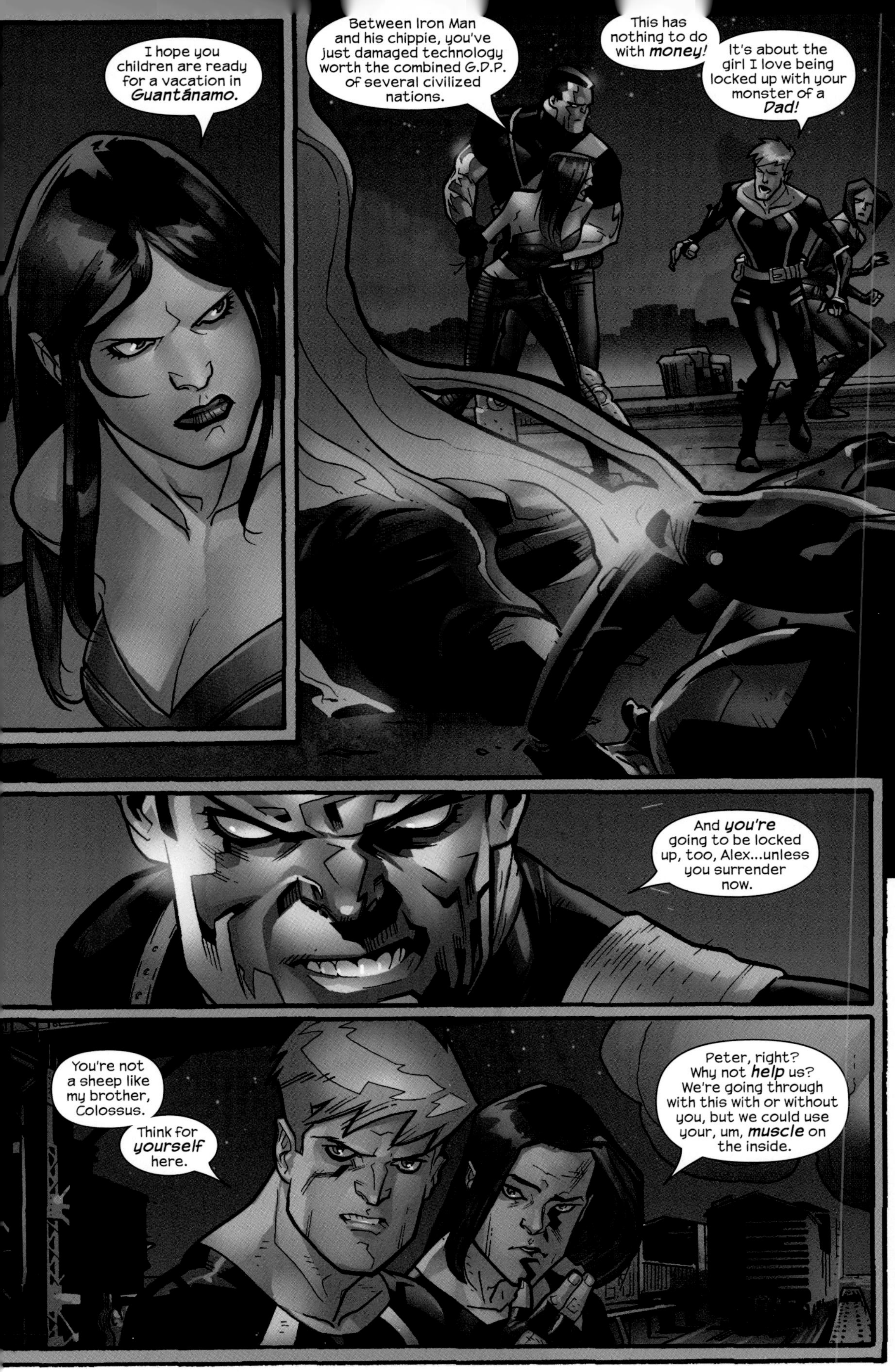
I hope you children are ready for a vacation in *Guantánamo.*
Between Iron Man and his chippie, you've just damaged technology worth the combined G.D.P. of several civilized nations.
This has nothing to do with *money!*
It's about the girl I love being locked up with your monster of a *Dad!*
And *you're* going to be locked up, too, Alex...unless you surrender now.
You're not a sheep like my brother, Colossus.
Think for *yourself* here.
Peter, right? Why not *help* us? We're going through with this with or without you, but we could use your, um, *muscle* on the inside.

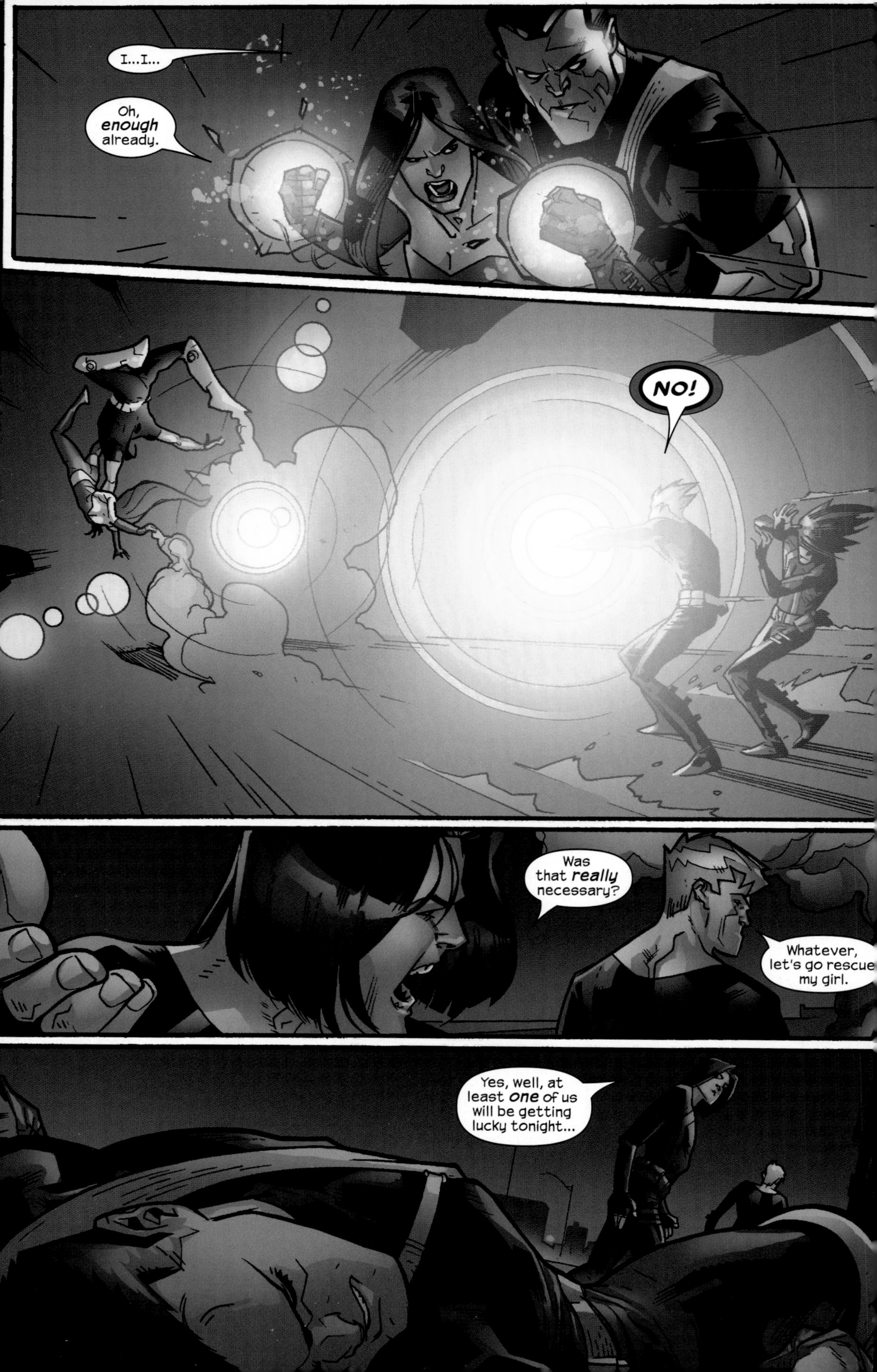

I...I...
Oh, enough already.
NO!
Was that really necessary?
Whatever, let's go rescue my girl.
Yes, well, at least one of us will be getting lucky tonight...

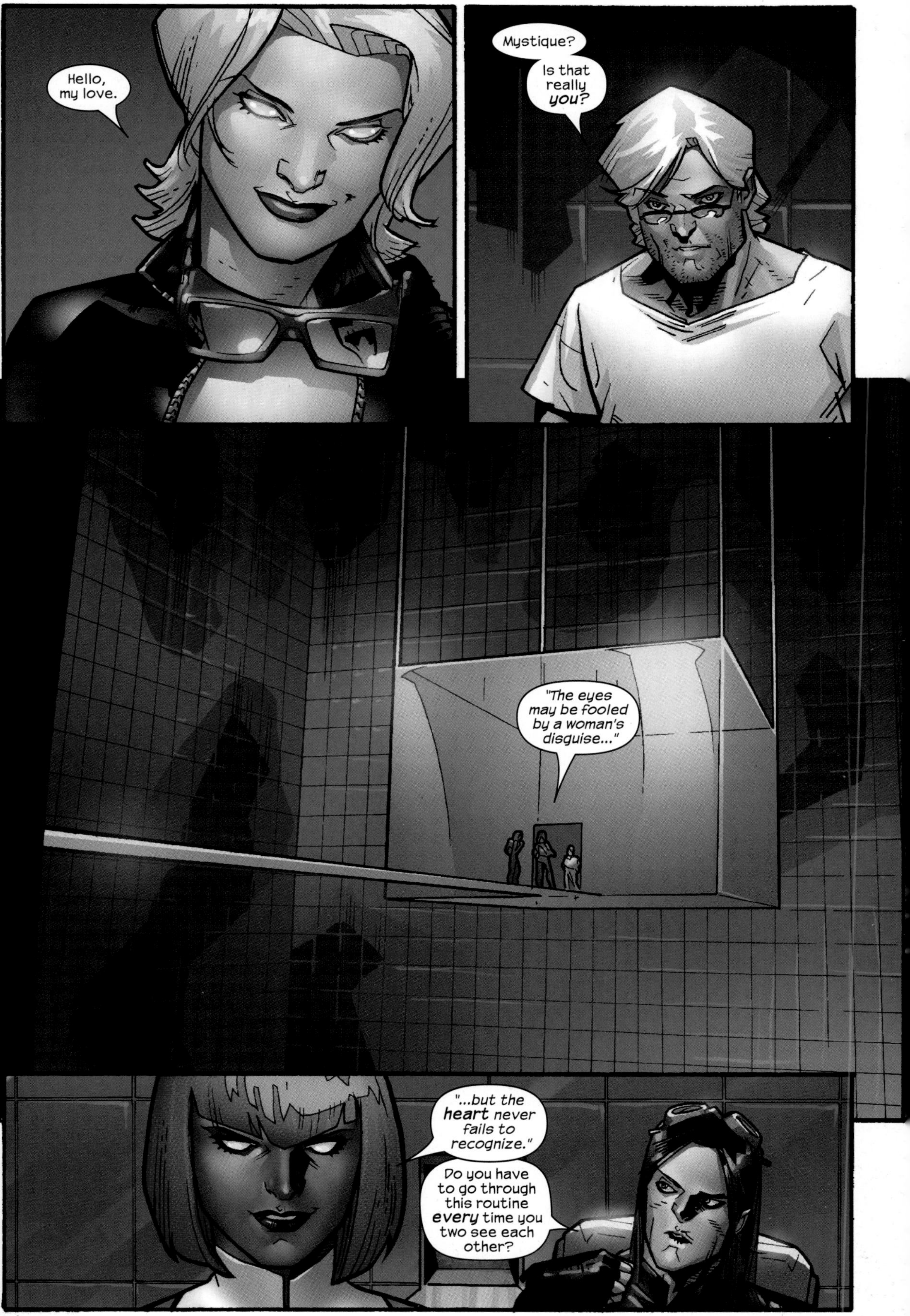
Hello, my love.
Mystique?
Is that really *you?*
"The eyes may be fooled by a woman's disguise..."
"...but the **heart** never fails to recognize."
Do you have to go through this routine ***every*** time you two see each other?

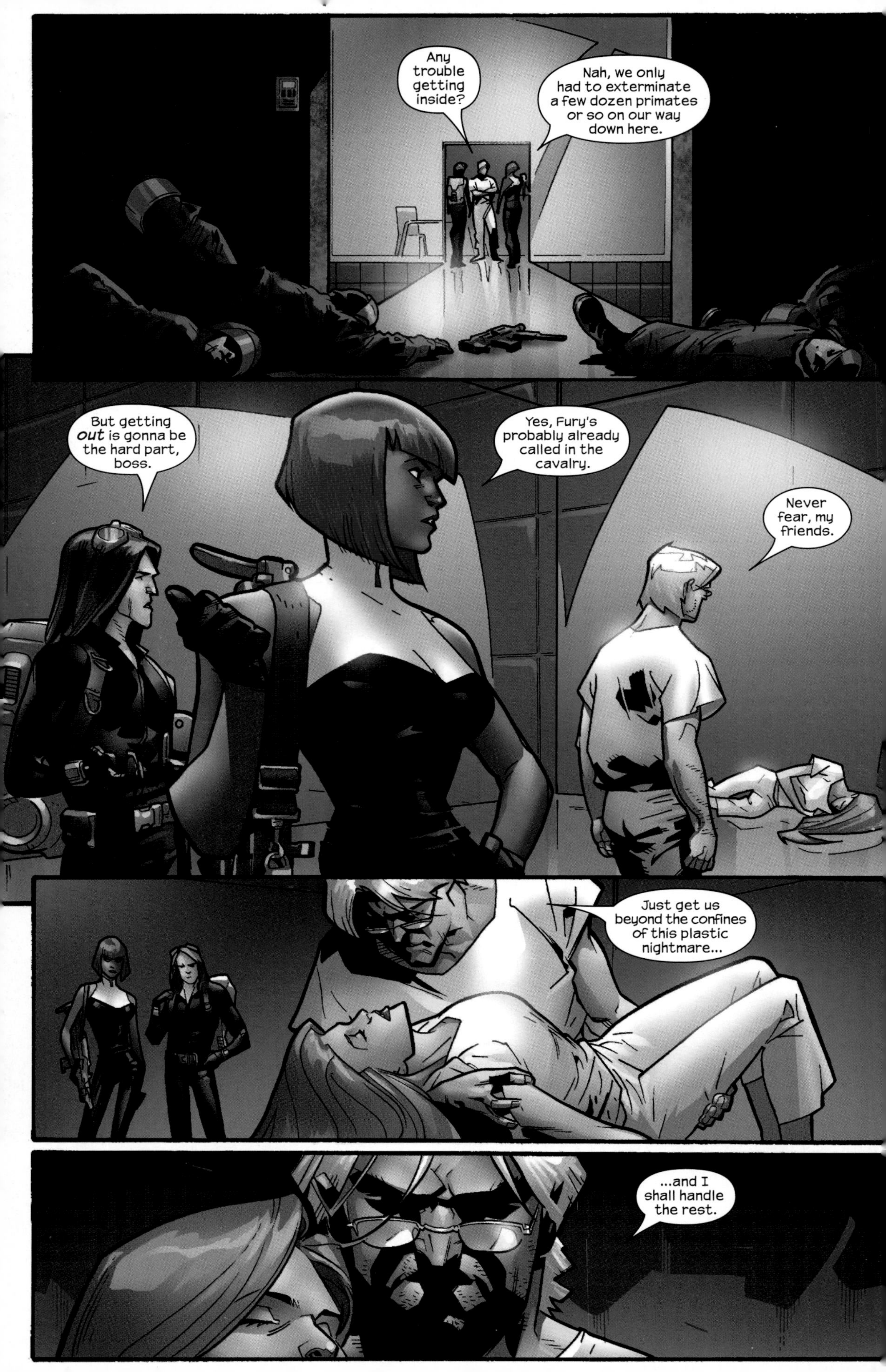
Any trouble getting inside?
Nah, we only had to exterminate a few dozen primates or so on our way down here.
But getting *out* is gonna be the hard part, boss.
Yes, Fury's probably already called in the cavalry.
Never fear, my friends.
Just get us beyond the confines of this plastic nightmare...
...and I shall handle the rest.

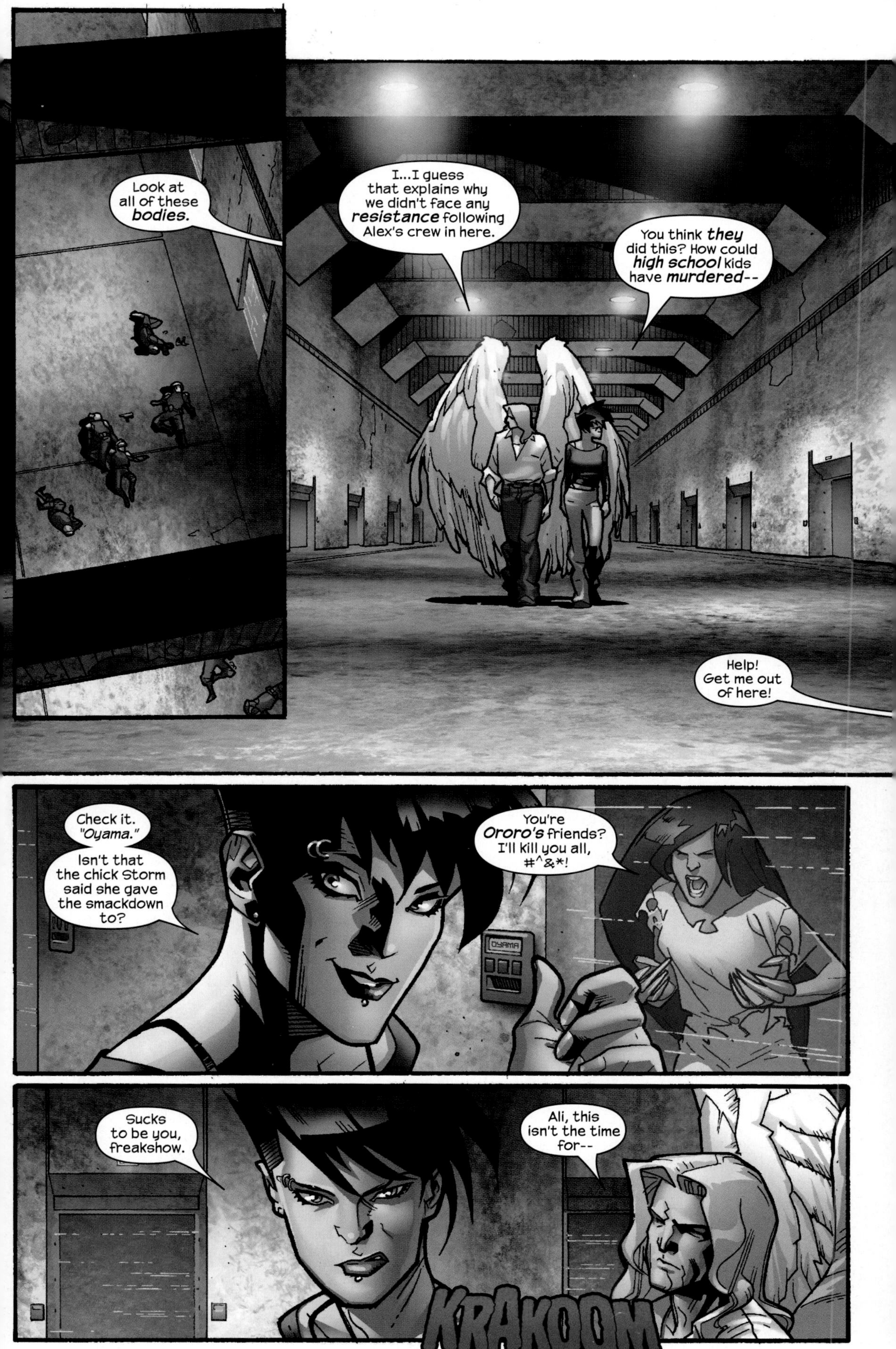
Look at all of these *bodies.*
I...I guess that explains why we didn't face any *resistance* following Alex's crew in here.
You think *they* did this? How could *high school* kids have *murdered*--
Help! Get me out of here!
Check it. *"Oyama."* Isn't that the chick Storm said she gave the smackdown to?
OYAMA
You're *Ororo's* friends? I'll kill you all, #^&*!
Sucks to be you, freakshow.
Ali, this isn't the time for--
KRAKOOM

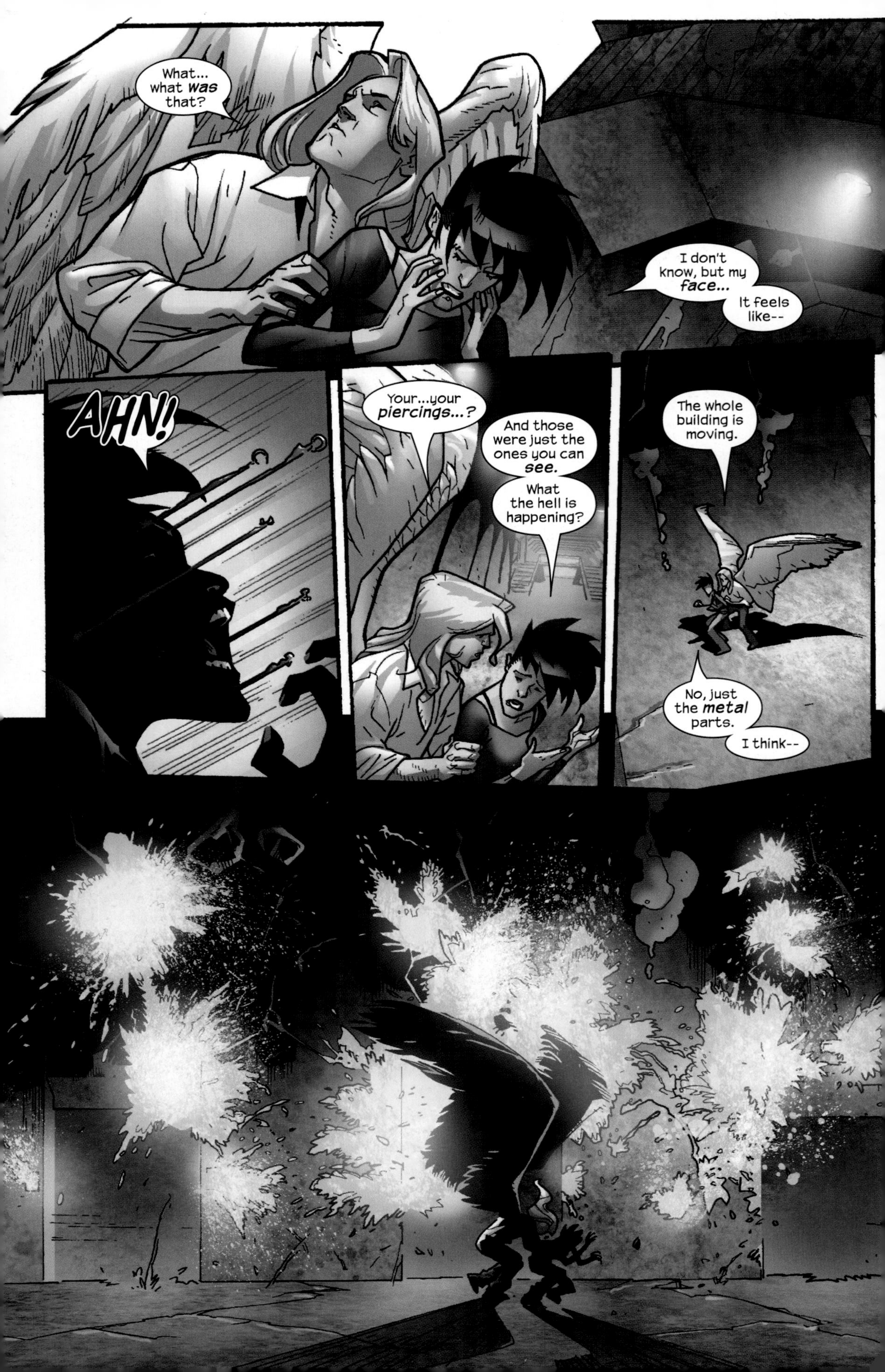
What... what **was** that?
I don't know, but my ***face...***
It feels like--
AHN!
Your...your ***piercings...?***
And those were just the ones you can ***see.***
What the hell is happening?
The whole building is moving.
No, just the ***metal*** parts.
I think--

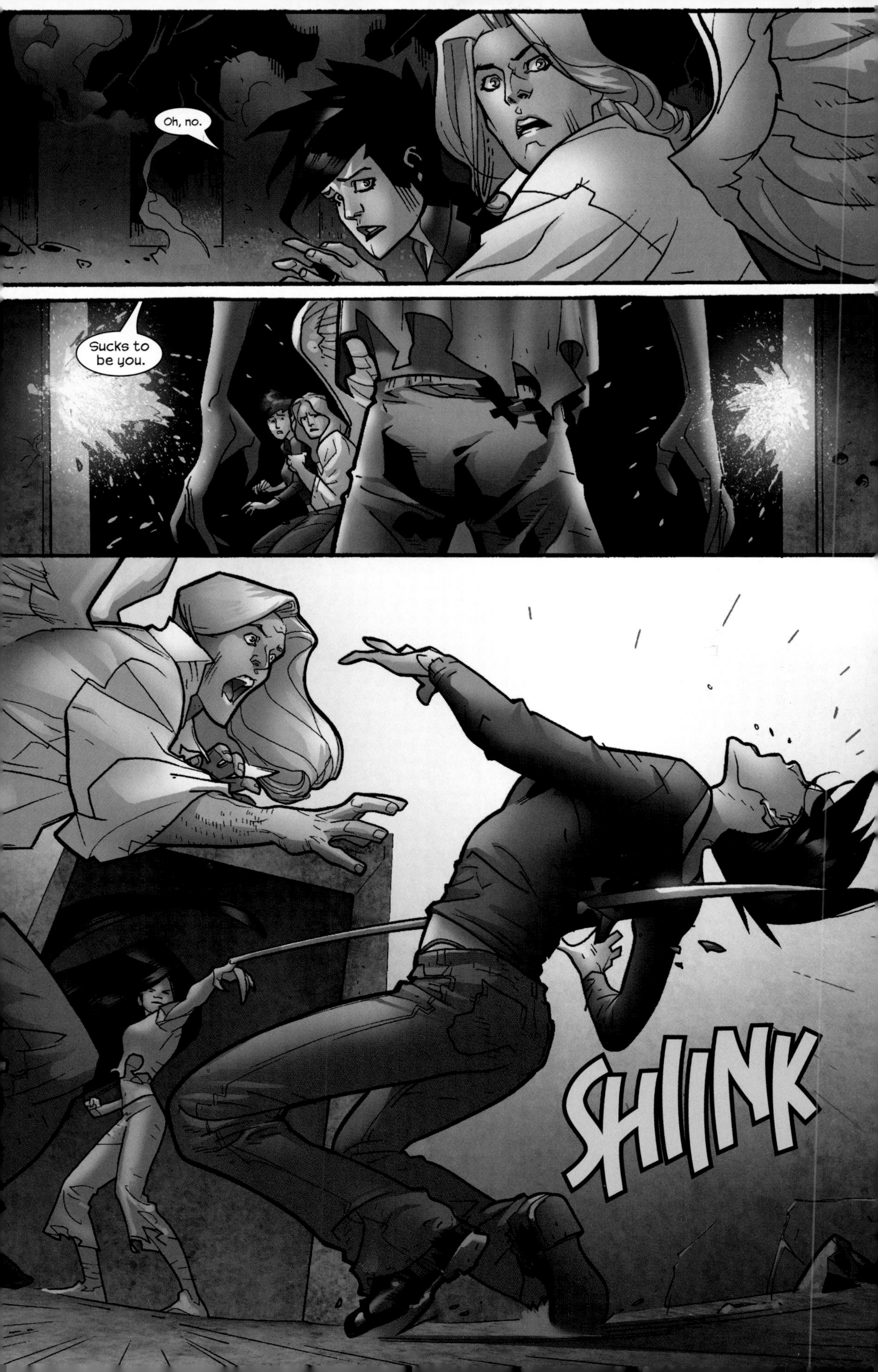
Oh, no.
Sucks to be you.
SHIINK

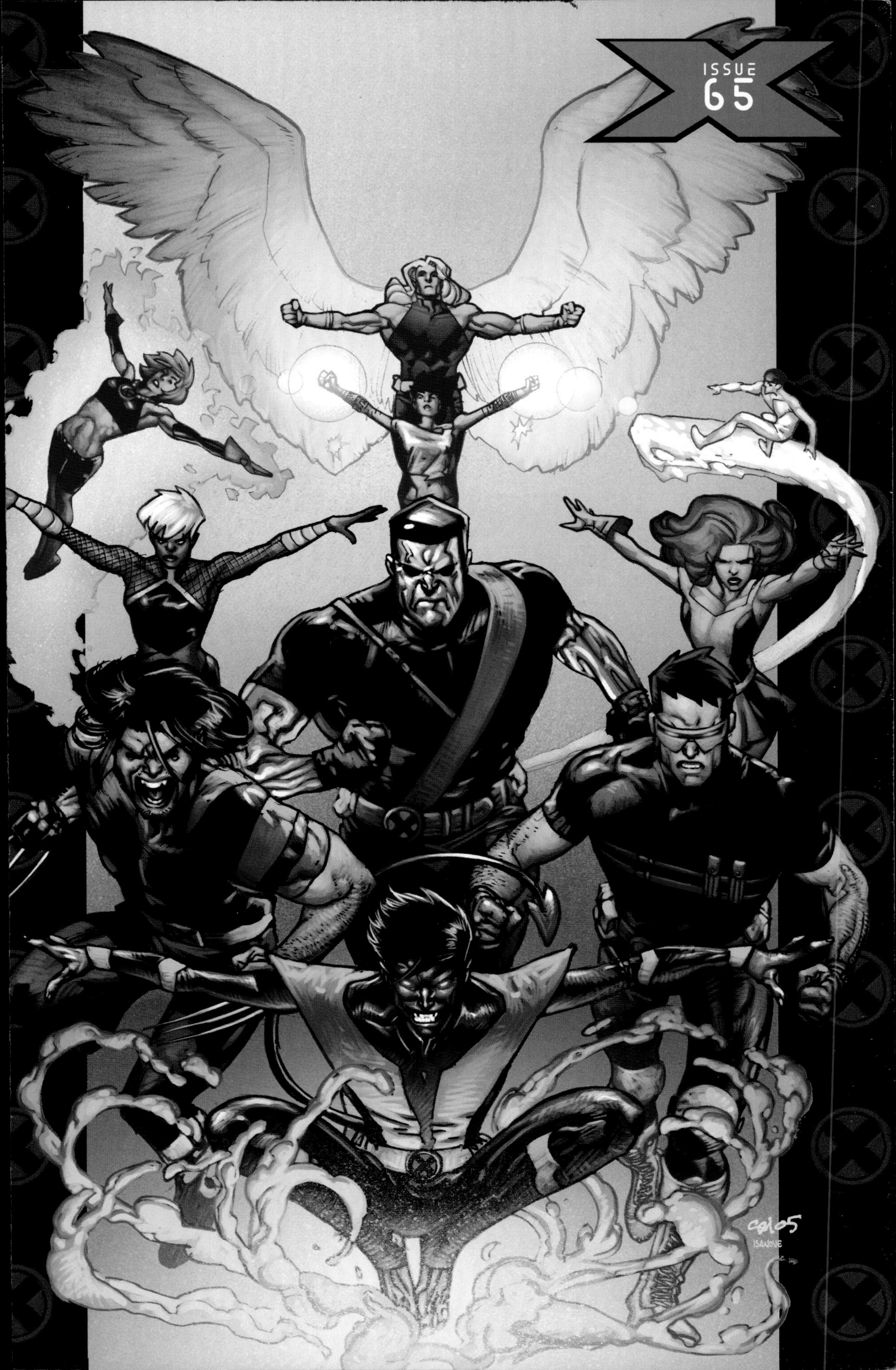
ISSUE
65

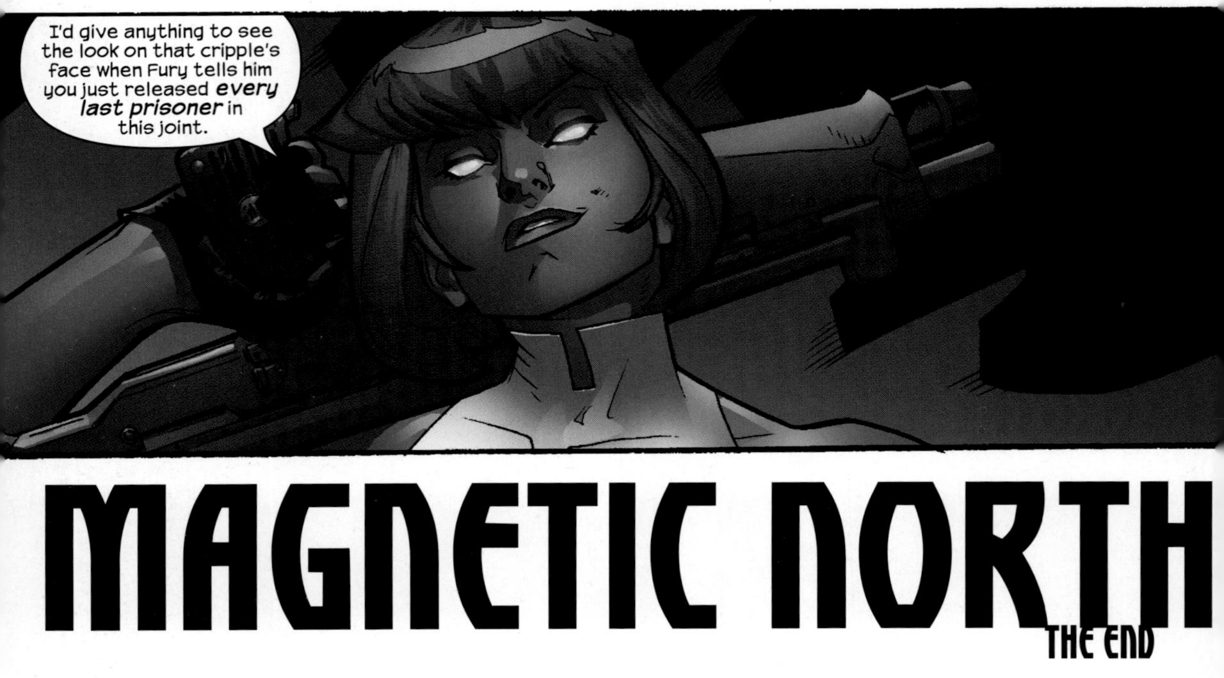
I'd give anything to see the look on that cripple's face when Fury tells him you just released *every last prisoner* in this joint.

MAGNETIC NORTH

THE END

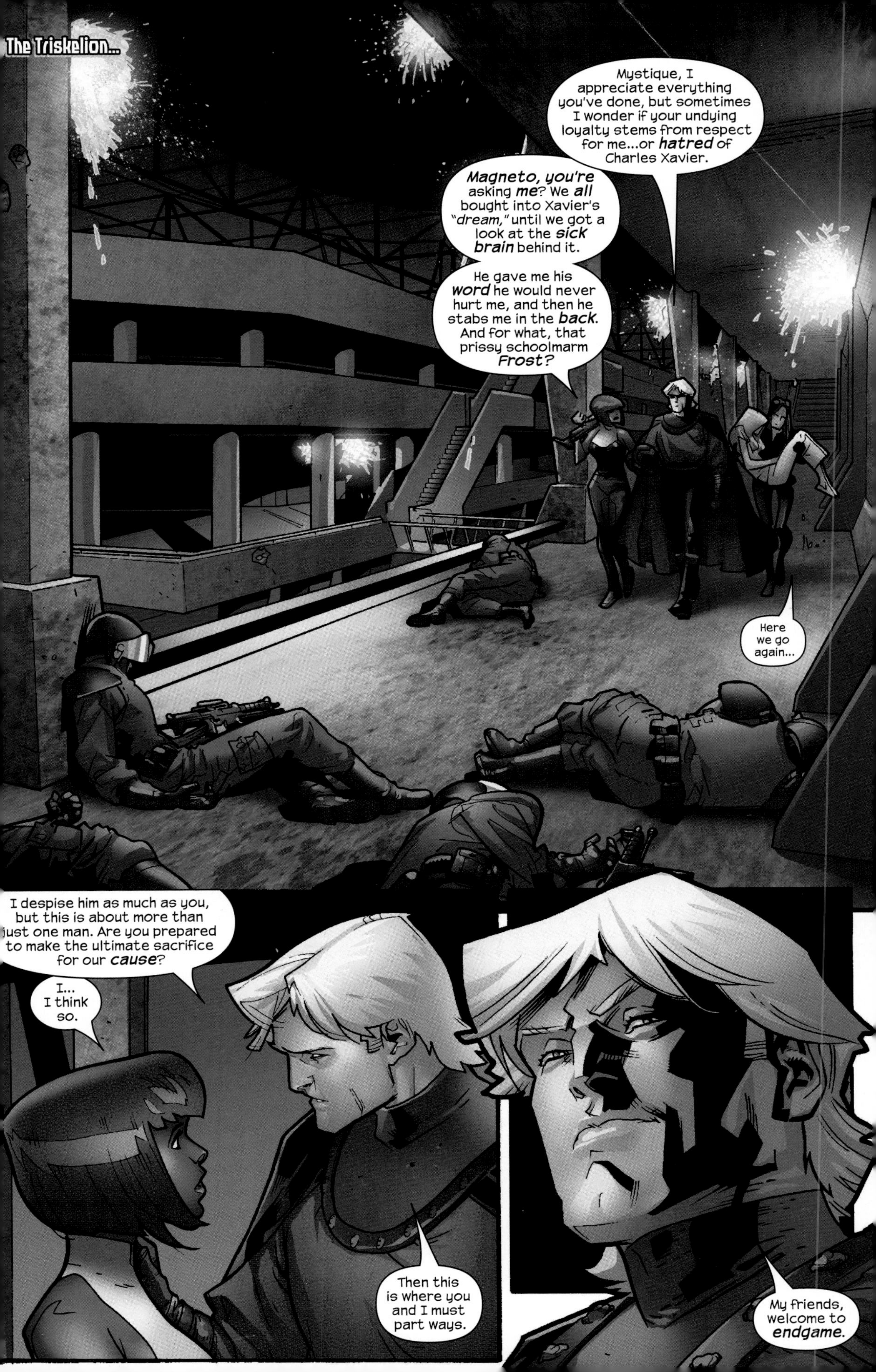
The Triskelion...
Mystique, I appreciate everything you've done, but sometimes I wonder if your undying loyalty stems from respect for me...or hatred of Charles Xavier.
Magneto, you're asking me? We all bought into Xavier's "dream," until we got a look at the sick brain behind it.
He gave me his word he would never hurt me, and then he stabs me in the back. And for what, that prissy schoolmarm Frost?
Here we go again...
I despise him as much as you, but this is about more than just one man. Are you prepared to make the ultimate sacrifice for our cause?
I... I think so.
Then this is where you and I must part ways.
My friends, welcome to endgame.

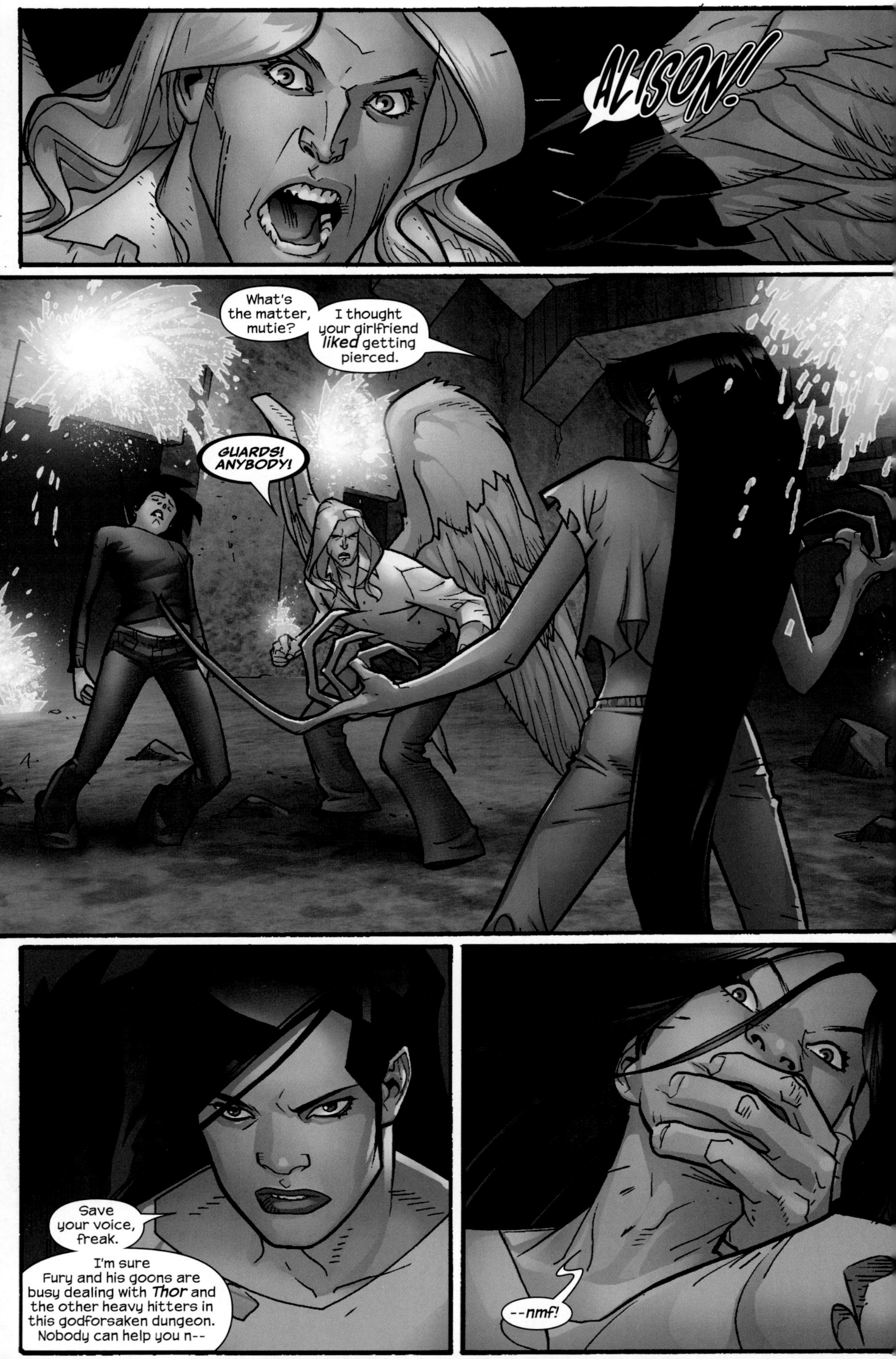
ALISON!!
What's the matter, mutie?
I thought your girlfriend *liked* getting pierced.
GUARDS! ANYBODY!
Save your voice, freak.
I'm sure Fury and his goons are busy dealing with *Thor* and the other heavy hitters in this godforsaken dungeon. Nobody can help you n--
--nmf!

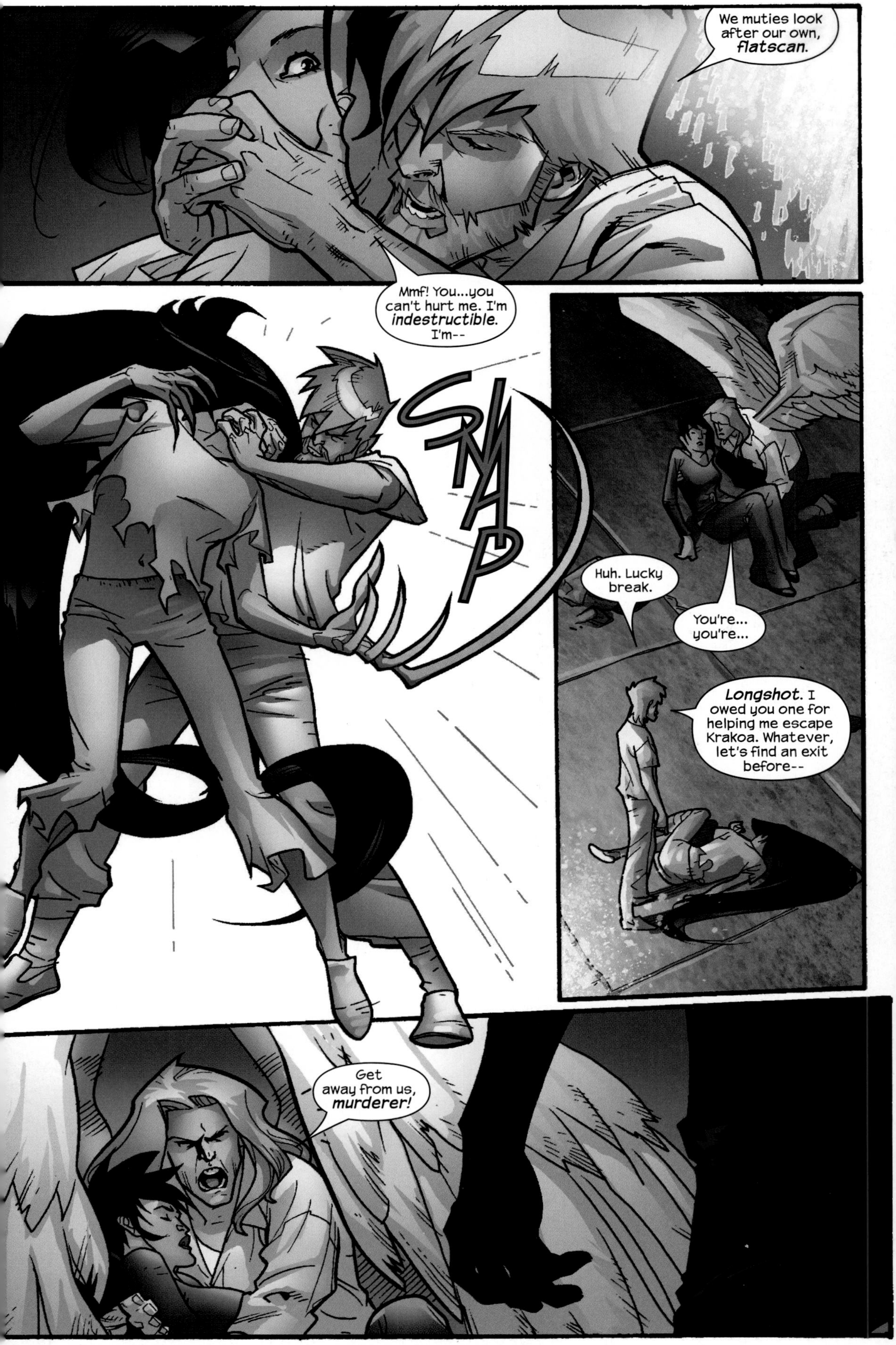
We muties look after our own, *flatscan*.
Mmf! You...you can't hurt me. I'm *indestructible*. I'm--
SNAP
Huh. Lucky break.
You're... you're...
Longshot. I owed you one for helping me escape Krakoa. Whatever, let's find an exit before--
Get away from us, *murderer*!

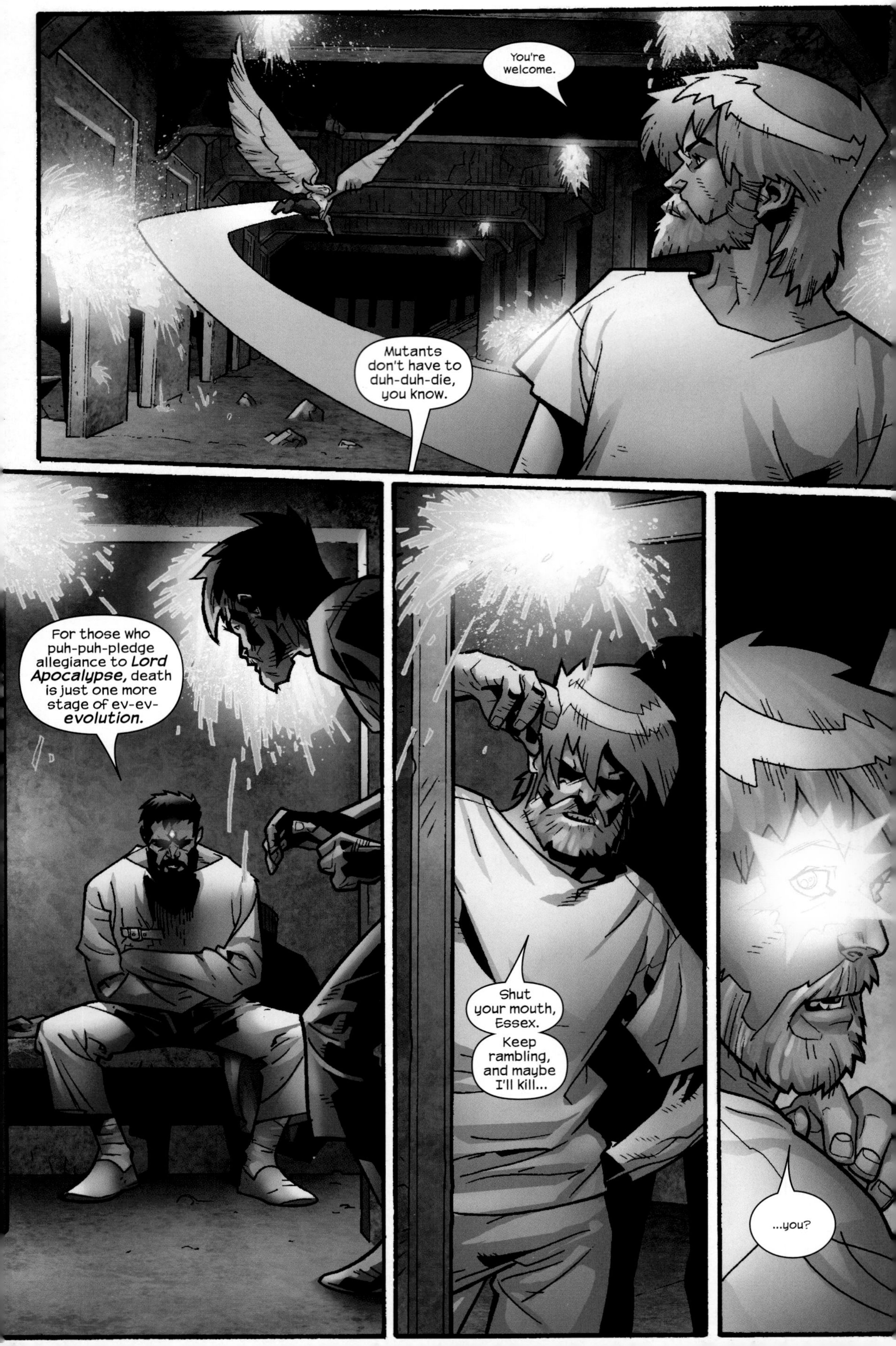
You're welcome.
Mutants don't have to duh-duh-die, you know.
For those who puh-puh-pledge allegiance to *Lord Apocalypse,* death is just one more stage of ev-ev-*evolution.*
Shut your mouth, Essex.
Keep rambling, and maybe I'll kill...
...you?

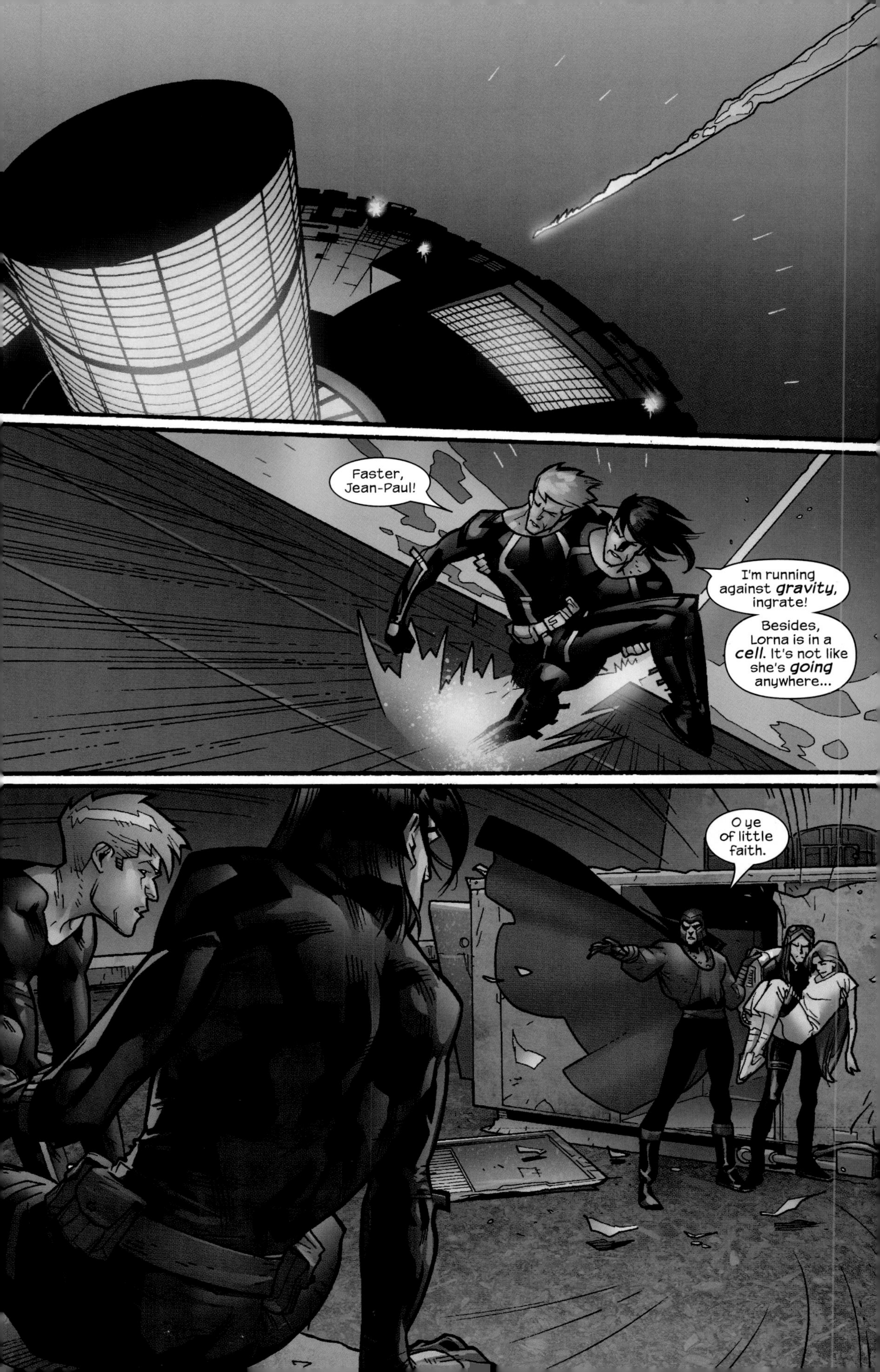

Faster, Jean-Paul!
I'm running against *gravity*, ingrate!
Besides, Lorna is in a *cell*. It's not like she's *going* anywhere...
O ye of little faith.

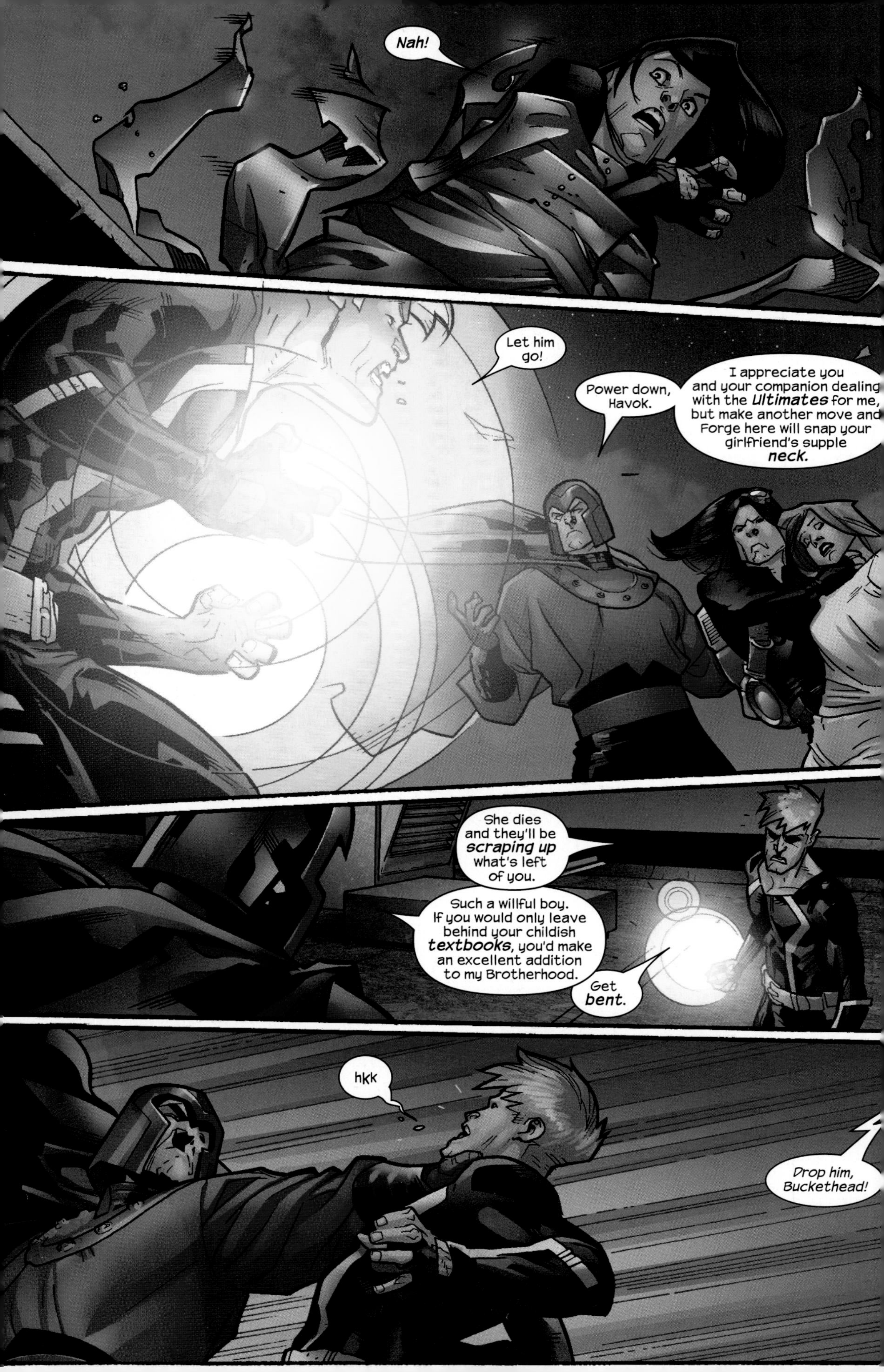
Nah!
Let him go!
Power down, Havok.
I appreciate you and your companion dealing with the Ultimates for me, but make another move and Forge here will snap your girlfriend's supple neck.
She dies and they'll be scraping up what's left of you.
Such a willful boy. If you would only leave behind your childish textbooks, you'd make an excellent addition to my Brotherhood.
Get bent.
hkk
Drop him, Buckethead!

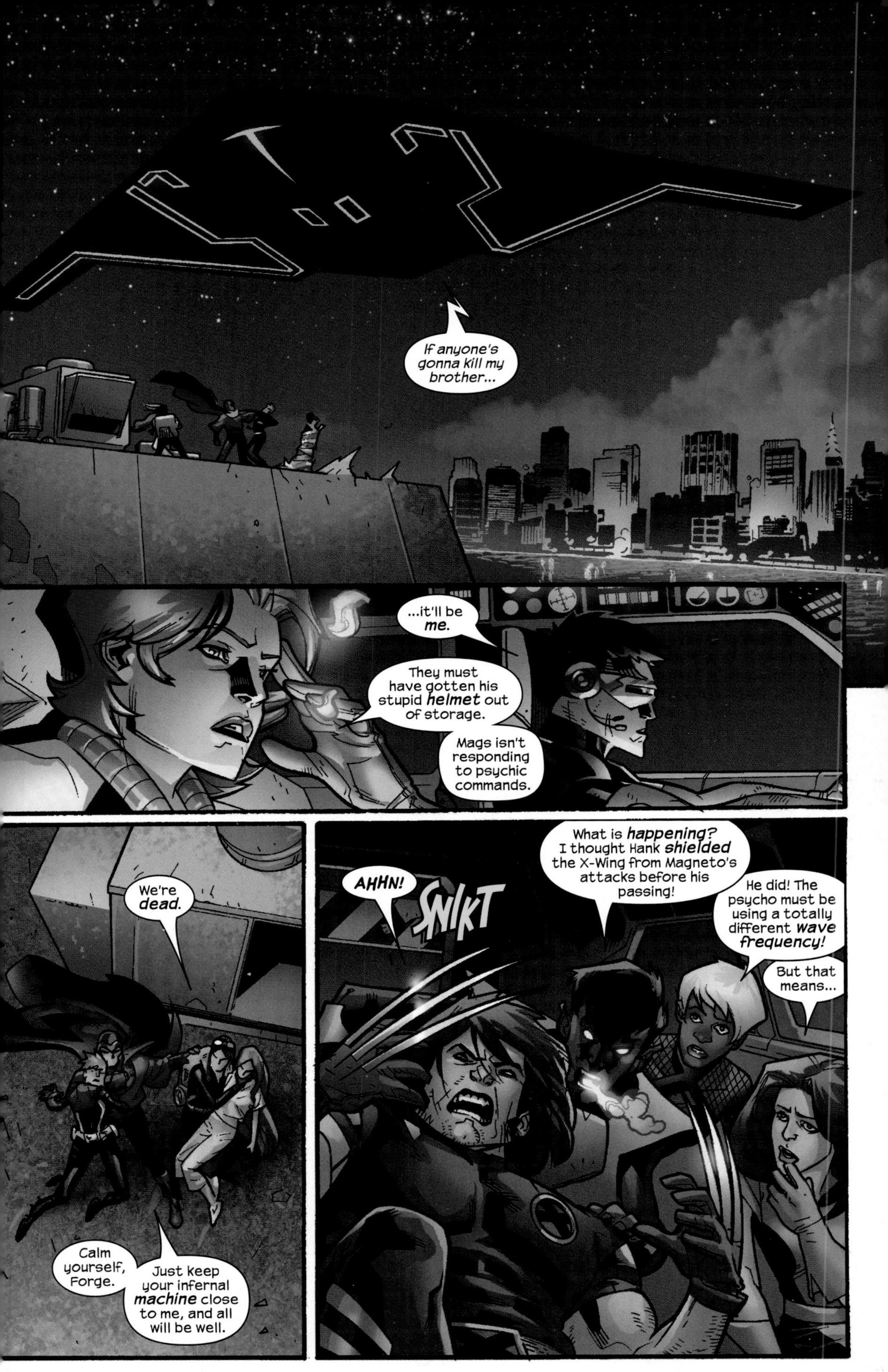

If anyone's gonna kill my brother...
...it'll be *me*.
They must have gotten his stupid *helmet* out of storage.
Mags isn't responding to psychic commands.
We're *dead*.
Calm yourself, Forge.
Just keep your infernal *machine* close to me, and all will be well.
AHHN!
SNIKT
What is *happening*? I thought Hank *shielded* the X-Wing from Magneto's attacks before his passing!
He did! The psycho must be using a totally different *wave frequency*!
But that means...

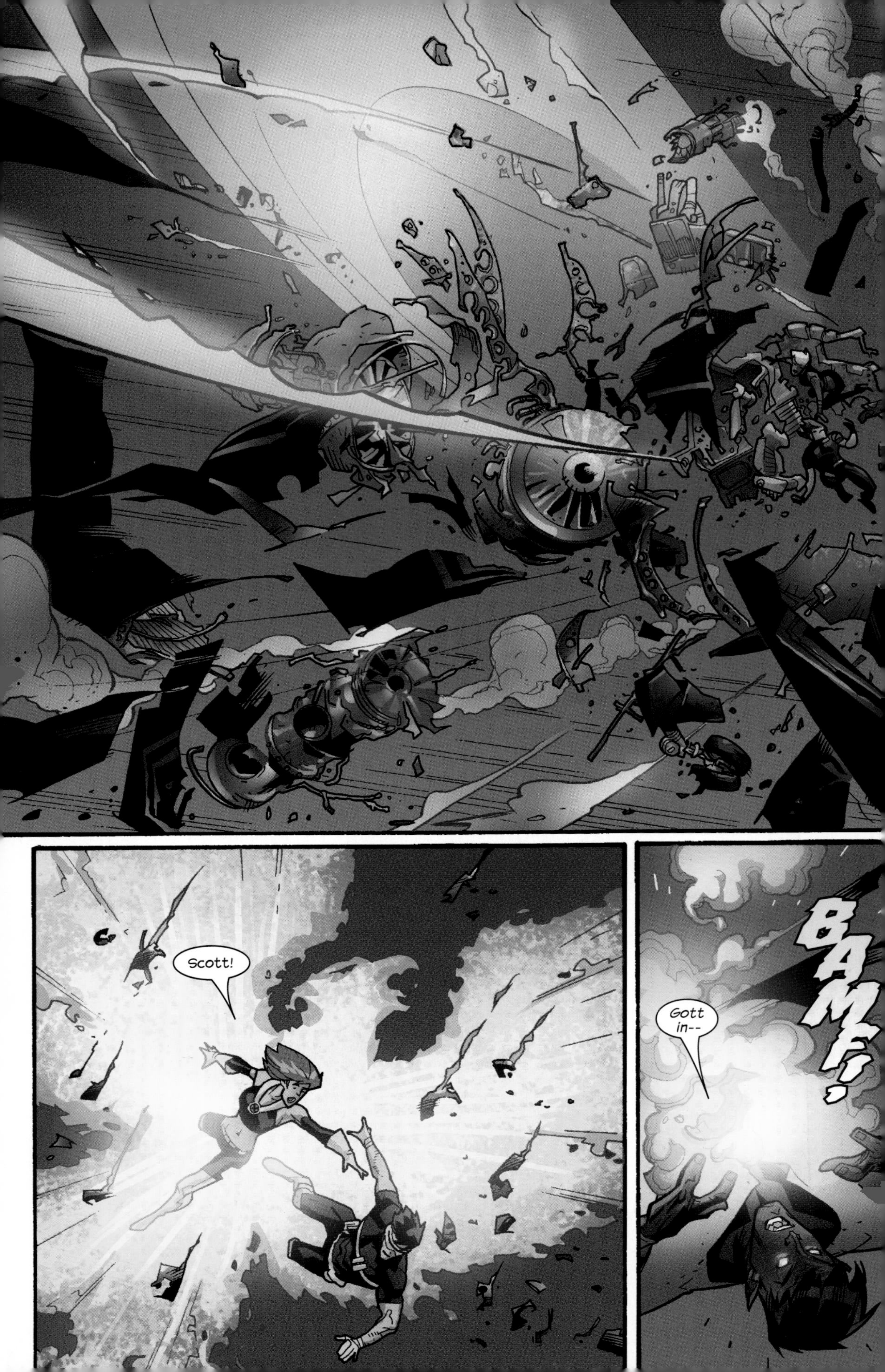
Scott!
Gott in--
BAMF!

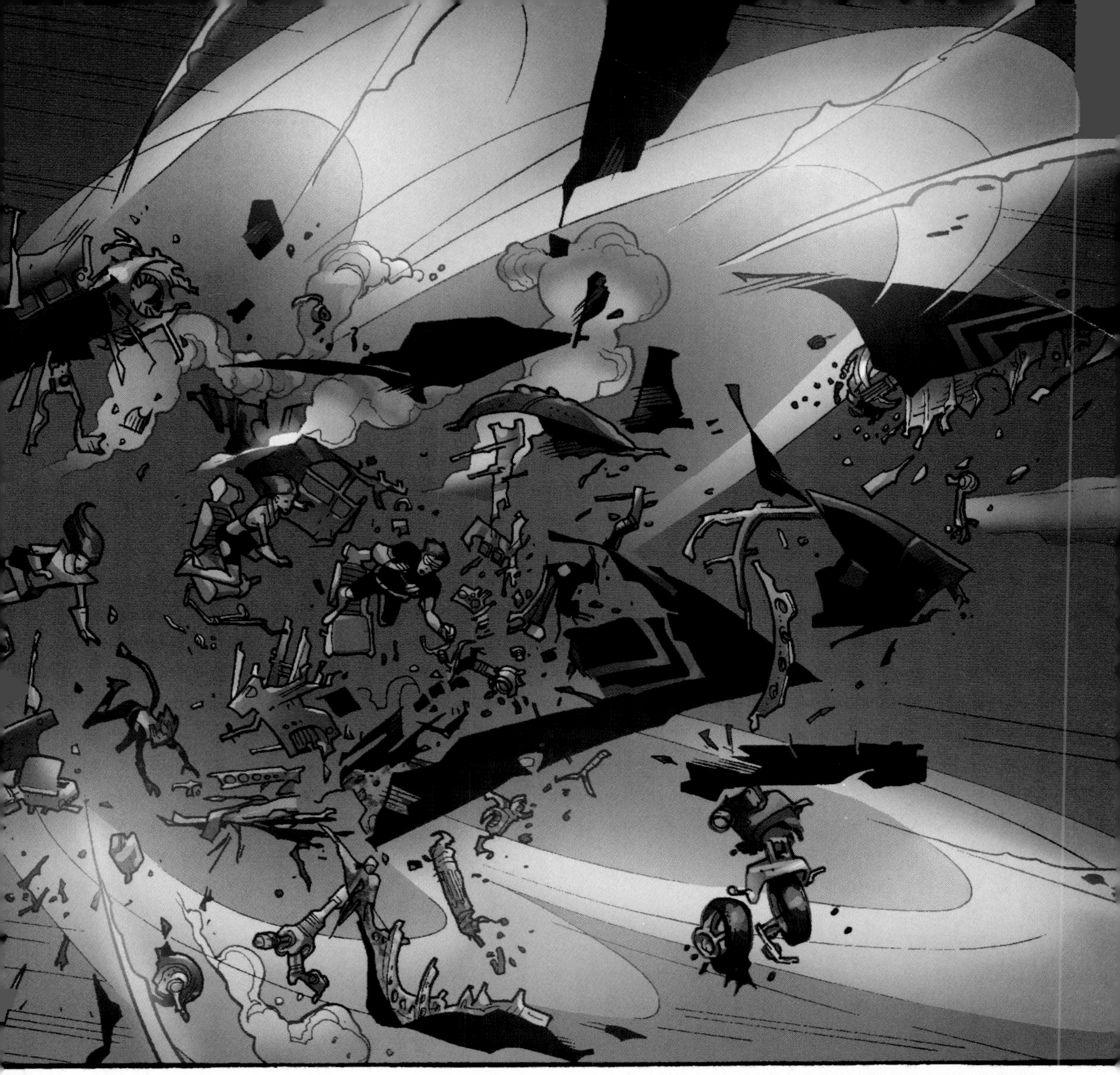

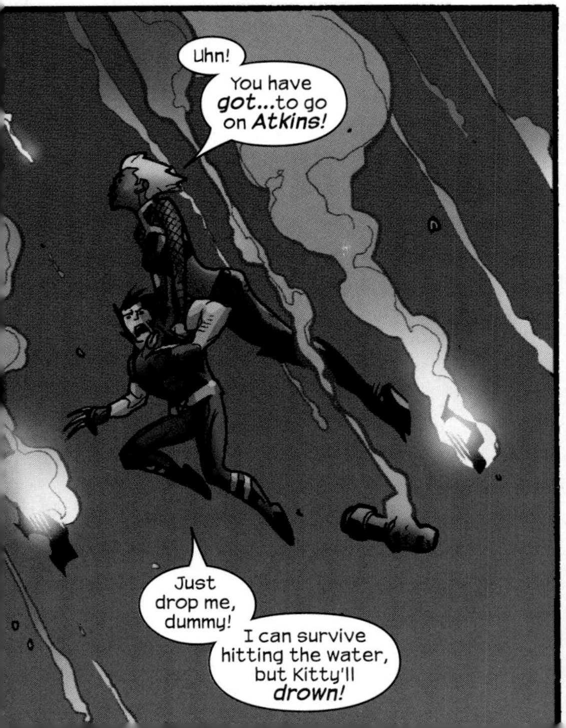
Uhn!
You have got...to go on Atkins!
Just drop me, dummy!
I can survive hitting the water, but Kitty'll drown!

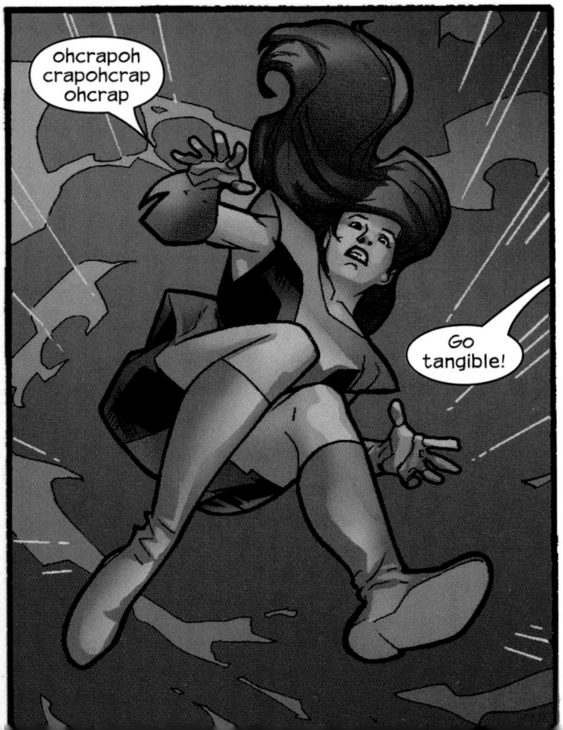
ohcrapoh crapohcrap ohcrap
Go tangible!

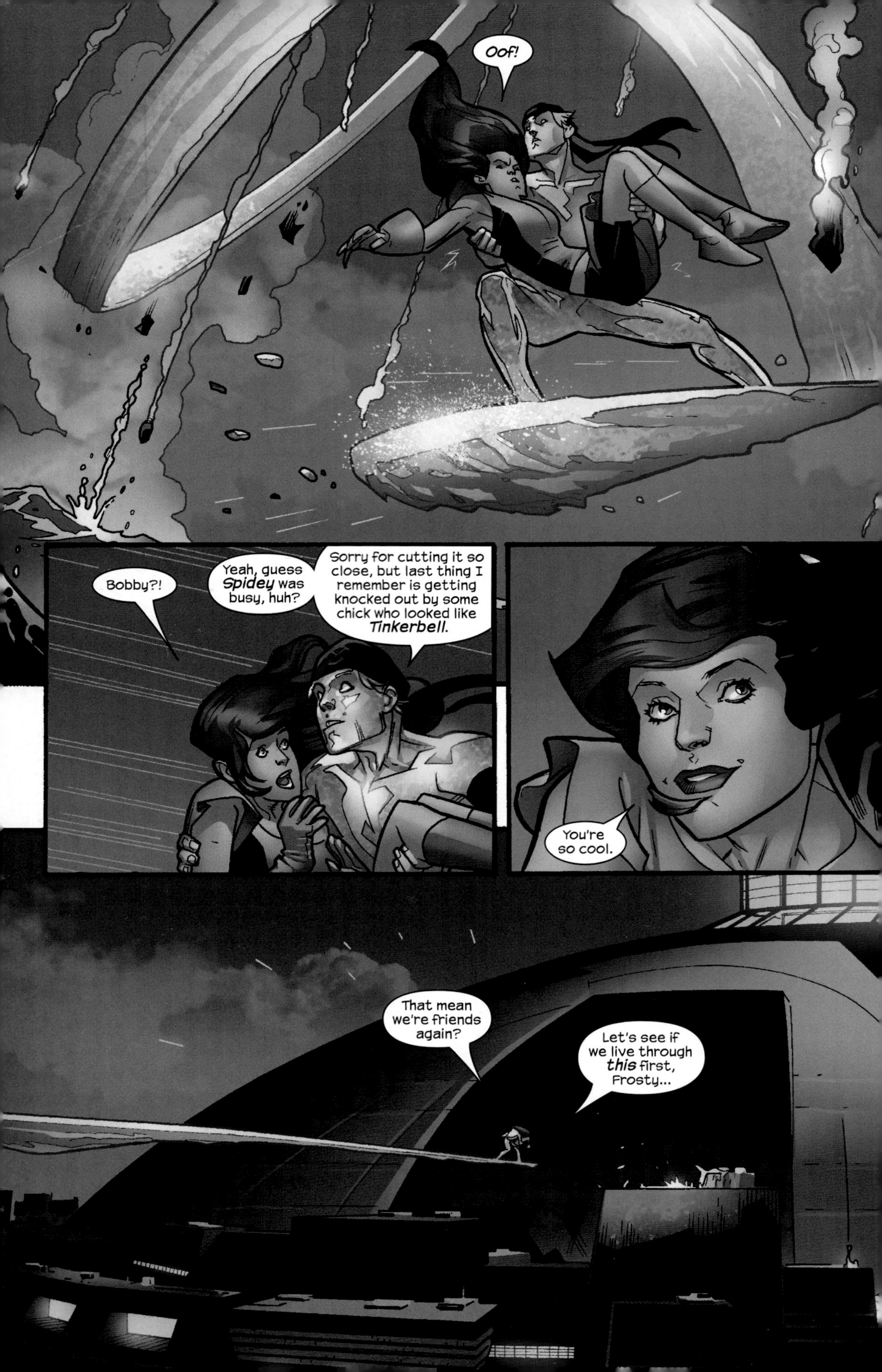
Oof!
Bobby?!
Yeah, guess Spidey was busy, huh?
Sorry for cutting it so close, but last thing I remember is getting knocked out by some chick who looked like Tinkerbell.
You're so cool.
That mean we're friends again?
Let's see if we live through this first, Frosty...

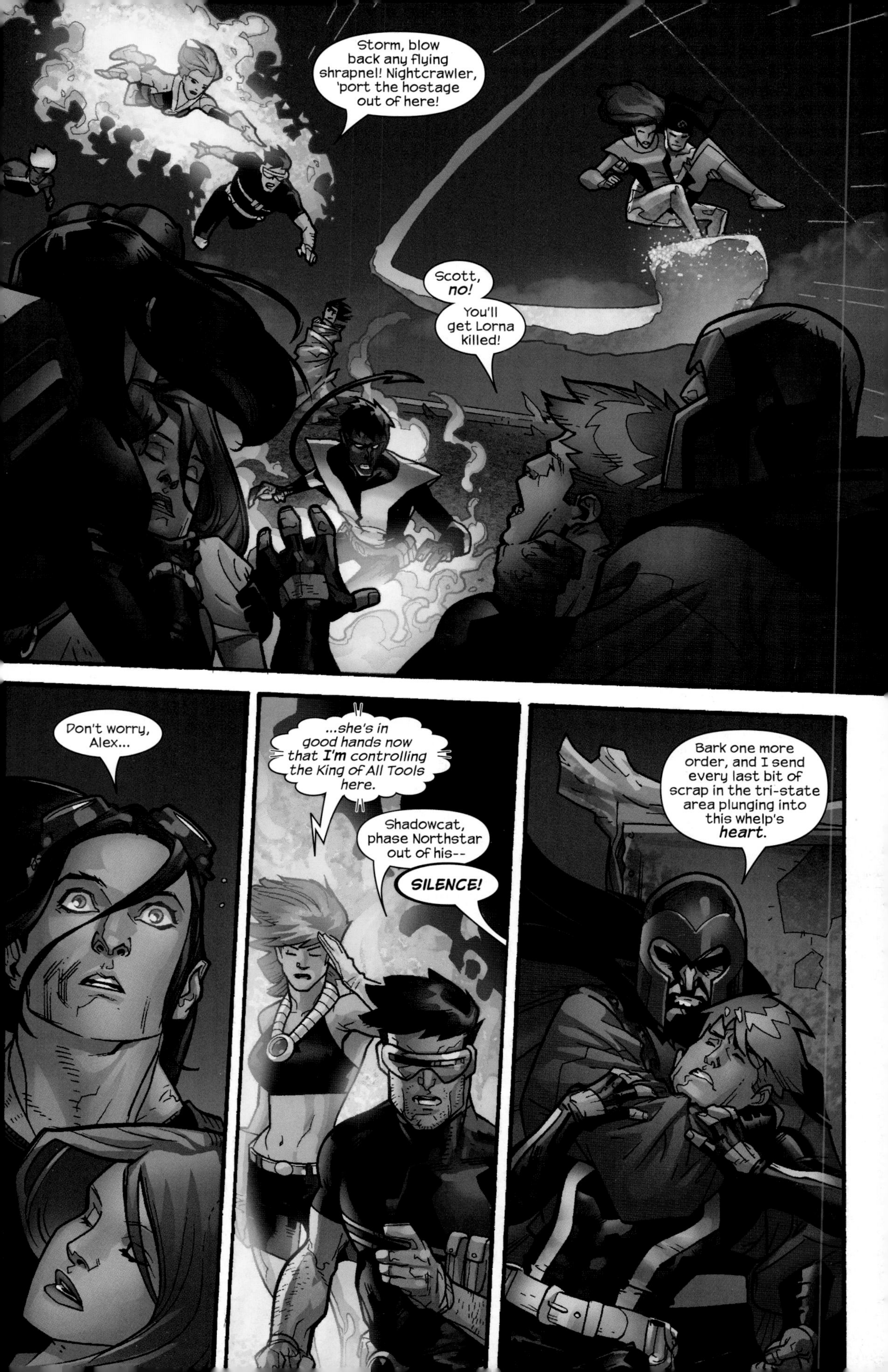
Storm, blow back any flying shrapnel! Nightcrawler, 'port the hostage out of here!
Scott, **no!**
You'll get Lorna killed!
Don't worry, Alex...
...she's in good hands now that **I'm** controlling the King of All Tools here.
Shadowcat, phase Northstar out of his--
SILENCE!
Bark one more order, and I send every last bit of scrap in the tri-state area plunging into this whelp's **heart**.

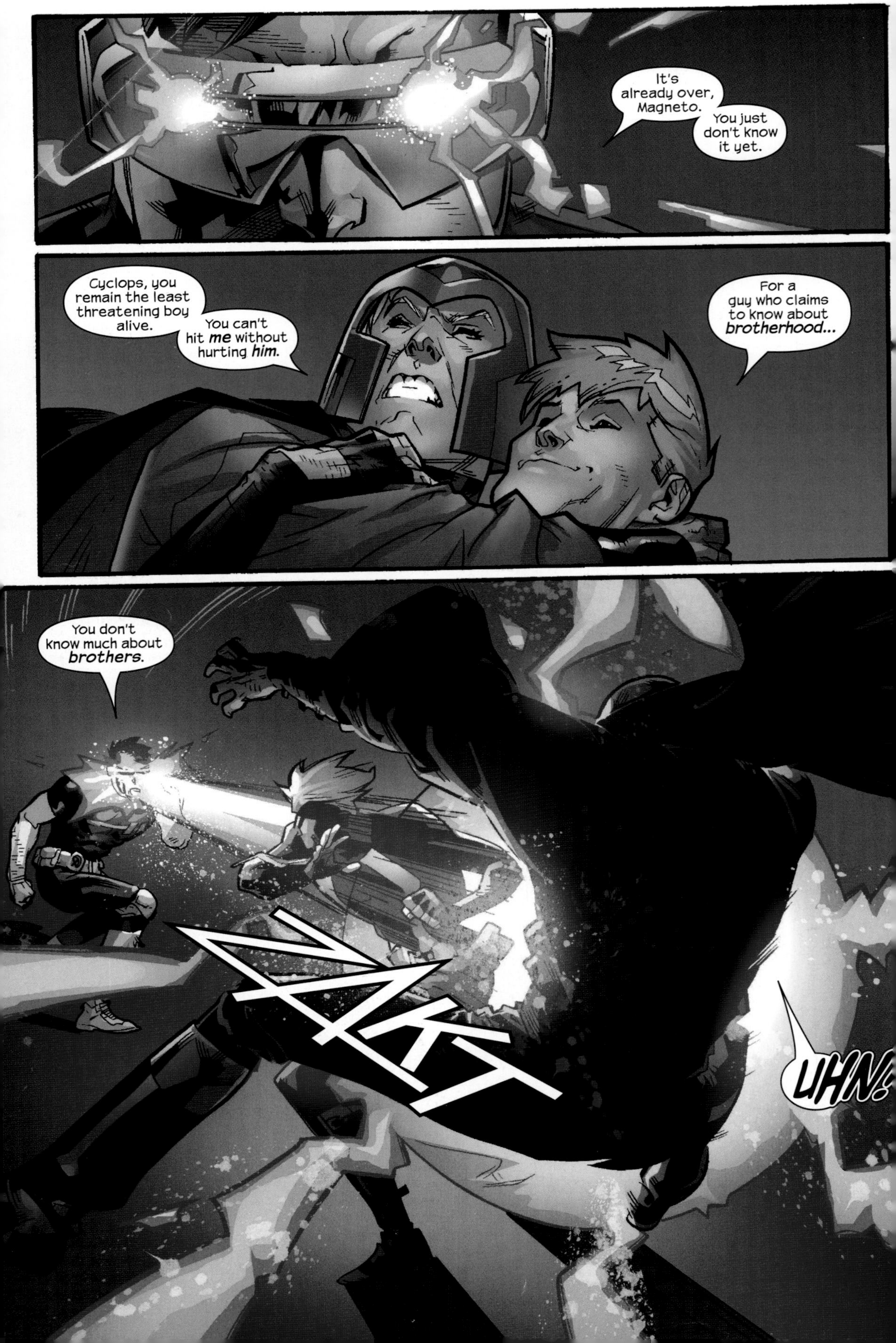
It's already over, Magneto.
You just don't know it yet.
Cyclops, you remain the least threatening boy alive.
You can't hit me without hurting him.
For a guy who claims to know about brotherhood...
You don't know much about brothers.
ZAKT
UHN!

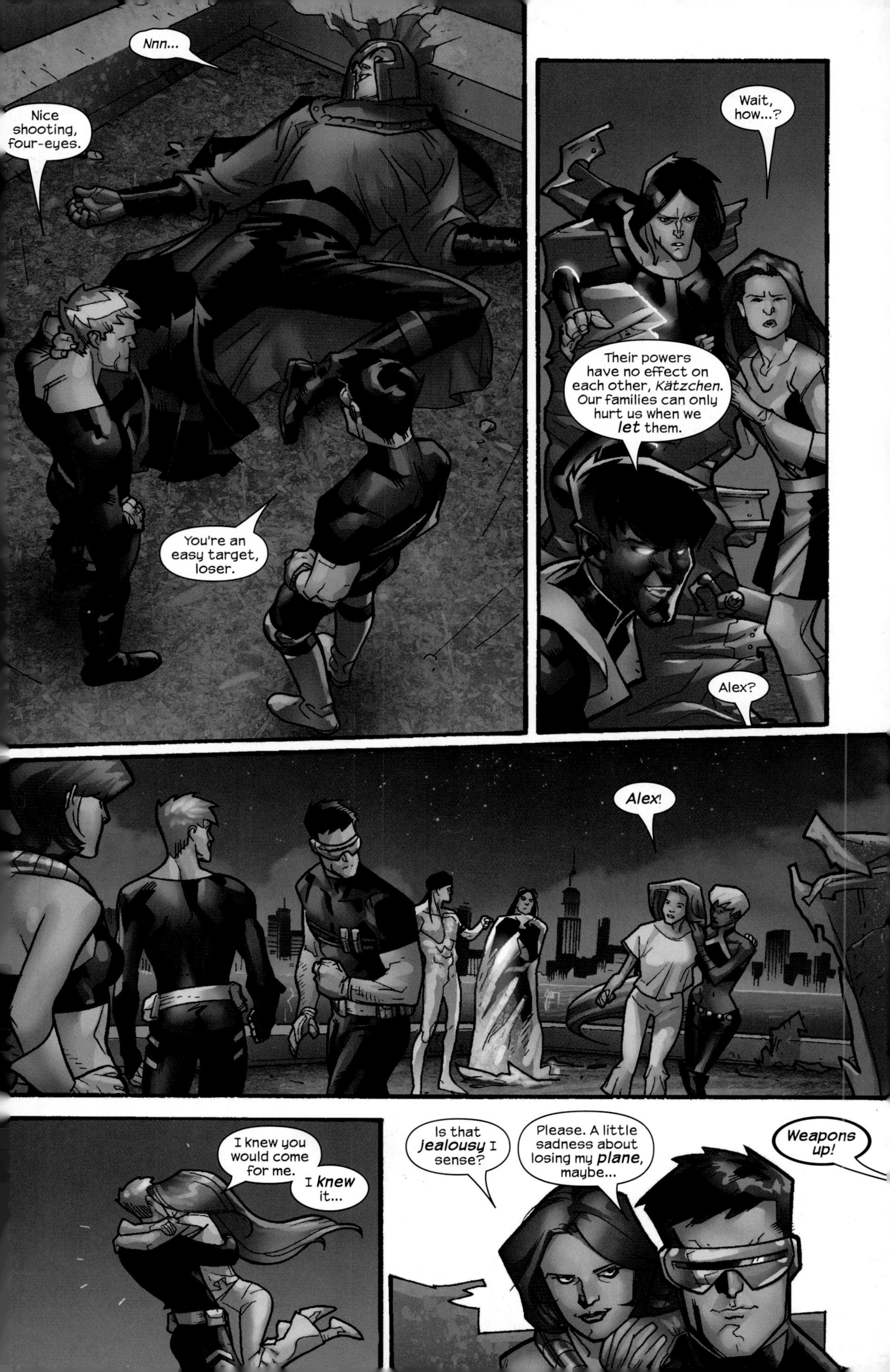
Nnn...
Nice shooting, four-eyes.
You're an easy target, loser.
Wait, how...?
Their powers have no effect on each other, *Kätzchen.* Our families can only hurt us when we ***let*** them.
Alex?
Alex!
I knew you would come for me.
I ***knew*** it...
Is that ***jealousy*** I sense?
Please. A little sadness about losing my ***plane***, maybe...
Weapons up!

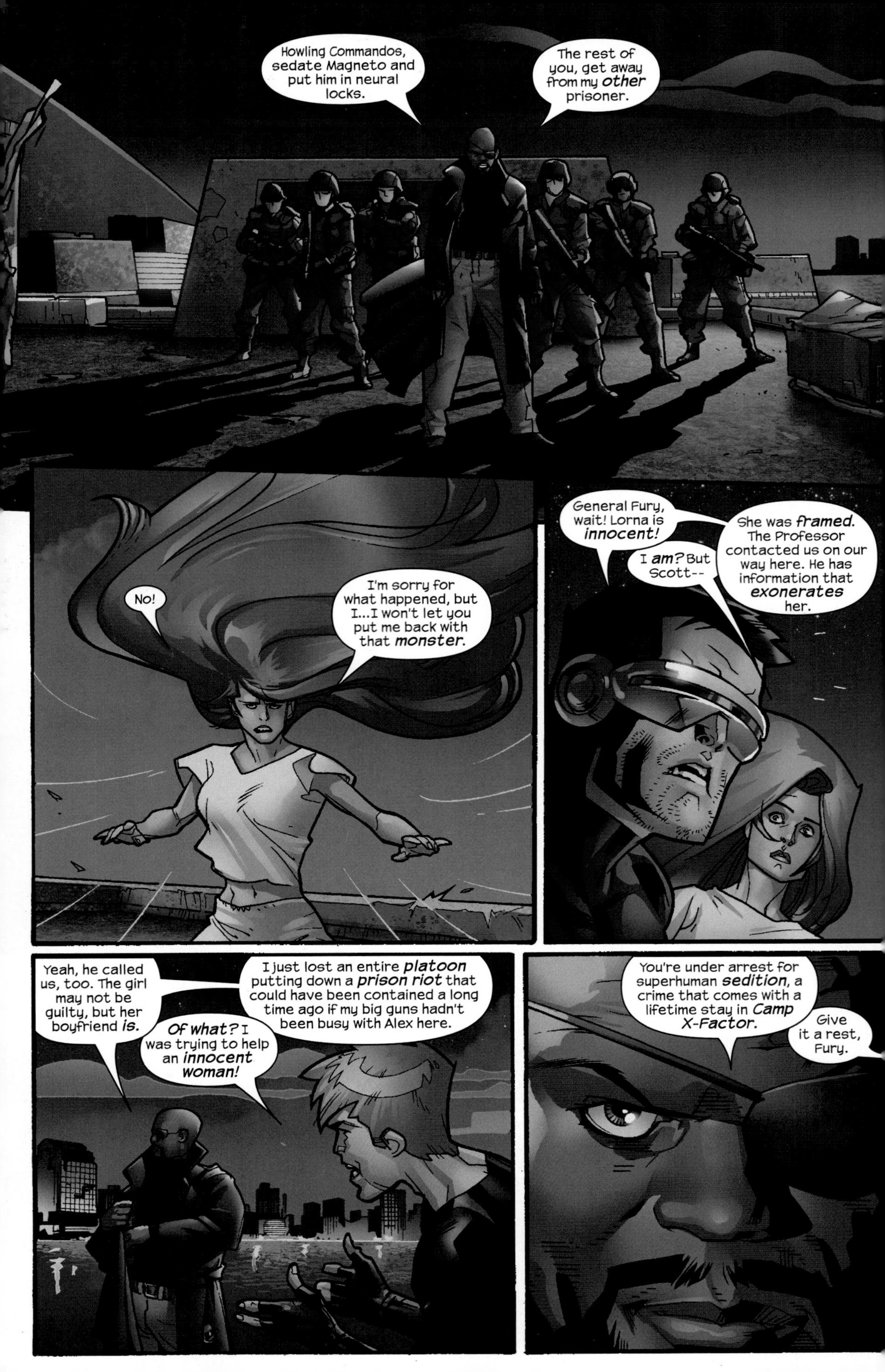
Howling Commandos, sedate Magneto and put him in neural locks.
The rest of you, get away from my *other* prisoner.
No!
I'm sorry for what happened, but I...I won't let you put me back with that *monster*.
General Fury, wait! Lorna is *innocent!*
I *am?* But Scott--
She was *framed*. The Professor contacted us on our way here. He has information that *exonerates* her.
Yeah, he called us, too. The girl may not be guilty, but her boyfriend *is*.
I just lost an entire *platoon* putting down a *prison riot* that could have been contained a long time ago if my big guns hadn't been busy with Alex here.
Of what? I was trying to help an *innocent woman!*
You're under arrest for superhuman *sedition*, a crime that comes with a lifetime stay in *Camp X-Factor*.
Give it a rest, Fury.

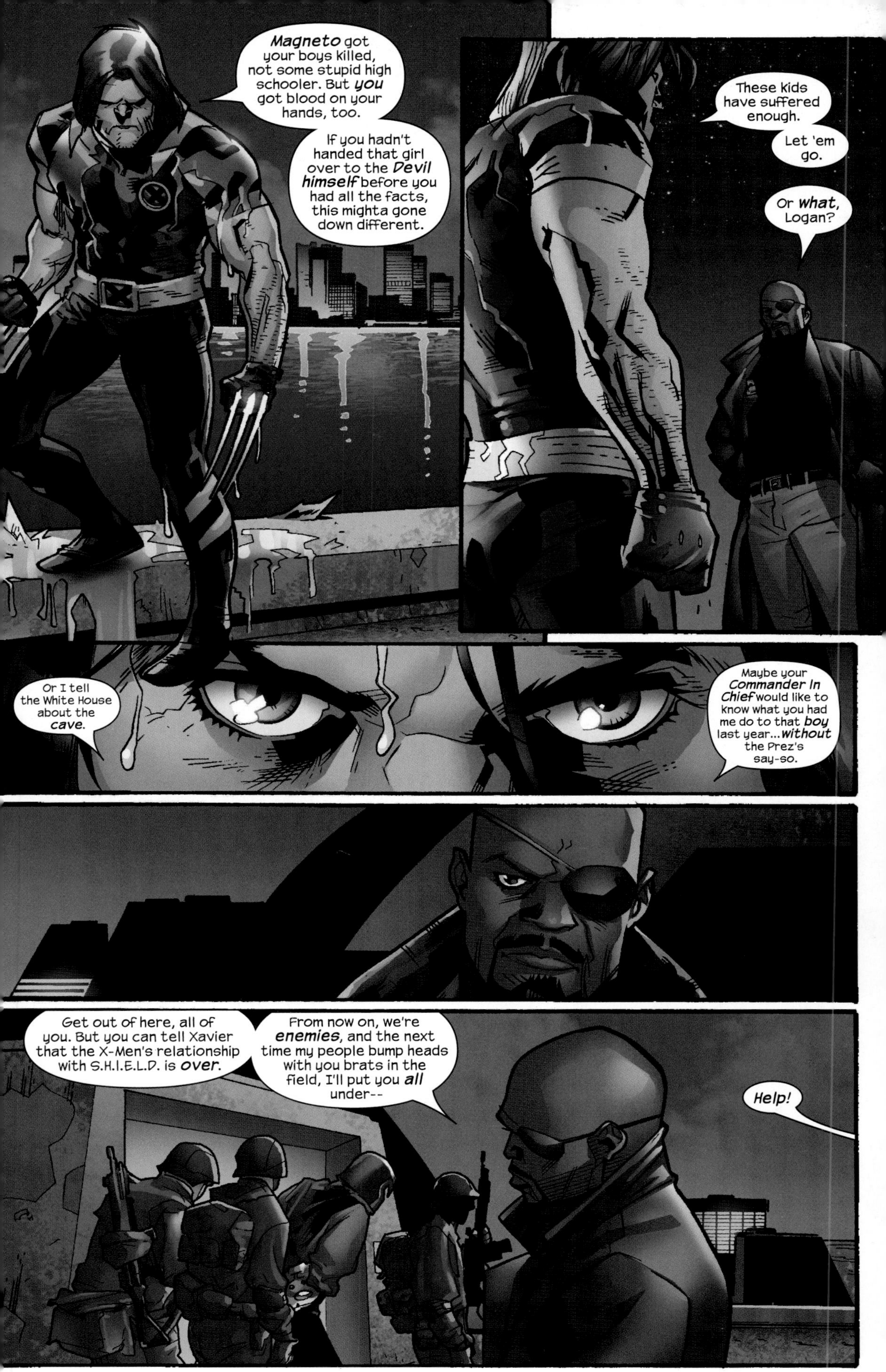
Magneto got your boys killed, not some stupid high schooler. But you got blood on your hands, too.
If you hadn't handed that girl over to the Devil himself before you had all the facts, this mighta gone down different.
These kids have suffered enough.
Let 'em go.
Or what, Logan?
Or I tell the White House about the cave.
Maybe your Commander In Chief would like to know what you had me do to that boy last year...without the Prez's say-so.
Get out of here, all of you. But you can tell Xavier that the X-Men's relationship with S.H.I.E.L.D. is over.
From now on, we're enemies, and the next time my people bump heads with you brats in the field, I'll put you all under--
Help!

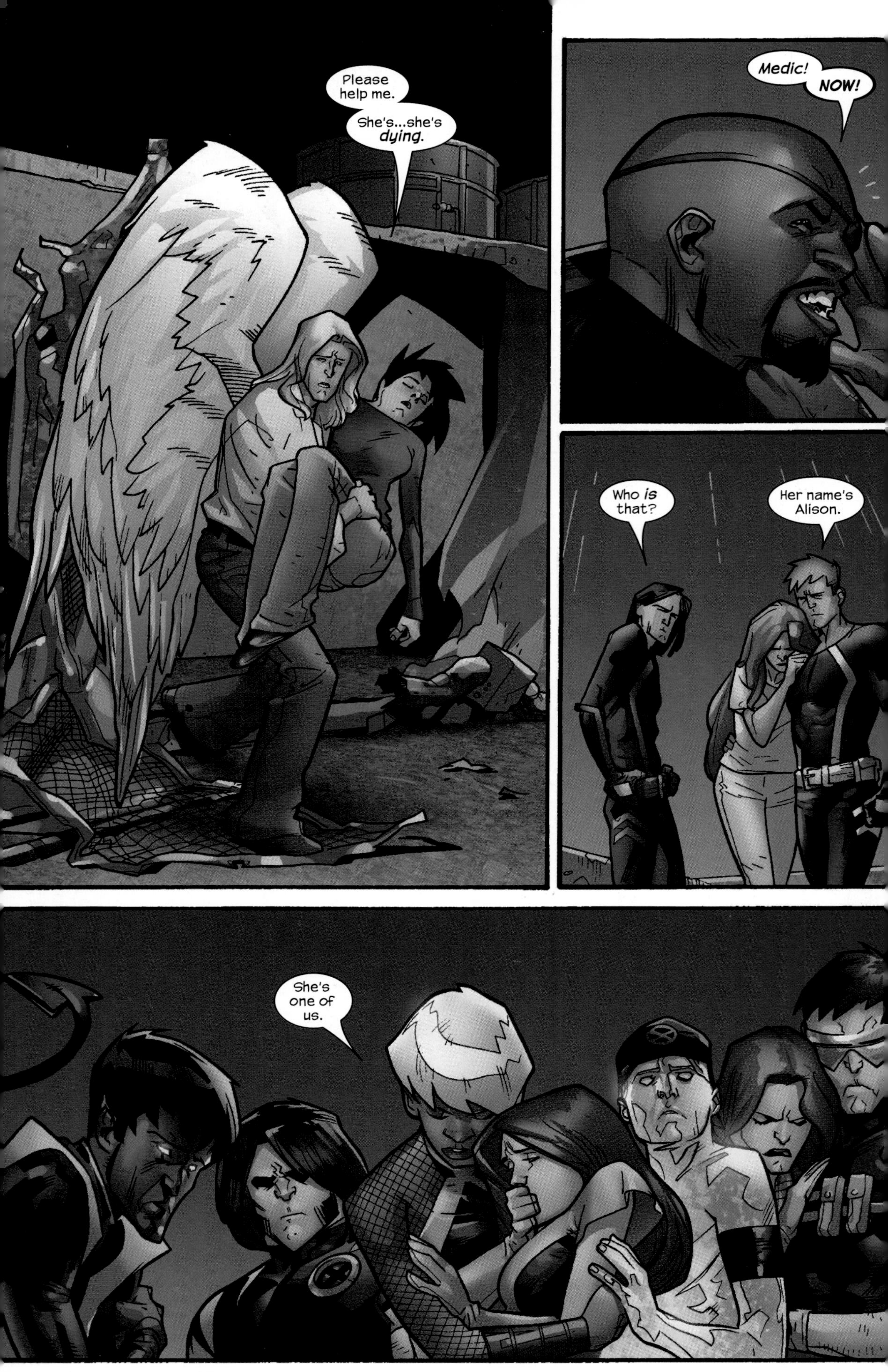
Please help me.
She's...she's *dying*.
Medic! **NOW!**
Who *is* that?
Her name's Alison.
She's one of us.

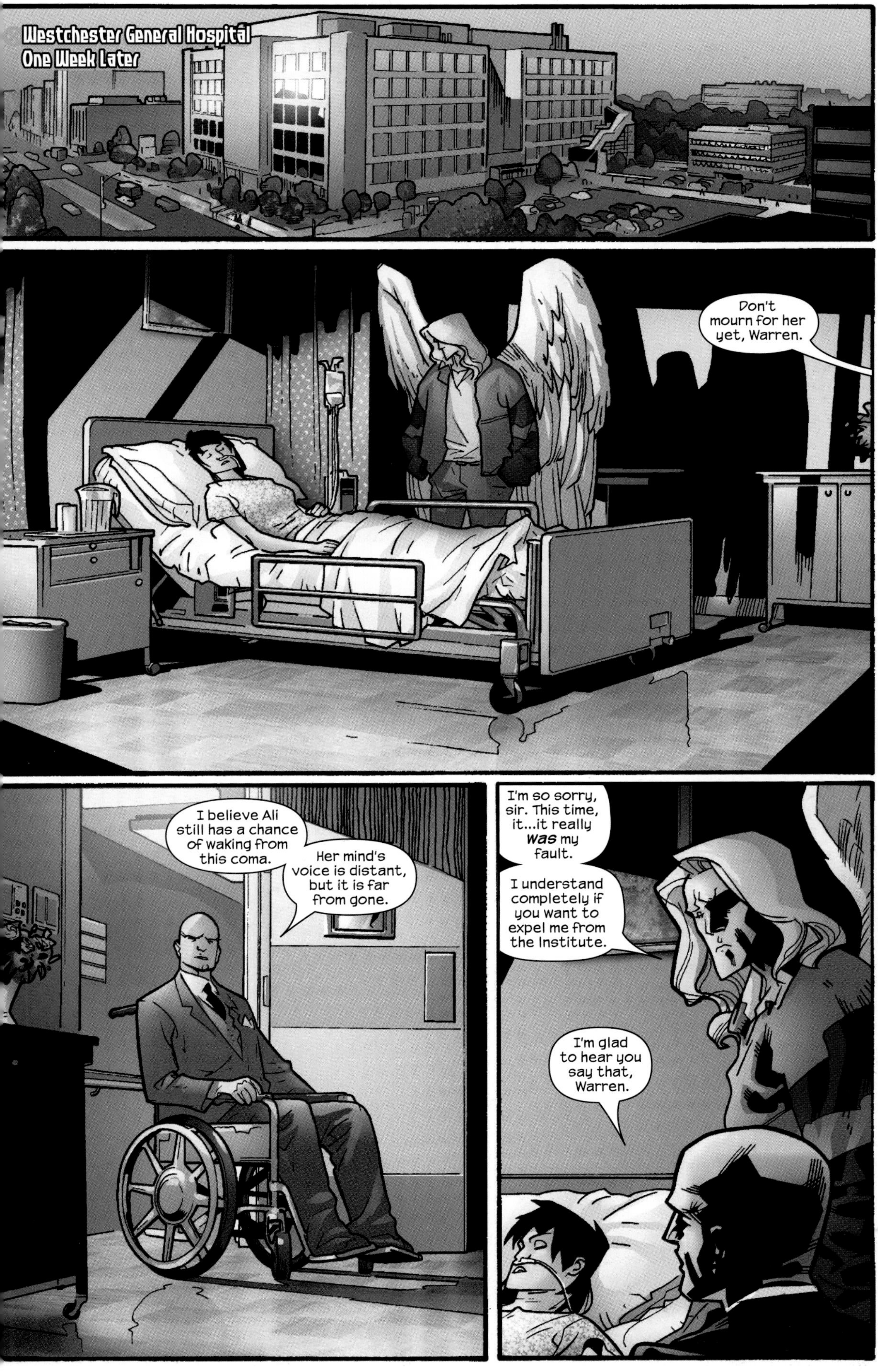
Westchester General Hospital
One Week Later
Don't mourn for her yet, Warren.
I believe Ali still has a chance of waking from this coma.
Her mind's voice is distant, but it is far from gone.
I'm so sorry, sir. This time, it...it really *was* my fault.
I understand completely if you want to expel me from the Institute.
I'm glad to hear you say that, Warren.

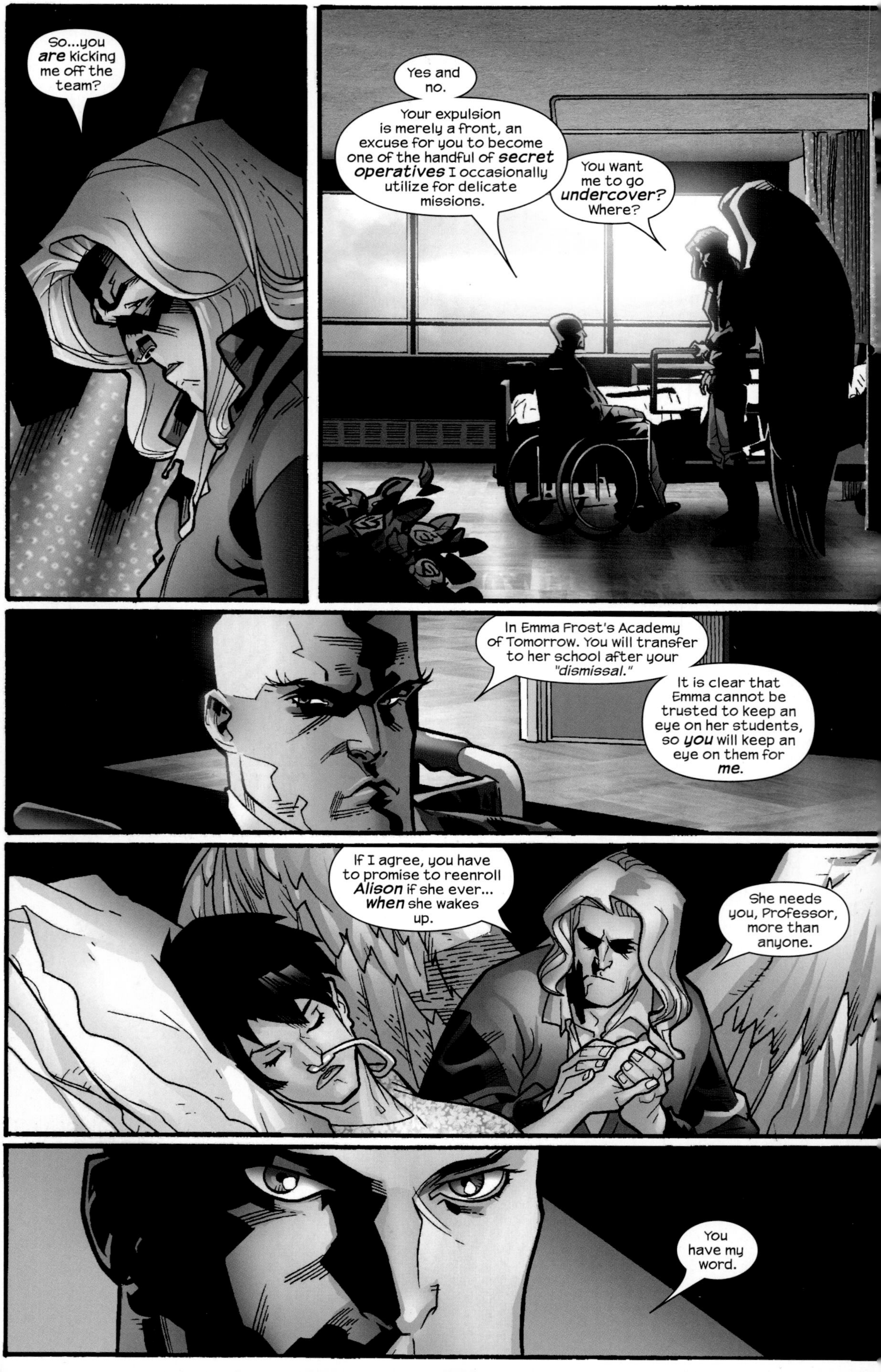
So...you are kicking me off the team?
Yes and no.
Your expulsion is merely a front, an excuse for you to become one of the handful of secret operatives I occasionally utilize for delicate missions.
You want me to go undercover? Where?
In Emma Frost's Academy of Tomorrow. You will transfer to her school after your "dismissal."
It is clear that Emma cannot be trusted to keep an eye on her students, so you will keep an eye on them for me.
If I agree, you have to promise to reenroll Alison if she ever... when she wakes up.
She needs you, Professor, more than anyone.
You have my word.

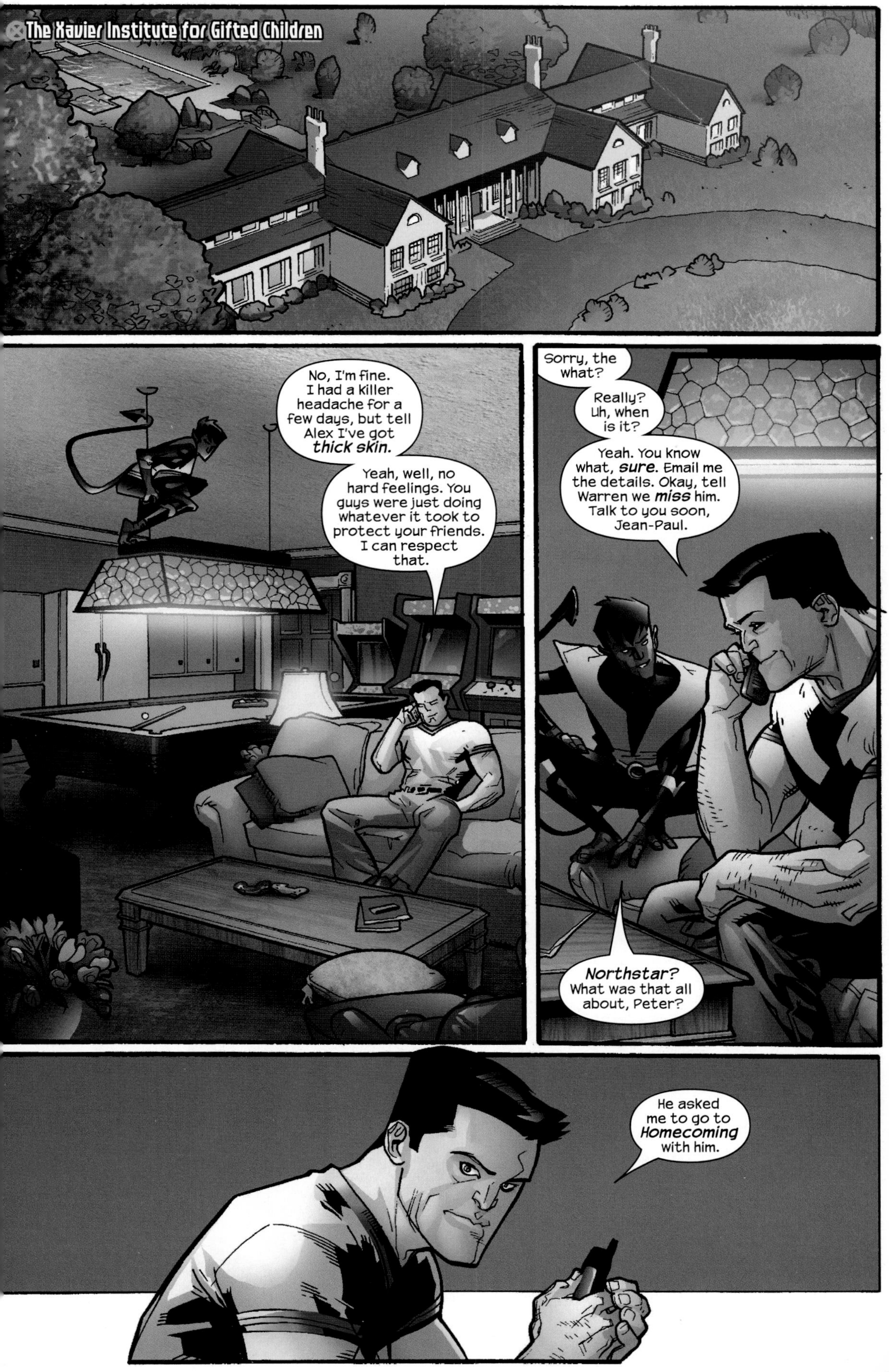
The Xavier Institute for Gifted Children
No, I'm fine. I had a killer headache for a few days, but tell Alex I've got *thick skin.*
Yeah, well, no hard feelings. You guys were just doing whatever it took to protect your friends. I can respect that.
Sorry, the what?
Really? Uh, when is it?
Yeah. You know what, *sure*. Email me the details. Okay, tell Warren we *miss* him. Talk to you soon, Jean-Paul.
Northstar? What was that all about, Peter?
He asked me to go to *Homecoming* with him.

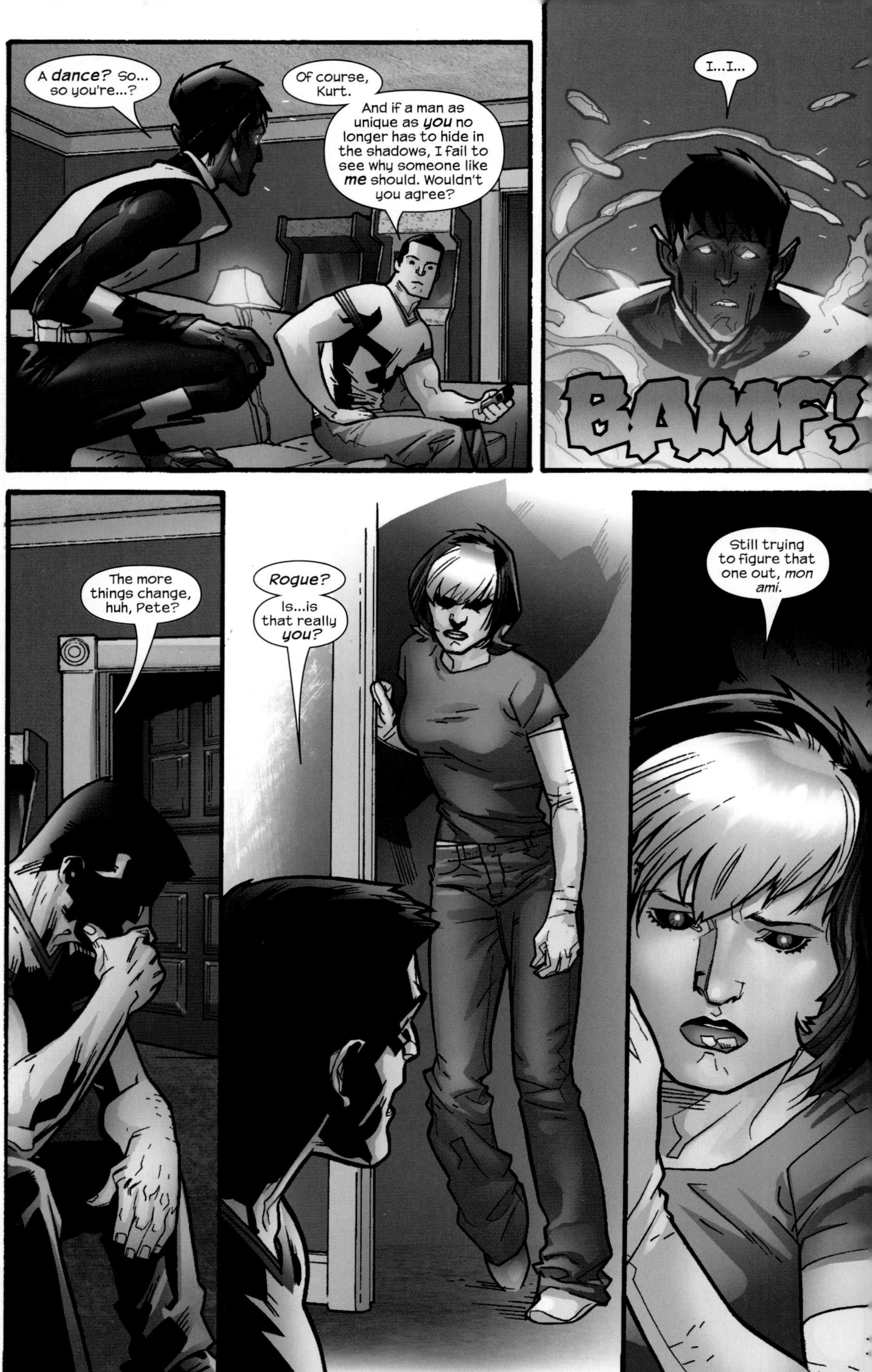
A *dance?* So... so you're...?
Of course, Kurt.
And if a man as unique as ***you*** no longer has to hide in the shadows, I fail to see why someone like ***me*** should. Wouldn't you agree?
I...I...
BAMF!
The more things change, huh, Pete?
Rogue?
Is...is that really ***you?***
Still trying to figure that one out, *mon ami.*

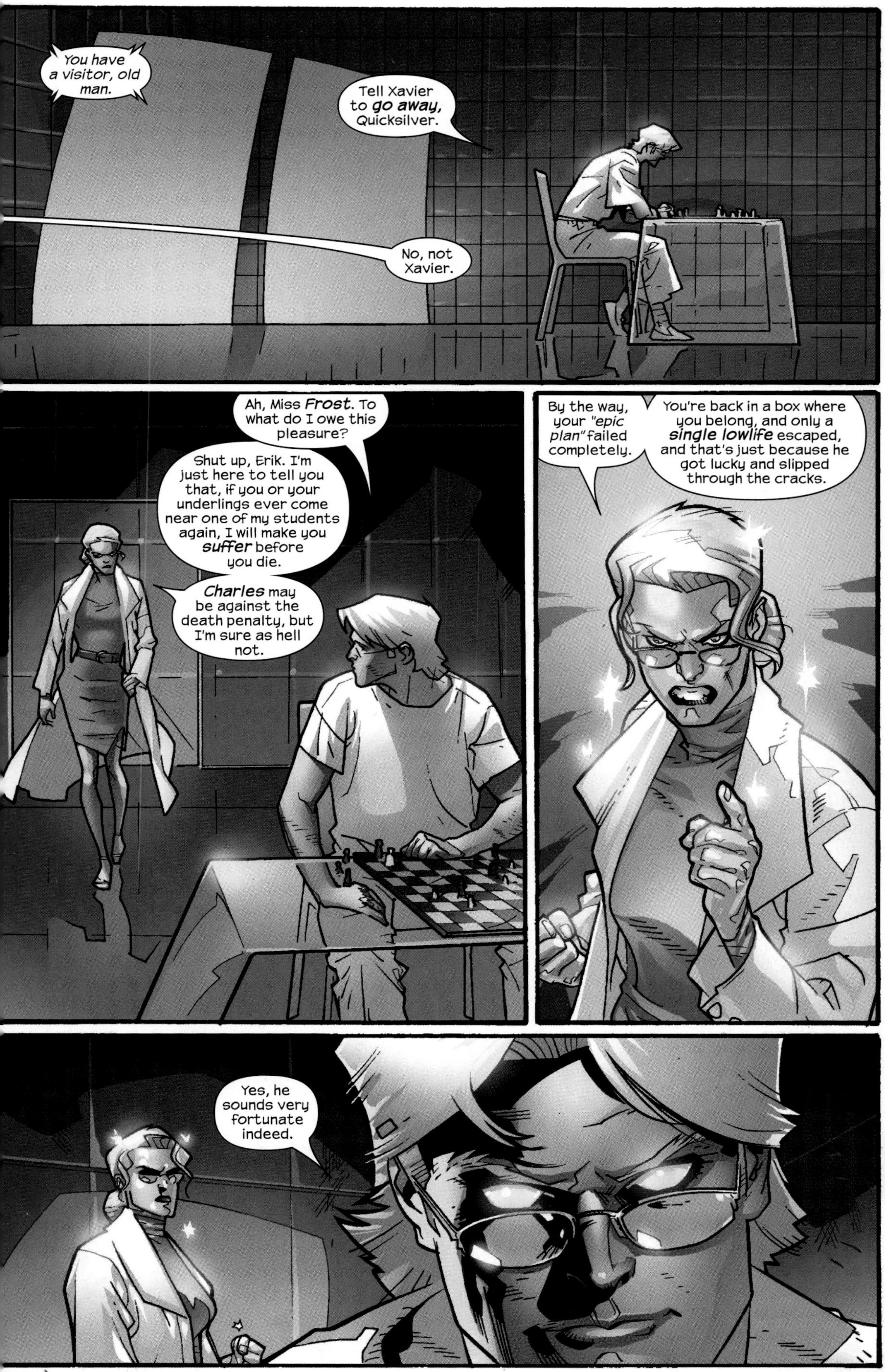
You have a visitor, old man.
Tell Xavier to go away, Quicksilver.
No, not Xavier.
Ah, Miss Frost. To what do I owe this pleasure?
Shut up, Erik. I'm just here to tell you that, if you or your underlings ever come near one of my students again, I will make you suffer before you die.
Charles may be against the death penalty, but I'm sure as hell not.
By the way, your "epic plan" failed completely.
You're back in a box where you belong, and only a single lowlife escaped, and that's just because he got lucky and slipped through the cracks.
Yes, he sounds very fortunate indeed.

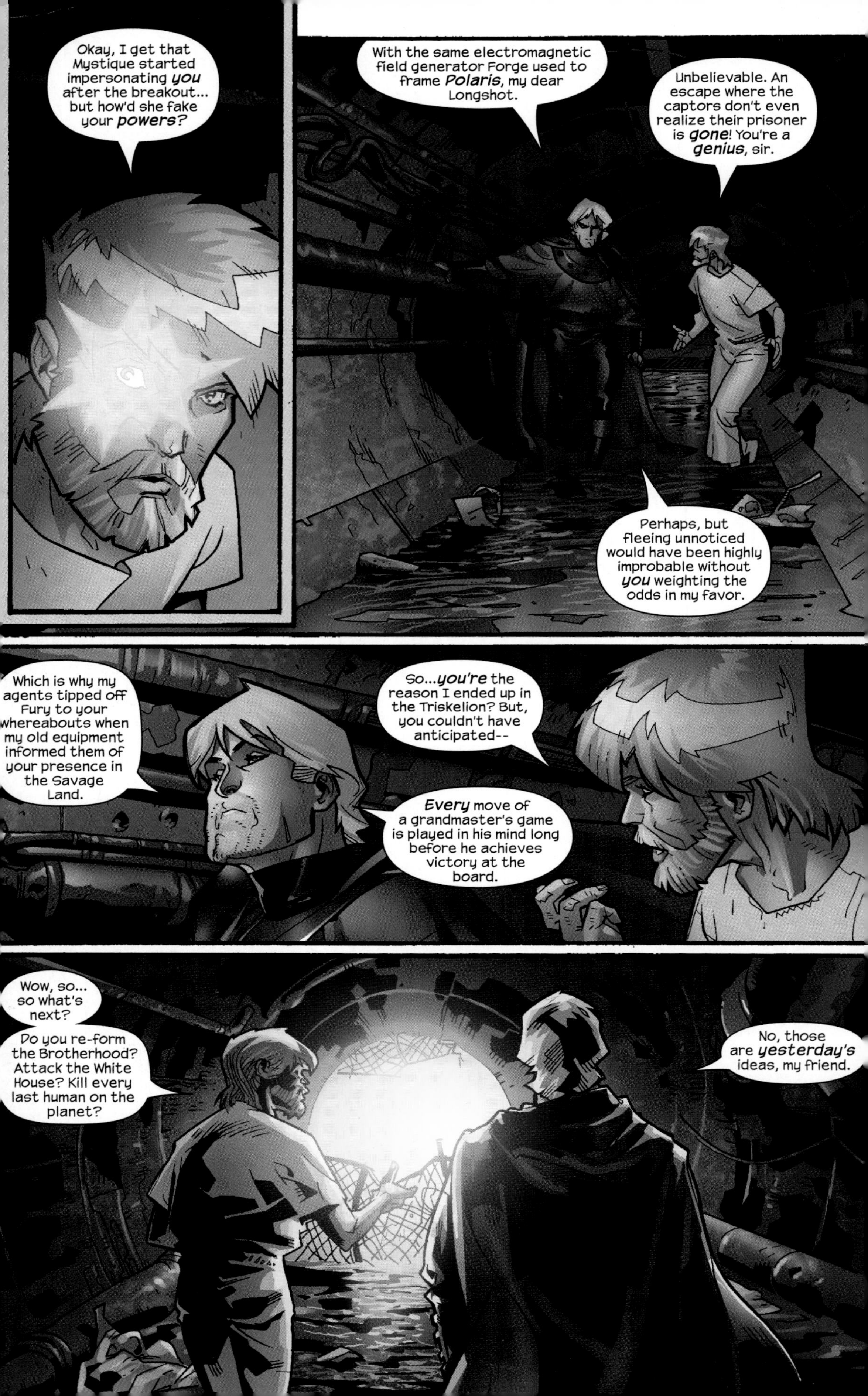
Okay, I get that Mystique started impersonating *you* after the breakout... but how'd she fake your *powers*?
With the same electromagnetic field generator Forge used to frame *Polaris*, my dear Longshot.
Unbelievable. An escape where the captors don't even realize their prisoner is *gone*! You're a *genius*, sir.
Perhaps, but fleeing unnoticed would have been highly improbable without *you* weighting the odds in my favor.
Which is why my agents tipped off Fury to your whereabouts when my old equipment informed them of your presence in the Savage Land.
So...*you're* the reason I ended up in the Triskelion? But, you couldn't have anticipated--
Every move of a grandmaster's game is played in his mind long before he achieves victory at the board.
Wow, so... so what's next?
Do you re-form the Brotherhood? Attack the White House? Kill every last human on the planet?
No, those are *yesterday's* ideas, my friend.

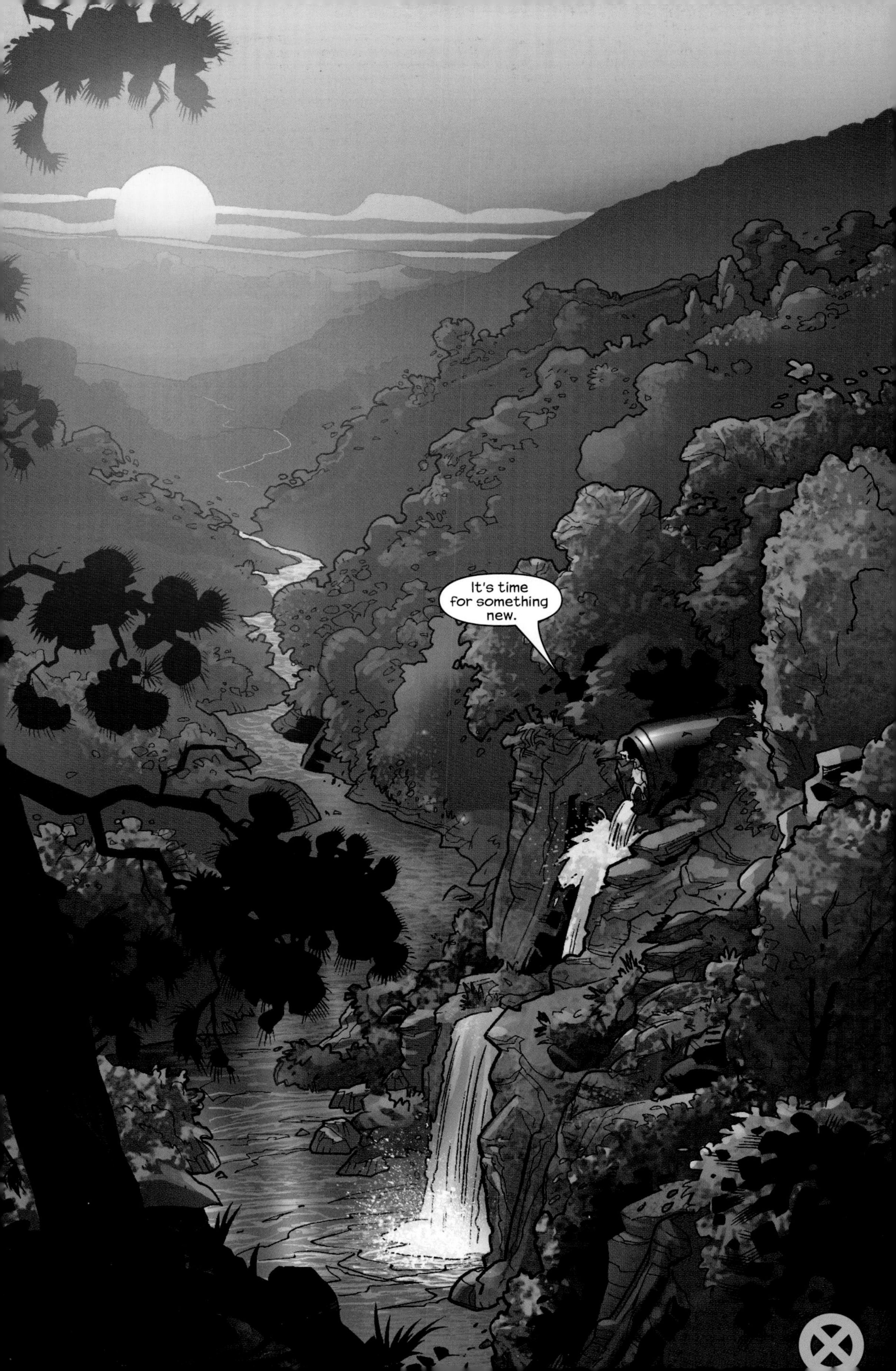
It's time for something new.

ACADEMY OF TOMORROW

CURRENT MEMBERS: Angel (Warren Worthington III), Cannonball (Sam Guthrie), Emma Frost, Havok (Alex Summers), Northstar (Jean Paul Beaubier), Polaris (Lorna Dane), Doug Ramsey, Sunspot (Roberto DaCosta)
FORMER MEMBERS: Beast (Henry McCoy), Dazzler (Alison Blaire), Karma (Xi'an Coy Mahn)
BASE OF OPERATIONS: Chicago
FIRST APPEARANCE: (as Emma Frost's "new mutants") Ultimate X-Men #44 (2004); (as Academy of Tomorrow) Ultimate X-Men #62 (2005)

HISTORY: Able to assume an unbreakable crystalline form, Emma Frost was a former student and lover of fellow mutant Charles Xavier. She broke up with him after disagreeing over Homo Superior's role in society. Charles felt mutants could avoid racial conflict with humanity by policing themselves, while Emma felt mutants must become role models and educators. Emma moved to Chicago, becoming a schoolteacher and running mutant education seminars. After the public debut of Xavier's X-Men, Emma approached the government with a proposal to create a group of popular, attractive mutant spokespeople from various backgrounds and ethnicities to win over public opinion and launch her education campaign. Though a number of her candidates were rejected, the President approved her plan. She recruited Alex Summers, elder brother to the X-Men's Cyclops, an energy generator who had turned down Xavier's school; Alison Blaire, lead singer of the punk band Dazzler, who could absorb sound and generate light; and Hank McCoy, a.k.a. Beast, a disenchanted Xavier dropout. At the President's behest, Emma also added S.H.I.E.L.D. Black Ops agent Xi'an Coy Mahn, codename Karma, who could possess people. However, at

the group's press launch on the Capitol steps, rogue government elements that feared mutants influencing the President unleashed Sentinels. Beast was killed saving others from the Sentinel attack. The X-Men intervened to destroy the Sentinels, and Karma revealed Nick Fury had placed her in the group to uncover the anti-mutant conspiracy within the President's inner circle. In the aftermath, Frost and her remaining charges moved into Xavier's estate to re-evaluate their mission.

After a brief stay, Frost and Alex departed for Chicago, still feeling the X-Men were taking the wrong path. Frost established the Academy of Tomorrow, which accepted all outstanding individuals, mutant or not. Among her new students were computer genius Doug Ramsey; mutant speedster Jean-Paul Beaubier, a.k.a. Northstar, son of the Canadian ambassador; Alex's magnetic-powered girlfriend Lorna Dane (Polaris); Sam Guthrie (Cannonball), able to generate a protective forcefield and fly; and Roberto DaCosta, known as Sunspot because he could generate solar blasts. While trying to rescue people from a fire, Polaris seemingly lost control of her powers, causing the deaths of three people. To prevent all her students being arrested, Emma handed Polaris over to S.H.I.E.L.D., who incarcerated her in the Triskelion. Her loss of control was actually due to a device planted by Brotherhood of Mutant's Forge, who knew that due to the similar nature of their powers, she would be imprisoned in same cell as Magneto. While Doug tried to figure out the real reason Polaris had lost control, the rest of her classmates decided to break her out. Learning of these plans, the X-Men moved to intercept the Academy students before they turned themselves into fugitives, but instead both groups ended up clashing with one another and the Ultimates, unwittingly providing a distraction which enabled the Brotherhood to free Magneto. In the aftermath of the Academy's incursion into the Triskelion Polaris was freed thanks to evidence found by Doug; Nick Fury would have imprisoned Havok for leading the break-in, but the X-Man Wolverine blackmailed Fury into dropping the charges. Angel joined the Academy, apparently expelled from Xavier's but in truth acting as an undercover operative for Professor X, who believed Emma could not be trusted to keep an eye on her students. And the openly gay Northstar asked Colossus to the Homecoming Dance, finally giving the metallic X-Man the courage to come out to his team-mates.

HISTORY: A magnetic-powered mutant (or "post-human"), Erik Lensherr approached mutant telepath Charles Xavier after hearing of his work saving young mutant patients with uncontrollable powers. Lensherr and Xavier found each other fascinating, neither having met an adult mutant before. They became close friends and developed an ideology regarding mutants as mankind's replacements. Eventually, both men left their wives to found the Brotherhood of Mutants, a safe haven for persecuted mutants. Erik took his mutant children with him, and would later deny he ever loved his human spouse. A few years later, the Brotherhood moved to a remote Pacific island, the Savage Land, to found a new civilization. Erik even devised a new language for this new world, and through genetic experimentation created dinosaurs to inhabit it. Increasingly convinced humanity would not peacefully relinquish the planet to Homo Superior, Erik became more radical, regarding the Savage Land's citizens as an army. Abandoning his human name, Erik took the title Magneto. Realizing that Xavier didn't agree with his views, a paranoid Magneto took to wearing a helmet to prevent psi intrusion into his mind. Xavier finally fled with a handful of followers, but Magneto decided to teach him a lesson and broke his spine, leaving him crippled. Soon after, Magneto led the Brotherhood in an anti-human campaign of political assassinations and terrorist bombings.

Following an attack on Washington, the U.S. government unleashed robotic Sentinels on the mutant population in retaliation. When Xavier's new students, the X-Men, interfered, Magneto learned Xavier had survived, and sent Wolverine to slay his former friend. He also had the President's daughter kidnapped, which halted the Sentinel campaign; the X-Men soon rescued her. American authorities located the Savage Land and launched a massive Sentinel attack, but Magneto used his powers to reprogram them, leading them back to assault Washington. While the Sentinels decimated the capital, Magneto dragged the President naked onto the Whitehouse lawn. The X-Men intervened, and Magneto was defeated when his son Quicksilver, convinced that genocide was going too far, removed his helmet, leaving him vulnerable to Xavier's powers. Xavier claimed to have killed Magneto, but had instead secretly brainwashed him, hoping to rehabilitate him. For several months the amnesiac Erik lived peacefully as a Manhattan social worker looking after disabled children; however, the Brotherhood eventually learned he was alive, and restored his memories. Magneto resumed the bombing campaign halted by his errant children, simultaneously gathering every mutant he could into a floating Arctic Citadel. His powers enhanced by a machine of

REAL NAME: Erik Lensherr
KNOWN ALIASES: None
IDENTITY: Publicly known
OCCUPATION: Terrorist
CITIZENSHIP: Unrevealed
PLACE OF BIRTH: Unrevealed
KNOWN RELATIVES: Father (name unrevealed, deceased), Isabelle (wife), Pietro (son), Wanda (daughter)
GROUP AFFILIATION: Brotherhood of Mutants
EDUCATION: Unknown
FIRST APPEARANCE: Ultimate X-Men #1 (2001)

Forge's design, Magneto intended to reverse Earth's magnetic field, leaving humanity to perish in the ensuing environmental chaos. The X-Men stopped him, and he was imprisoned in the Triskelion, home of S.H.I.E.L.D. and the Ultimates. He was recently freed by Mystique and Forge.

HEIGHT: 6'2"
WEIGHT: 195 lbs.
EYES: Blue
HAIR: Silver

ABILITIES AND ACCESSORIES: Magneto can manipulate magnetic fields to fly, create force fields, and move metallic objects at will.

POWER GRID	1	2	3	4	5	6	7
INTELLIGENCE							
STRENGTH							
SPEED							
DURABILITY							
ENERGY PROJECTION							
FIGHTING SKILLS							

THE ULTIMATES

ACTIVE MEMBERS: Black Widow (Natasha Romanov), Captain America (Steve Rogers), Hawkeye (Clint Barton), Iron Man (Tony Stark), Quicksilver (Pietro Maximoff), Scarlet Witch (Wanda Maximoff), Wasp (Janet Pym)
FORMER MEMBERS: Giant-Man (Hank Pym), Hulk (Bruce Banner), Lieberman (deceased reservist), Thor (allegedly Thorlief Golman)
RESERVES: The Four Seasons, the Goliaths, Intangi-Girl, Owen, O'Donohue, Rocketman One (Dexter), Rocketman Two, Rocketman Three, Rusk, Son of Satan (Damien), Thunderbolt, unspecified others
BASE OF OPERATIONS: The Triskelion, Upper Bay, Manhattan
FIRST APPEARANCE: Ultimates #2 (2002)

HISTORY: The world's foremost superhuman strike force, the Ultimates trace their origins back to World War II super-operative Captain America (Steve Rogers), whom the U.S. government empowered in part to oppose the Nazis' secret extraterrestrial Chitauri allies. Rogers appeared to die while helping destroy the Chitauri/Nazi war effort, and U.S. scientists tried for decades to duplicate his powers. In recent years, the super-soldier program's lead scientist was geneticist Bruce Banner, reporting to General Ross, head of the S.H.I.E.L.D. intelligence agency. Later, new S.H.I.E.L.D. director Nick Fury pushed through a multi-billion expansion of the super-soldier program, though Banner's temporary transformation into the monstrous Hulk resulted in his demotion to deputy under new head scientists Hank and Janet Pym, who did double duty as size-changing super-operatives Giant-Man and Wasp. Altruistic armored billionaire inventor Tony Stark soon joined as Iron Man. Enigmatic left-wing powerhouse Thor refused membership at first, but Captain America himself was found alive and revived from a state of suspended animation to join the team. Together, Rogers, Stark and the Pyms became the Ultimates, headquartered in the high-tech Triskelion complex and backed by a huge support staff, a large conventional military force and black ops agents. Banner's semi-estranged girlfriend Betty Ross (daughter of General Ross) was hired as Director of Communications and helped make the new team into celebrities while making Bruce's life miserable. The depressed Banner finally snapped and transformed into the Hulk again, embarking on a destructive rampage stopped by the Ultimates with the aid of Thor, who began working with the team thereafter.

The Hulk's true identity was concealed from the public, and the Ultimates became beloved national heroes. The group soon expanded: intelligence veterans Hawkeye and Black Widow and mutant ex-terrorists Quicksilver and Scarlet Witch were promoted from the black ops division to the core team. Meanwhile, Hank Pym nearly killed his wife during a violent domestic dispute and was himself beaten into traction by Captain America, who later began dating the Wasp. Pym's former assistant Dr. Eamonn Brankin became the new scientific head of the program. Despite losing Giant-Man, the Ultimates saved the world from a Chitauri plot with the unwitting aid of the Hulk and became bigger icons than ever. They went on to apprehend Kraven, Electro, Luther Manning, the X-Men and Norman Osborn's "Six." Later allied with the European Super-Solider Initiative, the Ultimates became more controversial as they began operating in foreign territory, notably the Middle East. Thor quit, and a traitor within the group outed Banner as the Hulk. Seemingly executed for the Hulk's crimes, Banner secretly survived with the aid of Hank Pym, who was soon fired from the Ultimates altogether. Meanwhile, apparently exposed as a madman, Thor was brutally arrested by the team. The global community grew wary as the Ultimates developed many more superagents as their reserves, and anti-Ultimates sentiment accelerated when the team stripped a small "rogue" Middle Eastern nation of its nuclear capability. The traitor within the Ultimates responded by murdering Hawkeye's family, framing Captain America for the crime, and helping a foreign super-army invade America. Assisted by Hank Pym, this foreign force destroyed the Triskelion and occupied major American cities, slaughtering the reserves and capturing the remaining Ultimates in the process.

Art by Bryan Hitch